# CHURCHWARDENS' ACCOUNTS OF CRATFIELD

## 1640–1660

# CHURCHWARDENS' ACCOUNTS
# OF CRATFIELD

## 1640–1660

Edited by
### L. A. BOTELHO

General Editor
### DAVID DYMOND

The Boydell Press

Suffolk Records Society
VOLUME XLII

A Suffolk Records Society publication
First published 1999
The Boydell Press, Woodbridge


ISBN  0 85115 759 9


Issued to subscribing members for the year 1998–9




The Boydell Press is an imprint of Boydell & Brewer Ltd
PO Box 9, Woodbridge, Suffolk IP12 3DF, UK
and of Boydell & Brewer Inc.
PO Box 41026, Rochester, NY 14604–4126, USA
website: http://www.boydell.co.uk


A catalogue record for this book is available
from the British Library


This publication is printed on acid-free paper

Printed in Great Britain by
St Edmundsbury Press Ltd, Bury St Edmunds, Suffolk

# Contents

# Illustrations

# Abbreviations

| | |
|---|---|
| Bodl. | Bodleian Library, Oxford |
| BL | British Library, London |
| CUL | Cambridge University Library |
| CWA | Churchwardens' Accounts |
| *EDD* | *The English Dialect Dictionary*, ed. J. Wright |
| fn | footnote |
| *MED* | *Middle English Dictionary*, ed. R. E. Lewis |
| MS | Manuscript |
| MSS | Manuscripts |
| SROI | Suffolk Record Office, Ipswich |
| TB | Town Book |

# Acknowledgements

I would like to express my thanks to a number of individuals and institutions who have helped me with this project. First of all I would like to thank the Suffolk Records Society and especially its general editor, David Dymond, for assistance at all stages of production and without whose help this volume could not have been completed. I am equally grateful to the staff and archivists of the Suffolk Record Office at Ipswich for their cheerful assistance with the Cratfield churchwardens' accounts, to Gillian Harvey for supplying a detailed map of the parish, to Phillip Judge for drawing three maps for publication, and to Nesta Evans for her detailed index. I would also like to thank my colleagues in the Department of History, Indiana University of Pennsylvania, for their support and the University's Senate Research Grant for financial assistance during the final stages of this work. Further thanks go to a number of individuals whose support and careful reading have saved me from innumerable errors: Jean-Yves Boulard, Michelle Doehring, Gillian Harvey, Geoff Hudson, Anne Kugler, Irwin Marcus, Elizabeth Ricketts, Holly Shissler, Brian Vivier and Tamara Whited. Finally, all errors that remain are solely my own.

*Key to Map 1*

1　Church
2　Vicarage or parsonage
3　Town House or Guildhall
4　Manor House of Cratfield Roos
5　The Bell, a sixteenth-century house which may have earlier origins. By 1713 it was the village's public house, although its use as such is probably much older.
6　The site of a windmill
7　Barets, *c.*1500, more recently known as Town Farm
8　Old Hall
9　Mill Farm, probably site of the mill of the Priory Manor
10　Benselyns, later Little Town Farm. Copyhold possession was given to the parish in *c.*1460.
11　Cratfield Hall. Probably built as a grander and larger successor to Old Hall after the hunting park was abandoned sometime before 1500.
12　Tye Cottage
13　Priory Manor, later called Church Farm[1]
14　Probably the tenement called 'Tongs'
15　Rose Farm today, probably the original 'Rose Larks'

A　North Green, also known as Northward or Norwood Green
B　Bell Green, earlier called Little Haugh Green
C　Silverleys Green
D　Swan Green, or Goosestead Green
E　A green of which the early name is uncertain; in 1783 called Barrile Green, now the Spong

---

[1]　The fact that both the property and advowson were held together, as late as 1839, suggests that this land was the Priory Manor. Mill Farm was also part of the same holding.

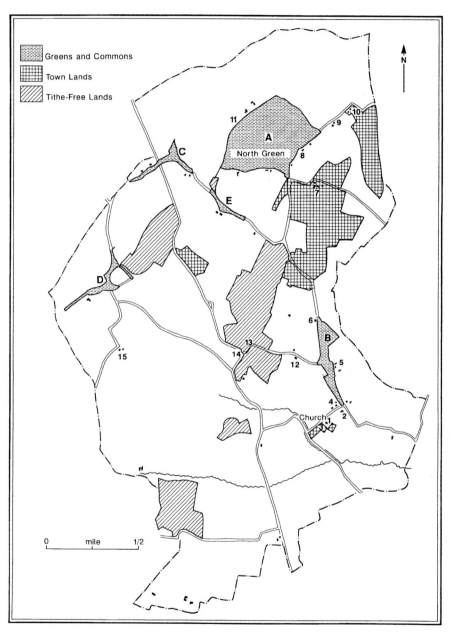

Map 1. Early Modern Cratfield
(based on the Tithe Map of 1839)

# Introduction

Viewed from the Roman road half a mile to the south, most of the modern village of Cratfield is hidden behind gently undulating fields and hedgerows. The medieval church tower, not surprisingly, dominates the view and marks the base of a 'T' which describes the pattern of village settlement. The supporting column of the 'T' is itself sparsely populated, and most of the village's buildings cluster at the top where several lanes join the former Bell Green.[2] Another larger green, North Green, lies further to the northwest, with Cratfield Hall standing beyond it. Scattered throughout the parish is a number of isolated farms, like the Hall and Rose Farm.[3] In fact, the general physical layout of Cratfield seems to have changed very little from the seventeenth century, when it had two to three hundred inhabitants (see p. xi, above).[4]

As the existence of a Roman road suggests, the area around Cratfield has been long cleared, settled and farmed. Its ancient past as a distinct community is implied in its Old English place-name, *Craetafelda*, under which Domesday Book in 1086 listed a church, two manors and 48 landholders.[5] More evidence comes from the regular, rectilinear and clearly planned layout of its fields which have been described as 'co-axial'. In other words, the principal axes of local fields run parallel to the Roman road, a fact which suggests that the whole system was planned in Roman times, or soon after.[6]

Not since Roman times has Cratfield been located directly on a major road or line of communication. Nonetheless, it lies between the rivers Blyth and Waveney, approximately five miles west of the market town of Halesworth, and just south of Christmas Lane, a significant sixteenth-century road. An anonymous seventeenth-century parliamentary scribe located Cratfield precisely but unhelpfully as 'a myle from Lynstead Magna and Huntingfield and a mile and a halfe from Ubbeston'.[7]

---

[2] Relatively isolated parish churches are a characteristic feature of eastern Suffolk and not necessarily a sign that the main site of the village has shifted. See N. Scarfe, *The Suffolk Landscape* (London, 1972), p. 177.

[3] J. Thirsk, 'East Anglia: Norfolk and Suffolk' in *The Agrarian History of England and Wales, IV: 1500–1640* (Cambridge, 1967), p. 46.

[4] For a full discussion of the calculation of Cratfield's population, see L. A. Botelho, 'Provisions for the Elderly in Two Early Modern Suffolk Communities', unpublished Ph.D. thesis (Cambridge University, 1995), pp. 118–23.

[5] A. Rumble, *Domesday Book: Suffolk*, 2 (1986), 33: 10.

[6] A. D. Mill, *A Dictionary of English Place-Names* (Oxford, 1991), p. 95; T. Williamson, 'Ancient Landscapes' in D. Dymond & E. Martin (eds), *An Historical Atlas of Suffolk* (Bury St Edmunds, 1988), p. 245. See also Williamson's 'Parish Boundaries and Early Fields: Continuity and Discontinuity', *Journal of Historical Geography*, 12 (1986), 241–48; and his 'Sites in the Landscape: Approaches to the Post-Roman Settlement of South Eastern England', *Archaeological Review from Cambridge*, 4 (1985), 51–64. At Yaxley, to the west of Cratfield, a major Roman road by contrast cuts at an angle across rectilinear fields. As a consequence it has been argued that Yaxley's fields are pre-Roman.

[7] D. MacCulloch, *Suffolk and the Tudors: Politics and Religion in an English County* (Cambridge, 1986), p. 14; Parliamentary Survey, 15 October 1650, Lambeth Palace Library MS, Comm. XIIa/15/520–22.

The early seventeenth-century commentator, Robert Ryece, described the region around Cratfield as having 'a naturall fatnes, and richnes in the soile; whereby each part is endowed most plentifully: for those parts inclining to the east [of Suffolk] having sufficient tillage, abound with all meadow and pasture by reason whereof their greatest commodities are raised by feeding and grasing'.[8] This, 'the Woodlande and High Suffolcke', was the largest and most significant region of Suffolk. Its heavy soils made it ideal for raising dairy cows.[9] An anonymous writer in about 1600 gave a similar picture:

> The nature of it [the soil] is divers as my selfe can testifye haveinge travayled in most parts of the same. That part of it which is called the Woodlande and High Suffolck is exceeding fruitfull comparable to any part of Englande for pasture for oxen and kine, not so good for sheepe ... The other parts westerlye of the contrye are very fruitfull also, but the woodland carryeth the chiefe creditt for goodnes of grounde.[10]

Farms in this area were mostly pasture and meadow, with relatively little arable land. Indeed, Ryece's impression was correct: most farmers concentrated on dairying and cheese making, forsaking the toil of the plough.[11] By the 1630s, the 'more enterprising farmers' of the Waveney valley grew carrots and turnips as cattle feed, in order to continue butter production over the winter months.[12] Even in the eighteenth century, according to Arthur Young, Cratfield remained at the heart of Suffolk's dairy region.[13] Dependency on any single market did have its drawbacks, as in the mid-1650s when 'the cheapness of comodityes and the hardness of times' proved too much for some who were given money by the churchwardens 'in regard of chepness of cheese and butter'.[14]

Cratfield, along with other established dairying parishes, had a long history of exporting vast quantities of cheese to London. According to Eric Kerridge, two types of cheese were produced in Suffolk at this time, a small cream cheese and a large hard cheese called 'bang'. The cream cheese was made from whole milk and had a reputation as 'excellent' table cheese. The large hard cheese was made from skimmed milk and was intended for poorer consumers. Kerridge tells us that contemporaries thought it 'so hard that pigs would grunt at it, dogs bark at it and none dare bite it'.[15] Contemporaries, in fact, were divided on this issue according, no doubt, to what they had

---

[8]  R. Ryece, *Suffolk in the XVIIth Century: The Breviary of Suffolk by Robert Reyce*, ed. Lord Francis Hervey (London, 1902), p. 26.

[9]  *The Chorography of Suffolk*, ed. D. MacCulloch (Suffolk Records Society, 19, 1976), p. 19.

[10] *Chorography*, pp. 19–20.

[11] There are four extant probate inventories, of which only one is of a person involved directly in agriculture: inventory of Robert Tallent, yeoman of Cratfield, 9 April 1702, SROI, FE1/4/117.

[12] Thirsk, 'East Anglia: Norfolk and Suffolk', p. 47.

[13] A. Young, *General View of the Agriculture of the County of Suffolk* (London, 1794), p. 38. For another 18th-century account of the county, see J. Kirby, *The Suffolk Traveller: or a Journey through Suffolk* (Ipswich, 1735). Defoe credits this part of Suffolk with being the first to employ such feeding techniques. D. Defoe, *A Tour thro' the Whole Island of Great Britain* (London, 1968), p. 58. See also B. A. Holderness, 'East Anglia and the Fens: Norfolk, Suffolk, Cambridgeshire, Ely, Huntingdonshire, Essex and the Lincolnshire Fens' in *The Agrarian History of England and Wales, V, I: 1640–1750* (Cambridge, 1984) pp. 231–4.

[14] Churchwardens' accounts of Cratfield (hereafter, CWA), SROI, FC62/A6/225, 235, 240 (1655, 1656, 1657–8).

[15] E. Kerridge, *The Agricultural Revolution* (London, 1967), p. 86.

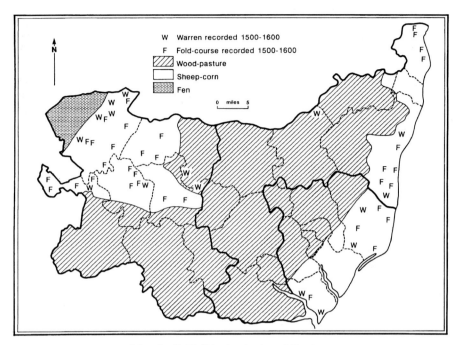

Map 2. Suffolk's Agricultural Regions
(based on D. MacCulloch, *Suffolk and the Tudors*, p. 17)

sampled. The chorographer described Suffolk cheese as of 'wonderfull goodness, comparable to any in the realme', while Defoe attacked it as 'perhaps the worst cheese in England'.[16] In 1735 the surveyor John Kirby echoed both the sixteenth-century chorographer of Suffolk and Daniel Defoe, when he claimed pride of place for Suffolk's cheeses as either the best or the worst in the country. He wrote, 'the cheese, if right made, none much better, and if not so, none can be worse'.[17]

Regardless of their relative merits, the butter and cheese of High Suffolk were two of the most important and widely marketed agricultural products of seventeenth- and eighteenth-century East Anglia. B. A. Holderness illustrates East Anglia's significant role as an exporter in terms of London's consumption:

London in 1730 apparently consumed 56,703 firkins of Suffolk and 74,918 firkins of Cambridge butter (3,029 tons), and 985 tons of Suffolk cheese. With the production of Essex and the northern fenland, East Anglia probably supplied about one-third of the capital's dairy produce in the early eighteenth century.[18]

[16] *Chorography,* p. 19; Defoe, *A Tour,* p. 53.
[17] Kirby, *Suffolk Traveller,* p. 2.
[18] Holderness, 'East Anglia and the Fens', pp. 231–2.

The importance of market-orientated agriculture grew throughout the period, and with it Cratfield's connection with the wider world of London and beyond.

Pig-keeping was often a lucrative side-line, so much so that it gave rise to the regional expression that the pig was 'tied to the cow's tail'.[19] Pigs, fed on skimmed-milk and pulse crops, provided bacon for the navy, the merchant fleet and the city of London.[20] Cratfield, however, seems not to have pursued this economic opportunity as aggressively as many other parts of the region. Wills and probate inventories reveal only small numbers of pigs. So great was the concentration upon dairying that in times of scarcity, grain was imported into the region from elsewhere in Suffolk and Norfolk. Cratfield, for example, purchased 'corn' on a number of occasions in the seventeenth century: ten bushels in September 1623; £7 16s. worth for the poor in 1630; 'wheate which was sould out to the pore' in 1631; and an unknown amount for the 'por pepell' in 1696.[21]

At first glance Cratfield seems surrounded by enclosed fields, a good number of cows, and a few pigs, seemingly isolated from other places by its 'narrow and fowle lanes'.[22] However, such an impression would be quite misleading. Cratfield was linked economically with the neighbouring parish of Laxfield and its local Saturday market, and with the much larger towns of Halesworth on the river Blyth and Beccles on the Waveney.[23] Boats and barges travelled the rivers and North Sea, connecting villages to regional markets, and provincial centres to London. Roads, too, ran along Suffolk's valleys and across its clay plateaux, expanding the corridors of communication into areas without navigable streams. However, the condition of Suffolk's roads was not always the most pleasant, prompting Ryece's cynical remark that the very 'impassablenesse' of Suffolk's country lanes might serve as a deterrent to any invading force, or to at least have given them 'just cause to repent their rashness'.[24]

The notion that early modern Cratfield possessed a healthy economy is confirmed in its records. The village possessed a guildhall, townhouse, schoolhouse, almshouse and bakehouse, all of which were maintained regularly and at the parish's expense.[25] In addition, the parish's frequent contribution to other villages and towns overcome by poverty or destroyed by fire speaks strongly of the overall wealth of the community and its relatively high level of disposable income. Cratfield contributed towards the relief of Blythburgh's poor on many occasions, including twice in 1599, once in 1602, and twice in 1603. Likewise the poor of Walberswick were assisted annually between 1631 and 1633, as well as in 1636. Lowestoft and Bungay received help at

---

[19] As quoted in Kerridge, *Agricultural Revolution*, p. 86.

[20] Holderness, 'East Anglia and the Fens', p. 233; Thirsk, 'East Anglia: Norfolk and Suffolk', p. 47.

[21] Thirsk, 'East Anglia: Norfolk and Suffolk', p. 47. Cratfield CWA, SROI, FC62/A6/147, 156, 159, 161, 361 (1623, 1630, 1631, 1696).

[22] Ryece, *Breviary*, p. 14.

[23] The Laxfield market was granted by royal charter in 1226 and was still in use during the seventeenth century: N. Scarfe, 'Medieval and Later Markets' in *An Historical Atlas of Suffolk*, p. 61.

[24] Thirsk, 'East Anglia: Norfolk and Suffolk', pp. 40–1; Ryece, *Breviary*, p. 14.

[25] The guild was dedicated to Saint Thomas the Martyr. Maintenance payments, for the guildhall and other structures, are scattered through the churchwardens' accounts; see Cratfield CWA, SROI, FC/A6/1–363. For parish property, see K. Farnhill, 'Religious Policy and Parish "Conformity": Cratfield's Lands in the Sixteenth Century' in K. L. French, G. C. Gibbs and B. A. Kümin (eds), *The Parish in English Life, 1400–1600* (Manchester UP, 1997), pp. 217–29.

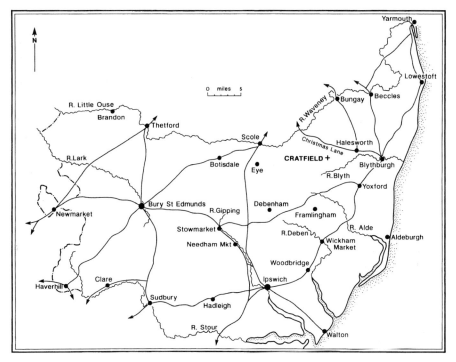

Map 3. Suffolk's Roads and Waterways
(based on D. MacCulloch, *Suffolk and the Tudors*, p. 14)

least once in 1636 and 1665, respectively.[26] Other examples of Cratfield's financial generosity include 2s. to help repair the hospital in Norwich in 1616, and a seemingly endless number of briefs for damage caused by fire, including those at Dorchester, 1614; Brundish, 1656; Bury St Edmunds, 1652; Glasgow, 1655; Hengrave, 1656; Peterborough, 1656; Saffron Walden, 1656; and a massive £10 to Southwold in 1659.[27] As the work of Robert Herlan (on Bristol and London) and of Valerie Pearl (on London) has shown, rates-in-aid were the sign of a prosperous parish.[28]

More significant and informative than these examples was the wide range of occupations and social status found within the parish. Its pastoral economy enabled Cratfield's inhabitants to pursue more than one trade at a time, and the local economy

[26] Cratfield CWA, SROI, FC62/A6/101–02, 107, 109, 111, 157, 159, 166, 169, 171, 275 (1599, 1602–03, 1630–1, 1634–6, 1665–6). See also a payment 'for relieving the inhabitants of the City of Lincoln who were much impoverished by the plague': W. Holland, *Cratfield: A Transcript of the Accounts of the Parish, from A.D. 1490 to A. D. 1642, with Notes*, ed. J. J. Raven (London, 1895), p. 167.

[27] Holland and Raven, *Cratfield*, p. 144; Cratfield CWA, SROI, FC62/A6/137, 210, 215, 239, 246, (1616, 1651–2, 1657, 1659).

[28] R. W. Herlan, 'Poor Relief in London during the English Revolution', *Journal of British Studies*, 18 (1979), pp. 37–9, 45; his 'Relief of the Poor in Bristol from Late Elizabethan Times to the Restoration Era', *Proceedings of the American Philosophical Society*, 126 (1982), pp. 223, 226; V. Pearl, 'Social Policy in Early Modern London' in H. Lloyd-Jones, V. Pearl and B. Worden (eds), *History and Imagination; Essays in Honour of H. R. Trevor-Roper* (London, 1981), p. 125.

became more diversified than the size of its population might initially suggest. Over the course of the sixteenth and seventeenth centuries, 192 individuals for whom either an occupation or status is known, represented 39 distinct social and occupational designations.[29] John Patten's work on Babergh Hundred provides a useful comparison. Using his criteria, one can see that Cratfield, with its high number of occupations of different types, was indeed a thriving and prosperous community, comparable to Boxford or Stoke-by-Nayland in the southern part of the county.[30] Ranging from woollen-draper to wheelwright, from baker to bricklayer, such occupations indicate a healthy economy, one which was stable and successful.

*Table 1. Status and Occupations in Cratfield, 1550–1700*

| Status/ occupation | Number of individuals | Status/ occupation | Number of individuals |
| --- | --- | --- | --- |
| Yeoman | 36 | Esquire | 2 |
| Gentleman | 28 | Mason | 2 |
| Tailor | 12 | Ironsmith | 2 |
| Goodman | 9 | Sawyer | 2 |
| Servant | 9 | Shoemaker | 2 |
| Master | 8 | Wheelwright | 2 |
| Carpenter | 7 | Armourer | 1 |
| Clerk | 7 | Baker | 1 |
| Schoolmaster | 7 | Bellfounder | 1 |
| Soldier | 7 | Captain | 1 |
| Butcher | 6 | Chaplain | 1 |
| Thatcher | 6 | Clock Keeper | 1 |
| Vicar | 5 | Linen Weaver | 1 |
| Husbandman | 4 | Oatmeal Maker | 1 |
| Bricklayer | 3 | 'Physicke' | 1 |
| Glazier | 3 | Singleman | 1 |
| Mister | 3 | Smith | 1 |
| Poor | 3 | Tanner | 1 |
| Preacher | 3 | Turner | 1 |
|  |  | Woollen Draper | 1 |

While obviously economically active, Cratfield was also outward-looking and functioned religiously and socially within a wider region. This was true both after the Reformation and before. For example, in 1509 Harry Francysse left not only a bequest of 6s.8d. for masses to be said at the high altar of Cratfield, but also gave a similar amount to Linstead Magna and bequeathed 3s.4d. to the churches at Linstead Parva, Cookley, Laxfield, Fressingfield, Ubbeston, Metfield and Chediston.[31] He, and others like him, obviously belonged to social and economic networks which embraced

---

[29] The occupations, status and titles of Cratfield people were collected from a wide range of documents: churchwardens' accounts (the most useful), overseers' accounts, town book, wills, deeds, grants, quit-claims, parish registers, ship-money payments, apprentice indentures, probate inventories, subsidy and hearth tax returns.

[30] J. Patten, 'Village and Town: An Occupational Study', *Agricultural History Review*, 20 (1972), p. 9.

[31] Will of Harry Francysse of Cratfield, 1509, SROI, IC/AA1/2/7/11.

6

many villages and towns: their lives were certainly not circumscribed by the parish boundary.

Membership of a wider community could be particularly helpful in moments of local tension as when, one night in 1650, a desperate mother abandoned her child in the church porch. The area immediately surrounding Cratfield responded promptly, with 'word of the woman which left the child in our church porch'.[32] A warrant was issued and a local man was sent 'to seek after the woman, and to find her'.[33] At this point the narrative becomes somewhat unclear. At first it appears that a woman, with other small children, was found and that the matter was concluded. We subsequently learn that it was not. Two years later, in 1652, the hue and cry was again called, and again the wider community responded to Cratfield's plea: a 'messanger . . . brought the towne word of a woman taken with the hue and crye uppon susspition to be the woman that left hir child in our towne'.[34] John Stannard was dispatched to Wood-bridge to retrieve her, and meanwhile Thomas Johnson's wife was paid to look after the infant. Finally, the parish paid a stranger 11s. to take the child off their hands.[35] Meanwhile, John Williams was sent to Bungay, once again in pursuit of this errant mother.[36] He was unsuccessful, but in the following year a beggar arrived with 'the woman that was taken uppon suspicion for leaveing hir child in towne'.[37]

The accounts, unfortunately, remain silent as to the ultimate fate of either mother or child. This example, however, while highlighting the desperate circumstances of the poor and the equally desperate bid of the community to avoid an awkward problem, also illustrates the functioning of the wider community and Cratfield's place within a regional network. Cratfield's neighbours, even those as far afield as Wood-bridge, were called upon to assist, and indeed they responded with goodwill to what was essentially a local problem.

By the early modern period, the community of Cratfield was no longer under the strong control of manors and manorial lords. The two relevant courts functioned only as *de facto* land registries, and by-laws passed in those courts were now less burden-some to local people.[38] By contrast, it is the town accounts which clearly reveal the actual administration of the parish, and confirm that the community governed itself through its vestry and under the leadership of its chief inhabitants.[39]

Joan Thirsk reached the same conclusion through different means. 'Like other pastoral, dairying regions of the kingdom', she explains, 'this was a thickly populated countryside of family farmers. The manor was a weak institution of little significance in ordering the lives of the inhabitants'.[40] She continues by explaining that in wood-pasture areas wealth was more evenly distributed, that social groups were less sharply defined, and that most people were better off than their counterparts in sheep-corn regions.[41] Likewise, the *Chorography* records 'very many yeomen of

---

[32] Cratfield CWA, SROI, FC62/A6/204 (1650).
[33] Cratfield CWA, SROI, FC62/A6/204 (1650).
[34] Cratfield CWA, SROI, FC62/A6/215 (1652).
[35] Cratfield CWA, SROI, FC62/A6/215 (1652).
[36] Cratfield CWA, SROI, FC62/A6/215 (1652).
[37] Cratfield CWA, SROI, FC62/A6/217 (1653).
[38] Cratfield manorial records, CUL Vanneck MSS.
[39] See Appendix 2, pp. 145–7.
[40] Thirsk, 'East Anglia: Norfolk and Suffolk', pp. 48–9; MacCulloch, *Suffolk and the Tudors*, p. 28.
[41] Thirsk, 'East Anglia: Norfolk and Suffolk', pp. 48–9.

good credit and great liberalitie, [and] good housekeepers' in High Suffolk.[42] Cratfield epitomises the descriptions of both the chorographer and Thirsk.

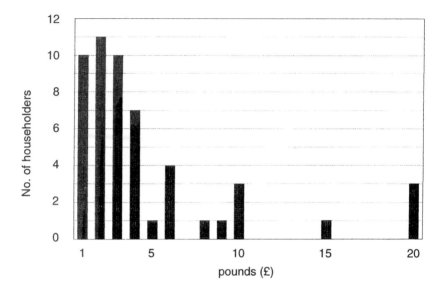

*Graph 1. Lay Subsidy of Cratfield, 1524*

As Thirsk predicted, its wealth was fairly equally distributed amongst those living in the village. Of those listed in the 1524 subsidy, most inhabitants were assessed at £10 or less, with the majority clustered between £2 and £4.[43] At first sight, and using Julian Cornwall's guidelines, Cratfield in 1524 seems more solidly populated by husbandmen than yeomen. However, in those wills which mention status we find thirty-three yeoman and only four husbandmen. One possible explanation is that in High Suffolk smallholding could be very profitable and thus support a greater number of yeomen on relatively smaller acreages. Cratfield may well be an example of this, but in the final analysis its farmers fell squarely within the yeoman/husbandman bracket. In the second half of the seventeenth century, Cratfield was still a prosperous parish for the Hearth Tax of 1674 shows the majority of its inhabitants possessing between two and four hearths.[44] Only two individuals resided in large dwellings,

---

[42] *Chorography*, p. 19.

[43] *Suffolk in 1524, Being the Return of a Subsidy Granted in 1523* (Suffolk Green Books, No. 10, Woodbridge, 1910), pp. 80–1.

[44] J. Cornwall, *Wealth and Society in Early Sixteenth Century England* (London, 1988), pp. 16–17. For average number of acres per taxpayer, see H. Todd and D. Dymond, 'Population Densities, 1377 and 1524' in *An Historical Atlas of Suffolk* (1988), p. 67. The large number of smallholdings also indicates long-established settlement where land had been repeatedly subdivided: see T. Williamson, 'Ancient Landscapes', p. 40.

Robert Meene with twelve hearths and John Fiske with ten. The rest of the community's wealth remained fairly evenly distributed.[45]

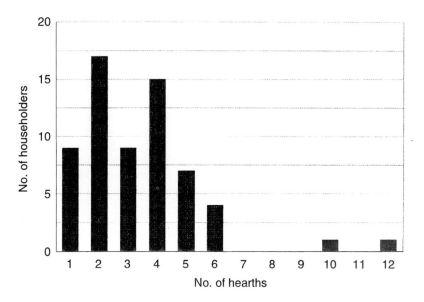

*Graph 2. Hearth Tax of Cratfield, 1674*

Yet despite this relative wealth and comfort, Cratfield could not escape the all-pervasive problem of early modern England: poverty at the bottom of the social scale. The sixteenth century witnessed an explosion in the number of poor people when factors such as population pressure, inflation, declining charity and the emergence of a cash economy combined to create conditions of uncertainty, insecurity and outright destitution. Many of these factors applied throughout the seventeenth century, when a 'new' category of impoverished people emerged, the labouring poor. These were relatively young families who were not only willing to work, and thus clearly not part of the unworthy poor, but whose heads were in fact working and still not able to maintain themselves or their dependants. Cratfield's thriving economy sheltered its weaker members from the worst effects of the early modern economic world, but by the closing years of the seventeenth century 11 per cent of its total population was considered poor and collecting parish relief. Another 15 per cent were marginally poor, surviving by makeshift strategies on the very edge of self-sufficiency and collecting occasional gifts from the parish. 'These [people]', according to contemporary opinion, 'are such (though they beg not) as are not able to abide the storme of one fortnights sickness but would be thereby driven to beggary'.[46] When in need, the poor turned to the rest of the population for practical help.

[45] *Suffolk in 1674, Being the Hearth Tax Returns* (Suffolk Green Books, No. 11, Vol. 13. Woodbridge, 1905), p. 85.
[46] As quoted in J. Pound, *Poverty and Vagrancy in Tudor England* (London, 1971), p. 93.

The evolution and eventual form of the Tudor and Stuart poor laws, and the role of the overseers of the poor, have long been subjects of historical discussion. The fundamental framework of the poor laws was established in 1601 by parliamentary statute. Simply stated, the worthy poor were to be housed and provided with a weekly pension; poor children and bastards were to be apprenticed; the labouring poor were to be given work; and the wilfully idle, those who according to common perception 'lick the sweat from the true labourers' brows', were to be punished and forcibly employed.[47] The entire structure of welfare and relief was to be underwritten by a weekly rate and managed by especially appointed officers called overseers of the poor.

Before statutory relief had been established, however, the parish and individual parishioners had already cared for the needy. Religious anniversaries, chantries, fraternities and other such endowments typically had subsidiary gifts to the poor attached to their foundation. As part of such religious bequests churchwardens were often named as executors of wills, but if not, responsibility generally fell into their hands nonetheless, as managers of the parochial purse. The tradition of giving bequests to the poor continued long after the Reformation, and certainly throughout the seventeenth century. The customary role of the churchwarden as distributor of aid continued as well, long after the separate office of overseers had been created. The accounts printed in this volume provide an exceptional view of the full range of non-pensioned assistance, while in some years they even list those given a parish pension (also known as the 'collection') with the amounts received.

During the seventeenth century, four general categories of assistance were available in Cratfield, all of which were recorded in the churchwardens' accounts: pensions (albeit incompletely), rents, firewood and medical treatment. The first decade of the printed accounts (1640–50) was a very difficult period for Cratfield, because 'of the cheapess of comodtyes and the hardness of the tymes'.[48] The number of full-time pensioners rose sharply in 1650 to eleven, then dropped precipitously for a few years, before rising sharply again. Under normal conditions roughly 50 per cent of Cratfield's poor relief took the form of weekly pensions, but in the 1650s the figure rose to 82 per cent. Significantly, the 1650s were a time of high mortality in the parish, with burials exceeding baptisms from 1654 onwards. Disease was probably responsible for both Cratfield's high mortality and extensive poor relief. Small pox struck East Anglia forcefully in the late 1640s and early 1650s, prompting the Essex clergyman Ralph Josselin to call it a 'wonderful sickly time'.[49] Ague or intermitting fever ravaged the south-east of England in the autumn of 1657, and a series of influenza epidemics followed at the end of the decade.[50] While the churchwardens clearly provided their traditional assistance during these years, the bulk of parochial relief was directed into weekly pensions and towards the very weakest members of the community. The 1660s, however, witnessed a return to more typical spending patterns

---

[47] As quoted in A. L. Beier, 'Vagrants and the Social Order in Elizabethan England', *Past and Present*, 64 (1974), p. 10.

[48] Cratfield CWA, SROI, FC62/A6/240 (1656).

[49] A. Macfarlane (ed.), *The Diary of Ralph Josselin, 1616–1683*, Records of Social and Economic History, New Series iii (London, 1976), pp. 116, 284.

[50] M. Dobson, *A Chronology of Epidemic Disease and Mortality in Southeast England, 1601–1800* (Historical Geography Research Series, 19, London, 1987), pp. 53–4.

with roughly one-half devoted to pensions and the remainder used for miscellaneous *ad hoc* relief.

The churchwardens' accounts also offer an extended view of the wandering poor, those who moved from place to place in search of work and food. The idle poor and vagrants, those travelling without a pass, were whipped and moved on, presumably to their home parish. Those travelling under a certificate were given food and a place to sleep for a single night, before they too were removed – lest they linger and become a permanent drain upon the parish purse. Poverty was a problem in Cratfield, just as it was everywhere in seventeenth-century England, yet the stability of the local economy and the organised response of the chief inhabitants meant that even in the troubled years of the 1650s the poor of their parish did not starve.

The Reformation in Cratfield was not a long and reluctant affair as it was in other parts of England, most notably in the north and west. The parish certainly seems to have accepted protestantism willingly, but it is difficult to agree with A. E. Nichols that 'Cratfield was radicalized early, wholeheartedly supported Edwardian reforms, and consistently strained at the leash of Elizabethan moderation'.[51] It was eager for reform, most certainly, but was not consistently straining against the established church. Its accounts reveal that, under the spiritual direction of the vicars Eland, father and son, Cratfield was sometimes ahead of official policy, and sometimes behind it. It welcomed protestantism, but the pace of that acceptance generally stayed within the bounds of religious conformity.

The spiritual leadership of incumbents such as Robert Thurkettle (1533–1548), John Page (1556–1561) and Thomas Plumpton (1561–1566) ensured that the parish conformed promptly to changes of religion in the mid-sixteenth century. Recent historians of the sixteenth century have turned to churchwardens' accounts as a way of understanding the theological stance of lay people and parochial responses to the Reformation. While Cratfield's accounts reveal little about parish life in the 1540s and 1550s, they re-appear in the 1560s with a thoroughness which becomes typical, and show a timely compliance in matters liturgical.[52] In fact, they intriguingly reveal the religious convictions of its inhabitants. They also serve as an excellent example of how such accounts may be used to examine one of the most pressing questions of the sixteenth century, the reception of protestantism in the localities.

Some historians, most notably David Underdown, have maintained that the contestants in the English Civil War were divided primarily along religious and cultural lines. While this interpretation has been seriously challenged, the role of religion in the early modern world was fundamental and Cratfield's religious path must be traced in some detail if we are to understand the community that produced the printed accounts which follow.[53]

---

[51] A. E. Nichols, 'Broken Up or Restored Away: Iconoclasm in a Suffolk Parish', in C. Davidson and A. E. Nichols (eds), *Iconoclasm vs. Art and Drama* (Early Drama, Art, and Music Monograph, no. 11, London, 1989), p. 165.

[52] See John Craig's work on religious change at parish level, also based on churchwardens' accounts from Suffolk. For example, 'Co-operation and Initiatives: Elizabethan Churchwardens and the Parish Accounts of Mildenhall', *Social History*, 18 (1993), 357–80. Compare D. M. Palliser, 'Popular Reactions to the Reformation during the Years of Uncertainty, 1530–70' in *The English Reformation Revised*, ed. C. Haigh (1987, reprint Cambridge, 1988), pp. 94–113.

[53] D. Underdown, *Revel, Riot and Rebellion: Popular Politics and Culture in England 1603–60* (Oxford, 1985). See also J. Morrill's critical analysis, 'The Ecology of Allegiance in the English Revolution', *Journal of British Studies*, 26 (1987), 451–67; and Underdown's reply in the same volume, pp. 467–79.

As has been said, the 1560s mark the return to detailed record-keeping by Cratfield's churchwardens. We see that the rood-loft was quickly taken down in response to the injunctions of Bishop Parkhurst of Norwich in May 1561 and to the Royal Order of October in the same year.[54] Lime and sand were brought into the church as part of general maintenance, which also included 'sowdynge of the church' and 'glassyn the churche windowes', prompted by the visitation articles of 1563.[55] Bishop Parkhurst's reputation as the slackest of disciplinarians accounts for what might otherwise look like a slow response to the new emphasis on the pulpit.[56] Only in 1566 did the churchwardens provide a pulpit, paying workers 'for helpeing downe the polpet and to sette it up'.[57] Underlining the parish's acceptance of the ministry of the Word, and Parkhurst's earlier laxness, was the prompt construction in 1569 of 'a decent and convenient seat in the body of the church, where the said minister may sit or stand, and say the Divine Service, that all the congregation may hear and be edified therewith'.[58]

After 1566 when Francis Eland arrived as vicar, Cratfield became markedly more protestant.[59] Except in a few isolated instances, however, it still did not persistently overstep the limits of official religion. One moment of undeniable transgression was Eland's removal of the elaborate 'seven sacrament' font in 1569. This action was in direct defiance of the Ecclesiastical Commission of 1561 which ordered 'that the font be not removed from the accustomed place, and that in parish churches the curates take not upon them to confer baptism in basins, but in the font customably used'.[60] Later, probably after 1660, the font was returned to its original place, but in a heavily defaced condition.[61] The reappearance of the font may reflect a personal compromise between the wishes of the Elands and those of the crown.

Francis Eland's commitment to reformed religion was demonstrated in 1583 when the church's wall paintings were whitewashed over and scriptural texts put up in their stead. An hour-glass was purchased in 1590, reflecting the importance of sermons by both Eland and visiting preachers, like 'the Scoote that preched hear' in 1599.[62] Nevertheless, preaching the word of God and timed sermons, while often characterised as a true sign of radical protestantism, were not, in fact, the sole preserve of puritans. As Diarmaid MacCulloch has convincingly shown, they were certainly well within the bounds of Elizabethan conformity.[63]

Still, Ann Nichols viewed the parish as radically protestant. In her article on iconoclasm in Cratfield, she asserts that the chalice was 'remade' into a communion cup as early as 1547, drawing her evidence from a printed nineteenth-century edition of the churchwardens' accounts. In the 1540s the use of the term 'communion cup' rather

---

[54] Cratfield CWA, SROI, FC62/A6/36 (1561); *Injunctions Exhibited by John, by Gods Sufferance Bishop of Norwich, in his First Visitation beginning the seconde daie of Maye in the thirde yeare of our Soveraign Ladie Elizabeth* (London, 1561); *Orders Taken the X Day of October for Rood Loftes* (London, ?1561).
[55] *Archbishop Parker's Diocesan Articles* (1563); Cratfield CWA, SROI, FC62/A6/43 (1565).
[56] J. Strype, *The Life and Acts of Matthew Parker*, Vol. I, (Oxford, 1821), pp. 289–90.
[57] *The Royal Articles of Queen Elizabeth* (1559); *Parker's Articles for Norwich Diocese* (1567); Cratfield CWA, SROI, FC62/A6/45 (1566).
[58] *Parkhurst's Injunctions for Norwich Diocese*, (1569); Cratfield CWA, SROI, FC62/A6/50 (1569).
[59] Francis Eland served as vicar from 1566 to 1602. His son Gabriel replaced him in 1602 and remained minister until he died in 1652.
[60] As cited in Nichols, 'Broken Up or Restored Away', p. 177.
[61] A pewter basin was still being used for baptisms in 1651. Cratfield, CWA, SROI, FC62/A6/211 (1651).
[62] Cratfield CWA, SROI, FC62/A6/103 (1599).
[63] D. MacCulloch, *The Later Reformation in England, 1547–1603* (Basingstoke, 1990), pp. 59, 70–77.

than 'chalice' would have been highly significant, representing a hotter protestant attitude to the Eucharist. Cratfield's actions in 1547 would therefore have been in anticipation of official policy. Yet, the actual churchwarden's entry reads, 'for makyng of the chalys'. In other words, a vessel was made which was large enough to administer wine to the whole congregation, who previously had received only bread at the Mass. The retention of the word 'chalice', however, indicates a very different and less precociously reformist position from that argued by Nichols.[64] While her general outline of religious life in Cratfield is correct, Nichols is perhaps guilty of searching for puritans in the archives and consequently overstates the degree of radical protestantism.[65]

The succession of Gabriel Eland (1602–1652), Francis's son, continued and furthered the commitment to a preaching ministry. Only in 1606 when the parish was fined at Blythborough for lacking the required book of homilies, do we learn that the reading of printed homilies had been replaced by preaching.[66] Furthermore, the churchwardens only installed communion rails *after* an archidiaconal visitation in 1636, prompted no doubt by Matthew Wren's installation as bishop of Norwich in the same year.[67] Suffolk, in general, resisted the implementation of Laudian Reforms, as Wren complained to Archbishop Laud.[68] Preaching continued during Gabriel's tenure, as it had under his father, and the pulpit and reading desk no longer suffered from neglect.[69] Sporadically, from the 1620s onwards, a succession of different preachers visited Cratfield – such as the 'blynd man wich preached here' in 1644.[70]

Between 1642 and 1651, however, the inhabitants of Cratfield had the opportunity of hearing a regular, probably weekly, sermon or 'lecture' delivered by Mr Thomas Crosby, a local minister and Cambridge graduate.[71] He received £20 a year for his labours, and the parish sexton, Rubin Tallent, was at the same time paid 17s.4d. 'for ringing the lecture bell'. After Crosby, Thomas Spatchet seems to have taken over as official lecturer. Unfortunately, nothing is known of the establishment and funding of this particular event, but it must be seen as part of a national movement which, in the period 1560 to 1660, gave conspicuous evidence of the

---

[64] It is unfortunate that Nichols has relied upon this printed source, as William Holland's nineteenth-century edition is riddled with errors.

[65] Nichols, 'Broken Up or Restored Away', p. 173, and fn. 33. See also E. Duffy, *The Stripping of the Altars: Traditional Religion in England 1400–1580* (New Haven, 1992), p. 569. Cratfield CWA, SROI, FC62/A6/13 (*c.* 1547); Nichols, 'Broken Up or Restored Away', p. 173; Holland and Raven, *Cratfield*, p. 73.

[66] This book was originally purchased in 1563. Cratfield CWA, SROI, FC62/A6/40 (1563).

[67] Cratfield CWA, SROI, FC62/A6/171 (1636); *Articles to be Enquired on in the Ordinary Visitation of the Right Worshipful Master Doctor Pearson, Archdeacon of Suffolk* (London, 1636). Wren was a noted lieutenant of Laud and, after the Archbishop's impeachment, was imprisoned in the Tower of London between 1642 and 1660: *The Concise Dictionary of National Biography*, Part I (Oxford, 1983), p. 1440 and J. Spurr, *The Restoration Church of England, 1646–1689* (New Haven, 1991), p. 160. For a more theoretical approach to Laudian worship and the Beauty of Holiness, see P. Lake, 'The Laudian Style: Order, Uniformity and the Pursuit of the Beauty of Holiness in the 1630s' in K. Fincham (ed.), *The Early Stuart Church, 1603–1642* (Basingstoke, 1993), pp. 161–85.

[68] C. Holmes, *The Eastern Association in the English Civil War* (Cambridge, 1975), p. 18.

[69] Cratfield CWA, SROI, FC62/A6/316, 317 (1674, 1675).

[70] Cratfield CWA, SROI, FC62/A6/215–275, 185 (1652–1667, 1644).

[71] Crosby was mentioned by name in all years, except 1648 and 1649 when Tallent continued to be paid for ringing the bell. It is highly likely that Crosby was paid in those two years, but that no record survives. See SROI, FC62/A6/181, 183, 185, 186, 192, 193, 197, 200, 203, and Biographies, pp. 132, 143.

protestant laity's determination to secure 'a godly, "painful", preaching ministry'.[72] Essentially, a local lecturership gave parishioners the opportunity of hearing regular preaching of the word of God, over and above the legally required minimum of quarterly or monthly sermons. In the words of Paul Seaver, 'not all lecturers were puritan nor all puritans lecturers, but there can be no question that the lecturership was essentially a puritan institution, that the impetus behind it was puritan in motivation, and that it was staffed predominantly by puritan preachers.'[73]

Like many English people in the sixteenth and seventeenth centuries, however, not all inhabitants of Cratfield were happy with the religious state of their parish. The first sign of a division between Francis Eland and a small number of parishioners occurred in 1584 when William Stubberb was fined 12d. for 'wearinge off his cappe' in church, a public and unmistakable sign of protest.[74] In the following year, Francis was fined 2s. for *not* wearing his cap, in clear violation of the Royal Injunctions of 1559 requiring the clergy to 'use and wear such seemly habits, garments, and such square caps'.[75] All appeared calm until 1592 when Eland was again ordered to pay a fine to the 'quenes balley for not wearing of capes'.[76] Eland managed to walk a fine line between conformity and religious insubordination without slipping completely into radical and prolonged disobedience. While he may not have worn his cap as directed by royal injunction, he did wear his surplice weekly, which was arguably a greater symbol of conformity.[77] Too religiously hot for some, Eland may have been a moderating influence on a number of his parishioners. George Milles was excommunicated in 1597 'because he will not resorte to church to devine service because the Booke of Common Prayer is there used', which demonstrates that the parish, at least in one man's mind, had not gone far enough with its godly reforms.[78] Religious division in the parish finally seems to have settled into a workable truce, or even agreement, as nothing further comes to light throughout the period. Even so, that was not the last time when Eland was at odds with a parishioner. Edmund Broadbank, churchwarden, accused Gabriel Eland of unlawfully cutting the tops off certain trees on the west side of the church 'to which he had no right'. On 30 April 1627, Eland formally admitted his fault in a signed and witnessed statement, and Henry Fiske paid his fellow churchwarden Edmund Broadbank 20s. 'to end the controversy between Mr Eland and himselfe by the consent of townes men'.[79]

The accounts printed in this volume give additional insights into the religious complexion of the parish. When the timing and expenses of Holy Communion are

---

[72] P. S. Seaver, *The Puritan Lecturerships: The Politics of Religious Dissent, 1560–1662* (Stanford, CA, 1970), p. 54.

[73] Seaver, *ibid.*, p. 22.

[74] Cratfield CWA, SROI, FC62/A6/71 (1584). See K. Wrightson, 'The Politics of the Parish in Early Modern England' in P. Griffiths, A. Fox, and S. Hindle (eds), *The Experience of Authority in Early Modern England* (Basingstoke, 1996), p. 29 for the wearing of caps as a specific form of protest against the Laudian reforms of the 1630s and 1640s.

[75] Cratfield CWA, SROI, FC62/A6/72 (1585); *The Royal Injunctions of Queen Elizabeth* (1559).

[76] Cratfield CWA, SROI, FC62/A6/89 (1592).

[77] For a sampling of evidence regarding the wearing of the surplice, see Cratfield CWA, SROI, FC62/A6/69,104 (1583, 1599).

[78] J. F. Williams (ed.), *Diocese of Norwich, Bishop Redman's Visitation, 1597: Presentments in the Archdeaconries of Norwich, Norfolk, and Suffolk* (Norfolk Record Society, 18, 1946), p. 128. For a discussion of the relationship between puritans and the *Book of Common Prayer*, see Patrick Collinson, *The Elizabethan Puritan Movement* (Oxford, 1967), pp. 356–9.

[79] SROI, FC62/G1/5 dated 30 Apr. 1627; Cratfield CWA, SROI, FC62/A6/153 (1627).

analysed, one can see that the leading men of Cratfield were generally in agreement with the religious directives issued by a puritan parliament. Yet they too found comfort in aspects of the earlier communion practice, or at least were willing to tolerate certain older forms of worship in an effort to maintain unity within the community.

John Morrill's work on the taking of the sacrament during the Civil War period shows that before 1642 most parishes held communion on a quarterly basis, including the three great feasts of Easter, Whitsun and Christmas.[80] Cratfield adhered to that pattern. Morrill further determined that, despite the ban in 1646, most parishes continued to offer quarterly communion between 1646 and 1650.[81] In other words, 'these ordinances were not only largely ignored but actively resisted'.[82] Cratfield, however, responded promptly to parliament's order, and communion was offered only once a year from 1646 to 1650. Unlike many parishes, Cratfield was not a centre of 'Anglican survivalism'.[83]

Another way in which these accounts illustrate the religious climate of the parish is through their record of the sums spent on bread and wine for communion. Again, Cratfield seems to keep closer to parliament's views than to those of most other parishes in the realm. In 1645, parliament sought to restrict access to communion, allowing only those with adequate knowledge and proper decorum to receive the sacrament. Nevertheless, most parishes continued to offer 'open communion', by accepting all parishioners at the Lord's Table.[84] Judging from the sums of money involved, Cratfield may well have begun to practice restricted communion in 1646, as the amount spent on a single communion dropped from roughly 5s. to just over 1s. It seems clear that significantly fewer people were receiving communion after parliament's directive of 1645. Cratfield's response was very similar to that of Ralph Josselin in Essex, who held no communion services whatsoever for a number of years, and then resumed the sacrament at a greatly reduced level.

In practice parishes did not meekly accept religious instruction, whether Laudian or puritan, without altering its practice to some degree. Despite the fact that communions at Christmas, Easter and Whitsun were declared illegal from 1644 to 1660, and despite Cratfield's speedy response to other aspects of parliament's order, the parish continued to celebrate Easter communion throughout most, if not all, of its proscribed period, as well as at least one Christmas communion in 1650.[85]

Determining the religious stance of a community is obviously complicated and difficult. Evidence for what looks like one specific theological position is offset by what appears to be evidence for the contrary, even in the same document. The difficulty of the historian's task is compounded by the passage of time; significant information may not have survived, or has not been discovered. Furthermore, the real possibility exists that historians may not fully understand the cultural 'code' of early

---

[80] J. S. Morrill, 'The Church in England, 1642–9' in J. S. Morrill (ed.), *Reactions to the English Civil War, 1642–49* (London, 1982), p. 105.
[81] Morrill, *ibid.*, p. 105.
[82] Morrill, *ibid.*, p. 90.
[83] Morrill, *ibid.*, p. 90.
[84] Morrill, *ibid.*, p. 106.
[85] Easter communion was administered in 1645, 1652, 1656, 1658 and 1659. Christmas communion was celebrated in 1650. One or both services may have been celebrated in other years for which the evidence is less precise.

modern society. As a result, the full meaning of the written word may at best be overlooked, or at worst mis-read.

The potential for mis-reading the evidence is perhaps nowhere greater than in documents generated during the Civil War. This national crisis often divided families in both politics and religion. It is small wonder then that small parishes could find themselves divided as well. Except in a few unusually unified communities, most parishes had a complex blend of beliefs. While one particular theological view may have set much of the tone, other points of view could have been publicly expressed. In a struggle for control groups of parishioners may have momentarily gained the upper hand, leaving their mark upon documents or on the fabric of the church. Another reason why conflicting evidence may be found in documents such as churchwardens' accounts is that many parishes underwent their own religious settlement, as they struggled to preserve communal unity and civic order, two extremely valued aspects of early modern life. As we have seen in Cratfield, one theological position seems to have predominated, but not entirely, and a compromise seems to have been struck and continued to prevail through the challenging decades of the 1640s and 1650s. The resultant balance was somewhat closer to the religious views of parliament than to those of the king.

A further split within the parish may have occurred during the divisive years of the Civil Wars. John Laney, patron of Cratfield, had a son called Benjamin who was a prominent high churchman. Having been Master of Pembroke Hall, Cambridge, between 1640 and 1644, Benjamin followed Charles I into exile and became one of his chaplains-in-ordinary. After the Restoration, he served as bishop of Peterbrough (1660–3), Lincoln (1663–8) and Ely (1668–75). Yet Benjamin's father married into the religiously radical Wentworth family.[86] The religious and political views of the son certainly did not seem to match those of the father, and such differences of opinion were, in fact, relatively common. 'Family connections are not necessarily as solid a basis for political and social alliances', explains B. Coward, 'as bonds based on patronage and clientage'.[87] Benjamin Laney was high church and royalist, while his father John appears to have been reforming and parliamentary. It is also an interesting fact that, throughout his time in the episcopate, Benjamin displayed a remarkable degree of leniency towards religious nonconformists.

In contrast to the religious convictions of his son, John Laney appointed as vicar of Cratfield the relatively reformist Gabriel Eland, who left an unmistakable mark upon the life of the parish.[88] He ensured that Cratfield pledged its support, with both men and money, to the parliamentary forces, according to the solemn vow and covenant of 1642 (facsimile opposite).[89] The churchwardens' accounts for these years illustrate the impact of Civil War upon a rural parish as it provided soldiers, armour and training, and even poor relief to the wives left behind.

As with many other communities across England, whether parliamentarian or royalist, Cratfield readied itself for war. Its commitment to parliament, particularly in the first Civil War, was deep: financially, personally and emotionally. Yet the king's writ continued to run during the early years of tension between crown and parliament.

---

[86] 'Lists of Manors in Suffolk with their Chief Inhabitants, 1655', Bodl. MS Tanner 324, fol. 26.

[87] B. Coward, *The Stuart Age: England 1603–1714* (2nd edn, London, 1994), p. 99.

[88] J. Venn and J. A. Venn, *Alumni Cantabrigienses*, part I, vol. III (Cambridge, 1922), p. 47.

[89] See also B. G. Blackwood, in his 'The Cavalier and Roundhead Gentry of Suffolk', *Suffolk Review*, 5 (1985), p. 7, and his 'The Gentry of Suffolk during the Civil War' in *An Historical Atlas of Suffolk* (1988), p. 85.

1. A copy of the Solemn Vow and Covenant of 1642, kept in the parish documents of Cratfield (SROI, FC62/A3/1).

In 1639 the parish sent men to Selby in south Yorkshire, to help meet the threat of a revolt in Scotland. In 1640, when the Scots rebelled, Cratfield paid William Aldus and Thomas Johnson for their 'serving in the towne armes', as well as for their clothing and equipment. Also in this year, the town spent the significant sum of £1 5s.4d. 'for oates for the king' when the royal purveyor made his demands.[90]

Cratfield assisted parliament with money and with men. It sent 2s.10d. to London, in response to demands for 'Poll Money'. In the following year, the parish committed 4s. towards the Propositions for Money and Plate, and sent four men to Yoxford who 'payde in the money and plate lent to parlement upon the propistions'.[91] Soldiers quickly followed money to Yoxford. Aldus and Johnson were given breakfast by Widow Broadbank and dispatched there, along with a horse to carry their arms. The village also contributed two nags and a mare, both with saddles and bridles, in 1642.[92]

The war effort was building to its peak in 1642–3. Another soldier was despatched, a musket rest was borrowed from Gregory Rouse, and the townsmen sent still more money, £3 8s.2d., 'beinge the second payment acording to the act of parlement'.[93] Soon afterwards a pike and sword, paid for by Widow Broadbank, were sent to the town soldiers. Johnson and Aldus served not only in Yoxford, but continued to train and be paid until the end of 1642.[94]

During 1643, the Eastern Association suffered a series of setbacks, and royalist troops drove deep into the heart of the region. Captain Poe appeared with a warrant and Cratfield responded with increased efforts. John and William Baxter and fifteen-year-old John Clark were sent to serve in parliament's forces, while volunteers were added to the regular complement of men and arms, and another belt and sword were provided. The cost of sending soldiers to Halesworth and mustering points like Sibton Green, as well as to the more distant Bury St Edmunds, was high. They needed to be provided with knapsacks, horses, powder and match. Those who did not fight shouldered the cost of those that did, as well as lending further support to the cause by buying 'a book to enter the Covenant and the Coventers' names', and taking the signed document to Beccles.[95]

Cratfield continued to provide soldiers in response to parliament's policy of conscription,[96] paying 'Tredeskin Coushall for charges for impressing souldiers and carying them in for the Parlement's service'. The high cost of the war continued when the parish paid 'Henery Worlich, constabell, and William Youngs, and Thomas Johnson and Samewell Cady and William Newson and other poore men for ther charges concerning the Parlement's cause, £3 8s.0d.'[97] New men continued to be

---

[90] Cratfield CWA, SROI, FC62/A6/179 (1640). Purveyance was the crown's right to collect supplies for a fixed price. It was one of the most resented royal prerogatives and was declared illegal in the years that followed.

[91] Cratfield CWA, SROI, FC62/A6/180 (1641), and footnote 84 on p. 48.

[92] Cratfield CWA, SROI, FC62/A6/181 (1642). For the parish's supply of horses, see Cratfield CWA, FC62/A6/183, 185, 193, 211 (1643, 1644, 1648, 1651).

[93] Cratfield CWA, SROI, FC62/A6/181 (1642). These are the Nineteen Propositions and represent Parliament's first attempt at raising money. For a discussion of the Propositions in Cheshire, see J. S. Morrill, *Cheshire 1630–1660: County Government and Society During the English Revolution* (London, 1974), pp. 96, 101–2.

[94] Johnson and Aldus were also sent to Bulcamp Heath, Peasenhall and Walpole at the parish's expense. Cratfield CWA, SROI, FC62/A6/182 (1642).

[95] Cratfield CWA, SROI, FC62/A6/183, 184 (1643).

[96] A Parliamentary ordinance authorised the raising of troops for the Eastern Association by conscription.

[97] Cratfield CWA, SROI, FC62/A6/185 (1644).

added to their number, still at the expense of the parish. Twelve shillings, for example, were spent in 1644 on 'Robert Keabell junior for trayning 7 dayes, and monny layd out for drume and collours'; and in the following year approximately the same amount was spent in bringing William Mingy into parliament's ranks.[98]

In 1645, the year when Charles surrendered to the Scots, Cratfield made up a rate of 4s.7d. to assist Scotland, another of 2s.2d. for 'the Scotts our well afected bretherin', and a third of 4s.4½d. for 'our good bretherin of Scotland'.[99] Furthermore, an additional rate was collected on behalf of the 'British armye', an unusually positive wording to describe the Anglo-Scottish forces in Ireland.[100] Generally, the town spent its extra money on co-religionists and political sympathisers, such as the shilling given to '21 poore pepell whose howses wer burnt in the borders of Walles by the Cavellers', or the money given to eleven poor people 'being fyred by the enemey in Hampshire'. All the while, Cratfield continued to finance both regular soldiers and auxiliaries, as well as five garrisons of the Eastern Association.[101] During the most intense phase of the Civil War, 1642–1645, the parish maintained up to five trained men ready to serve 'parliament's cause', in addition to supporting the 'good bretherin' of Ireland, Scotland, and Wales. After June 1646 and the end of the first Civil War, marked by the surrender of the royalists at Oxford, Cratfield was able to scale back its war efforts.

The political world of the 1650s had a very different effect upon the village. Cratfield remained in a state of readiness, training its soldiers, and repairing their weapons and the town's butts, but as the spectre of armed conflict began to fade, so too did the sense of urgency that had been so clearly conveyed in the earlier accounts. That was until 1659. In that year, Thomas Johnson, William Aldus, Robert Pacy and Edmond Mills, the knacker, were all sent to Blythburgh as soldiers. Cratfield readied itself to put down any royalist uprisings that might occur in East Anglia, such as those in Cheshire. Up to this point in the hostilities, Cratfield had fielded a total of thirteen men who served a combined eighteen years in arms. But this was not to prove a long, protracted affair. Following the political machinations of General Monck, and indeed his certificates, Cratfield welcomed the restoration of Charles II with bells, 'ringing that the king was com into England'.[102]

While Cratfield and Suffolk may have had a lucky escape from the Civil Wars, being neither burnt nor the site of open conflict, the real cost of this war was not confined to the movement of soldiers. The true expenses ran much deeper. Simply outfitting a soldier did not end a parish's obligation to him. Weapons needed to be

---

[98] Cratfield CWA, SROI, FC62/A6/185, 186 (1644–5).

[99] In fact, in the previous year, John Rouse went 'to Burry [Bury St Edmunds] for the town for the Scotts advance': Cratfield CWA, SROI, FC62/A6/185 (1644). See also F. D. Dow, *Cromwellian Scotland, 1651–60* (Edinburgh, 1979).

[100] See below, accounts 186 and 187. In fact, the support of Irish travellers is a constant theme throughout these accounts. In the 1640s large numbers of poor, displaced Irish people are mentioned. This coincides with the Irish rebellion of 1641–3 when Protestants were massacred and driven from their homes. Rather more puzzling are large numbers of Irish refugees mentioned in Cratfield's accounts in the 1650s, when the political situation was reversed and much of Ireland was being given to Protestants. For the impact of Cromwellian government in Ireland, see T. C. Barnard, *Cromwellian Ireland, 1649–60* (Oxford, 1975).

[101] Cratfield CWA, SROI, FC62/A6/187, 188, 190 (1645, 1646). The parish also contributed to the 'demollishing of the garisones': Cratfield CWA, SROI, FC62/A6/191 (1647).

[102] Cratfield CWA, SROI, FC62/A6/251 (1660). General Monck was a central figure in the political manoeuvrings of the Restoration. See also R. Hutton, *The Restoration: A Political and Religious History of England and Wales, 1658–67* (Oxford, 1985).

maintained, muskets needed to be trimmed and swords needed 'scowring'.[103] In fact, merely keeping a musketeer in shot was a sizeable achievement. Cratfield spent £2 7s.7d. 'for powder and bulletes and match which every musketter was to have: too pounds pouder, 2 pounds bullets and a pound of match'.[104] More significant still was the human cost. The absence of a husband, even on a short-term basis, could condemn a family to poor relief, as it did when 3s. was 'given to Paces wife in time of soulgren [soldiering]'.[105] If a man was injured, as was the 'solldier [who] lost his hand in the Parlements service', poverty and public relief would be his fate.[106]

Furthermore, Cratfield's thirteen soldiers were drawn overwhelmingly from the ranks of the destitute or marginally poor. In fact, only two participants were rate-payers, and one of these, Robert Keable who was fifty-seven years old, served only as an auxiliary. The fighting of wars was as hierarchical as other aspects of English life: those who carried the brunt of it were the poor. The very poverty of these fighting men meant that if they were injured, they had little else to see them through their dificulties than a parish or county pension. In the words of a Suffolk man, Sexby, who had been a soldier in Cromwell's troop: 'there are many thousands of us soldiers that have ventured our lives; we have had little property in the kingdom as to our estates'.[107] Many were killed in the conflict, often leaving wives and families destitute and wandering the countryside in search of relief. Good examples are the '6 poore widows and 7 small chilldrin whose fathers wer killed in the warres', who were relieved by Cratfield's churchwardens in 1643 and 1645.[108] Consequently, Cratfield maintained a steady stream of payments, at 17s.4d. a time, to maimed soldiers under the Marshalsea and Maimed Soldier ordinance, and gave various sums to those who passed through the parish.[109]

During these years, the pension system for ex-servicemen and war widows functioned at two levels: a central system established by parliament in 1643, and a county scheme set up in 1593. The parliamentary system consisted of a central fund, designed to operate for only six months, and intended to relieve approximately 765 needy individuals. Instead, it operated for seventeen years, relieved thousands of men, women and children, and provided monies for the two national military hospitals, the Savoy and Ely House which were established in 1644 and 1648 respectively. The fund was fed by excise and prize monies, at a rate of £26,260 a year, rising to £38,270 in 1654.

---

[103] Cratfield CWA, SROI, FC62/A6/185, 214 (1644, 1652). For the maintenance and replacement of weapons, see Cratfield CWA, FC62/A6/178, 182–3, 185–6, 188–90, 193, 200, 204, 210–11, 214, 220, 232, 235, 251 (1640, 1642–5, ?1646, 1648–52, 1654, 1656, 1660).
[104] Cratfield CWA, SROI, FC62/A6/182 (1642).
[105] Cratfield CWA, SROI, FC62/A6/211 (1651).
[106] Cratfield CWA, SROI, FC62/A6/183 (1643). Maimed soldiers and the payments they received appear throughout these accounts.
[107] As quoted in Holmes, *The Eastern Association*, p. 173.
[108] The plight of war widows is explored in detail in G. L. Hudson, 'Negotiating for Blood Money: War Widows and the Courts in Seventeenth-Century England' in J. Kermode and G. Walker (eds), *Women, Crime and the Courts in Early Modern England* (London, 1994), pp. 146–69.
[109] The churchwardens of Cratfield recorded payments for Maimed Soldiers at 8s.8d. a quarter, and for Marshalsea at 8s.8d. a quarter, making a total sum of 17s.4d. The payment of Marshalsea is recorded less consistently than that for Maimed Soldiers. Of interest is the payment in 1644–5 of £3 0s.8d. arrears for the double account.

The county scheme had a more direct bearing on the inhabitants of Cratfield. The act of 1593 provided for nationwide compulsory rates, assessed at the level of the parish, to provide disabled soldiers with a pension. While amended several times during the period covered by the accounts in this volume, the basic format of 1593 was maintained. Geoff Hudson's work on ex-servicemen and war widows has done much to illuminate the workings of this system. The act of 1593 ordered that all parishes in England and Wales pay a rate of not less than one penny, but not more than sixpence, to the relief of poor and maimed soldiers. It was to be gathered by parish officers, and at every quarter session turned over to the high constable of the relevant hundred. In turn the high constables transferred the money to a Justice of the Peace appointed to serve as County Treasurer for disabled soldiers. He was responsible for collecting the revenue, distributing pensions and keeping accounts.

To collect his pension, a maimed soldier needed a certificate from his captain, listing his injuries and detailing his service record. This document, in an effort to prevent forgery, needed to be counter-signed by the general muster-master or by the treasurer of the navy. At this point the ex-serviceman received enough money to travel to the county where he had been impressed or, if a volunteer, to the county in which he had served for three years, or to the county of his birth. Once at his final destination he received immediate relief until the next quarter session when he was awarded, and began to collect, his pension. Alterations to this basic system in 1598 and 1601 raised the amounts to be levied from parishes, as well as the sums awarded as pensions. Significantly, the act of 1601 stipulated that these pensions were to be life-long, and could not be arbitrarily revoked. Although the act was not renewed in 1610 under James I, the system continued to operate as if it were still in force. A number of ordinances in the late 1640s and early 1650s supplemented the 1601 act. By the early 1650s both the royalists and parliamentarians had their own versions of this scheme.[110]

Cratfield's regular payments for Marshalsea and Maimed Soldiers illustrate the complicated details which must be sifted by historians who wish to distinguish between personal conviction and civil obligation. The composite picture of Cratfield's inhabitants, drawn not only from the churchwardens' accounts, is that they were not passive bystanders of the conflict between king and parliament. Their prompt response to parliament's directives, both in terms of religious practice and military support, as well as their generous charity to those who suffered for their protestant or parliamentary allegiance, suggest, at least to my mind, that Cratfield was not like the neutral and obstinately conservative villages portrayed by John Morrill and Robert Ashton as characteristic of the 1640s.[111] Nor were they part of a semi-autonomous county, with little interest in the happenings at Westminster, as Alan Everitt's intriguing work suggests.[112] Instead, these villagers were engaged in an intense interaction between local and national politics. Since no resident gentry influenced their

[110] The above discussion is based on G. L. Hudson's 'Ex-Servicemen, War-Widows and the English County Pension Scheme', unpublished D.Phil. thesis (Oxford, 1995), Ch. 1. I would like to thank Dr Hudson for permission to cite his thesis, and for his invaluable help on the question of Cratfield's maimed soldiers.

[111] J. Morrill, *The Revolt of the Provinces: Conservatives and Radicals in the English Civil War, 1630–50* (1976, revised 1980), and R. Ashton, *The English Civil War: Conservatism and Revolution, 1603–49* (London, 1989).

[112] A. Everitt (ed.), *Suffolk and the Great Rebellion* (Suffolk Records Society, 3, 1961).

behaviour, they considered and decided for themselves an appropriate response – they chose to fight against the king.[113]

Parliamentarian in politics, outwardly conformist in matters of religion, though decidedly reformist within that wide spectrum of conformity, early modern Cratfield was prosperous and well integrated. Politically dominated by its own 'chief inhabitants', rather than by manorial lords or neighbouring gentry, it participated in regional and national networks.[114] The village that produced the following documents was in many ways a typical High Suffolk community. Its inhabitants were deeply involved in the affairs of their region and their nation, whether the issues were to do with economics, religion or war.

---

[113] See the following revisionist historians and their response to Everitt's work: J. Morrill, *Cheshire, 1630–1660*; D. Underdown, *Somerset during the Civil War and Interregnum* (Newton Abbot, 1973); A. Hughes, *Politics, Society and Civil War in Warwickshire, 1620–1660* (Cambridge, 1987); and Holmes, *The Eastern Association* (1975).

[114] See also H. French, 'Chief Inhabitants and their Areas of Influence: Local Ruling Groups in Essex and Suffolk Parishes, 1630–1720', unpublished Ph.D. thesis (Cambridge University, 1993).

# Note on the Manuscripts

The manuscripts printed in this book form part of the parish records of Cratfield in Suffolk, and are in the custody of the Suffolk Record Office at Ipswich. Other extant documents from this period include wills, parish registers, deeds, overseers' accounts, town books, and constables' and surveyors' accounts. Churchwardens' accounts, however, form the core of any parish's written history, as they are not only an account of ecclesiastical expenses, but also of much of the community's civic affairs. An excellent example of the historian's growing awareness and use of these documents is found in Reformation studies. In recent years scholars of England's religious changes have shifted their methodological attention away from parliamentary acts and bishops' articles to local wills and parish records, particularly churchwardens' accounts.[115]

The role of the churchwarden, while originally ecclesiastical in nature, was also vital to the functioning of the secular community. His activities were divided into two primary components: 'the enforcement of set policy and the provision of information'.[116] Cratfield's churchwardens were particularly detailed in their recording, and the parish particularly careful in their preservation. In this parish, two churchwardens were normally elected each year, and each submitted a 'reckoning' of their activity to the chief inhabitants on 25 March or Lady Day, at the end of the Julian year.[117] Upon verification and approval of each officer's collection and distribution of funds, the two accounts were combined and summarised in a town book, and the signatures of the chief inhabitants were affixed to the foot of the page, signifying their approval on behalf of the community. Most extant churchwardens' accounts are in this synthesised form. Cratfield is indeed fortunate in that not only does its town book survive, but in most years the individual accounts for each churchwarden as well. It is the individual accounts that are printed below.

There are, however, a few deviations from the general pattern of two accounts a year, one from each churchwarden. For example, we only have a single account surviving for the years 1653 and 1655. At the other extreme, John Smith of Norwood Green himself left two accounts in 1645, and Robert Smith of Coulshall did the same in 1650. The churchwardens' returns for these years, while less consistent than in the

---

[115] For example, see R. Whiting, *The Blind Devotion of the People* (Cambridge, 1990); Duffy, *The Stripping of the Altars*; C. Haigh, *English Reformations* (Oxford, 1993).

[116] J. S. Craig, 'Co-Operation and Initiatives: Elizabethan Churchwardens and the Parish Accounts of Mildenhall', *Social History*, 18 (1993), p. 359.

[117] The Julian, or Old Style, calendar was introduced by Julius Caesar in 45 B.C. It remained in effect in England until the passing of 'Chesterfield's Act' (24 Geo. II, c. 23) in March 1751, which established that the following 1 January would begin the year 1752, and that 2 September would be followed by 14 September. Generally, Roman Catholic countries adopted the New Style, or Gregorian Calendar, in the sixteenth century, Protestant countries in the eighteenth century, and Greece and Eastern Europe in the twentieth century. See C. R. Cheney, *Handbook of Dates for Students of English History* (Royal Historical Society, London, 1978), pp. 1–11.

periods on either side, are remarkably straightforward for a community at war – and especially for an historical era reputedly characterised by the collapse of civic life.[118]

The documents themselves conform to no standardised form, apart from a crude separation of expenses and revenue, but instead reflect the individuality of their author. While some churchwardens kept their accounts on small scraps of paper, using a barely legible script, most detailed their spending on large sheets of paper, roughly 12 by 16 inches, employing obviously practised and clear hands. In most cases, it appears that each churchwarden was the scribe of his own documents, although the parish did seek the services of a professional for the writing of the town book and other, more 'official' records.[119] The length of the accounts varied widely, from one short sheet of paper to three full sheets pinned together. In general, each churchwarden filled somewhere between one and two full-sized sheets.

The actual documents are loose and stored in archival boxes, mixed with a variety of other parish records, including constables' accounts,[120] records of the monthly assessments,[121] acknowledgements of debts,[122] and undefined 'bills' presented to the town.[123] The accounts transcribed below are catalogued as FC62/A6/176–253.

---

[118] The fact that local government did not break down during these years is discussed for the country as a whole by D. H. Pennington, 'The Accounts of the Kingdom, 1642–1649' in F. J. Fisher (ed.), *Essays in the Economic and Social History of Tudor and Stuart England in Honour of R. H. Tawney* (Cambridge, 1961), p. 183.

[119] For example, Cratfield CWA, SROI, FC62/A6/138, 210, 240 (1617, 1651, 1656–57).

[120] For example, SROI, FC62/A6/233 (1656–57).

[121] For example, SROI, FC62/A6/228 (1656).

[122] For example, SROI, FC62/A6/251 (1660).

[123] For example, SROI, FC62/A6/238 (1657).

# Editorial Conventions

Original spelling has been retained. Obvious abbreviations have been extended without comment (though 'Mr' and 'Mrs' have been retained). The ampersand has been changed to 'and'. Where two words are obviously elided (e.g. 'apasse'), they have been separated.

Deletions are shown thus: < >

Insertions are shown thus: \ /

Light punctuation has been added as an aid to the reader, but never where it might impose a questionable meaning. Similarly the use of capital letters has been modernised. Where the reading of any word or number is in doubt, it is preceded by a question-mark.

In sums of money the abbreviation 'li' has been modernised as '£'. The abbreviations 's.' for shillings and 'd.' for pence have been retained. Although some accounts used Roman figures, all sums of money in this transcription appear in Arabic, and are mostly tabulated on the right-hand side of the page.

Throughout the text editorial comments are put in italics within square brackets, such as [*damaged*], and extra biographical details are put in square brackets without italics, such as [Thomas]. To retain the original layout of the documents, one blank line represents a page break, and also a break within an account (when it moves, for example, from income to expenditure). Two blank lines indicate the beginning of a completely new account.

The accounting year of the parish of Cratfield was from 25 March to 24 March. In other words, the accounts are in Old Style with each year beginning on Lady Day, 25 March. As a help to the modern reader, however, New Style dates (starting the year on 1 January) are added in square brackets at the head of each account. Each time, therefore, two modern-style years are straddled, thus March 1640–March 1641.

Footnotes have been appended to explain the significance of entries when they first appear, or to put them into broader historical context. Words no longer in current use, or of technical significance, have been defined and further explained in a Glossary on pp. 155–61.

# CHURCHWARDENS' ACCOUNTS
# OF CRATFIELD
## 1640–1660

Suffolk Record Office, Ipswich

FC62/A6/176–253

xxiij° die Marcij anno domini 1639
The receyts of William Fiske junior, one of the churchwardens of Cratfeild, as
followeth [*for the year March 1639 to March 1640*]

|  | £ | s. | d. |
|---|---|---|---|
| Imprimis reeived the rent for one whole yere, for the Towne Meadowes |  |  |  |
| which was due \at/ Michaellmas last past the some of | 6 | 10 | 0 |
| received the rent for one whole yere for the towne fearme,[1] where |  |  |  |
| Gregory Rous senior late deceased dwelt, the some of | 40 | 0 | 0 |
| Some in all received is | 46 | 10 | 0 |

xxiij° die Marcij anno domini 1639
The layinges out of William Fiske junior, one of the churchwardens of Cratfeild, as
followeth [*for 1639–40*]

|  | £ | s. | d. |
|---|---|---|---|
| Imprimis remayne due to me from the towne, as appeareth by |  |  |  |
| the towne booke,[2] the some of | 6 | 2 | 8 |
| Item laid out to Gregory Rous by the consent of the townesmen | 1 | 0 | 0 |
| Item laid out the xxx<sup>th</sup> day of March <*illeg.*> for bread and wyne[3] |  | 3 | 4 |
| Item laid out the vj<sup>th</sup> day of Aprill for a surplis,[4] and to Richard |  |  |  |
| Powes for bringeinge of it to towne, the some of | 1 | 17 | 2 |
| Item laid out to Ruben Tallent for his quarters wages due at |  |  |  |
| Our Lady [*day*] last past,[5] the some of |  | 10 | 0 |
| Item laid out to him more for his attendence at the reckoninge daye[6] |  | 1 | 0 |
| Item laid out the vij<sup>th</sup> of Aprill to John Smyth of Norwood,[7] constable, |  |  |  |
| towards a warrent for the soulgers paye | 5 | 0 | 9 |
| Item laid out the same day for bread and wyne |  | 7 | 4 |
| Item laid out the xiiij<sup>th</sup> of Aprill for bread and wyne |  | 7 | 7 |
| Item laid out the xxvij<sup>th</sup> of Aprill at the generall[8] at Yoxford for our |  |  |  |
| charges in the courte and our expences their |  | 13 | 6 |

---

[1] Cratfield's endowed property was extensive. It included the Church Close, with its church house and two acres; Barretts, worth £3 6s.8d. annually in the late 15<sup>th</sup> century; a schoolhouse; guildhall and lands; Sallow Pightle; Rose Larks; and a number of other meadows, fields and closes. See Farnhill, 'Religious Policy and Parish Conformity' (1977), pp. 217–29; Botelho, 'Provisions for the Elderly' (1995), pp. 229–36.
[2] The 'town book' of this period has not survived.
[3] This is a payment, which recurs regularly, for bread and wine used in the Holy Communion. Cratfield offered quarterly communion, which included the three great feasts of Easter, Whitsun and Christmas, until 1646 when their celebration was banned by Parliament (see Introduction, pp. 14–15).
[4] The parish bought a surplice for its vicar.
[5] Ruben Tallent was sexton, and was paid 10s. quarterly.
[6] The 'reckoning' or 'pulvering' day was on or about the 25<sup>th</sup> March (Lady Day), the beginning of a new year and one of the regular quarter days. On this busy occasion the parish accounts were presented, town lands were re-distributed and a meal was provided, with pipes and tobacco.
[7] Norwood (later Northward or North) Green, lay in the north-western corner of the parish of Cratfield; see Hodskinson's map of Suffolk, 1783 (1972). For John Smith, see Biographies, p. 141.
[8] The 'general' was the six-monthly archdeacon's court, this time held at Yoxford, 6 miles south-east of Cratfield.

|  | £ | s. | d. |
|---|---|---|---|
| Item laid out the xiiij[th] day of May to M[r] [Thomas] Beddingfeild towards the conducketinge of souldiers to Selby in Yorkesheire,[9] the some of | 4 | 10 | 0 |
| Item laid out to him more for the Marshallseas[10] |  | 8 | 8 |
| Item laid out to Gregory Rous for his charges at Ipswich with the souldiers their, the some of | 2 | 14 | 0 |
| Item laid out to Edmond Brodbancke[11] for keppinge of the preast souldiers and for their dyett, the some of | 2 | 0 | 0 |
| Item laid out the first day of June for bread and wyne |  | 6 | 4 |
| Item laid out the vij[th] of July to John Smyth of Norwood for releife of the prest soulger, by the consent of the townesmen |  | 10 | 0 |
| Item laid out the x[th] of July for our dynners when the vissiters[12] were in towne, the some of | 1 | 10 | 0 |
| Item laid out to Thomas Kempe for dismission fees[13] |  | 2 | 4 |
| Item laid out the xiiij[th] of July to John Mylls senior, constable, for repayeringe of bridges and for a load of faggott, byllett, tale wood or blockes as appeare by the warrent, the some of | 1 | 3 | 0 |
| Item laid out to Ruben Tallent for halfe a yeares wages due at Michaellmas next, by the consent of the townesmen | 1 | 0 | 0 |
| Item laid out to Francis Barrowe for his charges at Ipswich with the souldiers | 1 | 4 | 0 |
| Item laid out the xxiij[th] of September to John Smyth of Norwood for his disbursements in the tyme of his constableshippe, as appeare by his bill, the some of | 8 | 13 | 7 |
| Item laid out the xxvj[th] of September to M[r] [Thomas] Beddingfeild for Marchallseas and maynned[sic] souldiers[14] for twoe quarters due at Michaellmas next, the some of |  | 17 | 4 |
| Item laid out the xiij[th] of October to Francis Aldus senior, <one of the> constable, for the mustermasters and souldiers paye | 3 | 6 | 10 |
| Item laid out the xxix[th] of October to Francis Barrowe for his disbursments in the tyme of his constableshippe, as appeare by his bill |  | 10 | 8 |

---

[9] Soldiers were sent to Selby in south Yorkshire. The accounts of 1639–40 contain many references to soldiers, their pay, feeding, provisioning, training and movements. See Introduction, p. 18.

[10] See Note 14, below.

[11] Edmund Broadbank kept a local inn or alehouse, and was often paid for drink, food, fire and accommodation.

[12] The 'visitors' refer to an ecclesiastical visitation, by either the local archdeacon or the bishop and their agents. Such visitors were sent regularly to assess the condition of parishes, both in terms of the church fabric and religious orthodoxy.

[13] 'Dismission fees' (or 'dimission') was paid at ecclesiastical courts.

[14] Pensions for soldiers and mariners injured in war were codified by Parliament in 1601 under 43 Eliz. c. 3. This act stipulated that money was to be raised weekly from every parish, collected by high constables and distributed by specially appointed county treasurers. Related closely was the relief of prisoners in the King's Bench and Marshalsea prisons, as required in 'An Act for the Relief of the Poore' (43 Eliz. c.2). Both systems of relief were administered at a county level and were typically known as 'Marshalsea and Maimed Soldiers'. The cost of these two rates for Cratfield was 8s.8d. per quarter. See also Hudson, 'Ex-Servicemen, War Widows' (1995), passim, and Introduction, pp. 20–1.

|  | £ | s. | d. |
|---|---|---|---|
| Item laid out the xij[th] of November to Samuell Hudson for a yeres rent for Rose Larkes,[15] which was due at Michaellmas last past to the hundred of Blithinge |  | 2 | 4 |
| Item laid out the xxv[th] of December to Ruben Tallent for his quarters wages |  | 10 | 0 |
| Some is | 45 | 12 | 5 |
|  |  |  |  |
| Item laid out the xxv[th] of December for bread and wyne |  | 6 | 0 |
| Item laid out the vij[th] of January to M[r] [Thomas] Beddingfeild for the Marshallseas and maynned souldiers paye for the quarter due at Chrismas last past, the some of |  | 8 | 8 |
| Item laid out the last day of January for dismission fees and my expences at the courte at Yoxford |  | 3 | 4 |
| Item laid out the xj[th] of March to M[r] [Gabriel] Eland by the consent and appointment of the townesmen, the some of | 3 | 0 | 0 |
| Some is | 3 | 18 | 0 |
|  |  |  |  |
| Sum' in tot' | 49 | 10 | 5 |

[unnumbered]

The account of John Newson, on of the churchwardens of Cratfeild, for the yeere of Our Lord 1639 [for 1639–40]

|  | £ | s. | d. |
|---|---|---|---|
| Aprill the 2. Inprimus laid out at the reckoninge for our diners, and for beere and fireinge | 1 | 8 | 4 |
| laid out to M[r] [William] Aldus for teachinge the 4 poore cheildren for the half yeere[16] | 1 | 0 | 0 |
| more laid out to him for repearing of the scoalhouse windowes[17] |  | 1 | 6 |
| Aprill the 10th, laid out to Edmond Miles for rent due for the towne land these sumes: |  |  |  |
| first for the Towne Close |  |  | 7 |
| more for the towne land |  | 3 | 2 |
| more for halfe & aker [sic] in Shaddowe Pightle[18] |  |  | 1½ |

---

[15] 'Rose Larks' was land belonging to the parish of Cratfield (see Note 1). It was named after the original benefactor, and carried an annual rent due to the local Hundred of Blything. Rose Lark's original endowment of 1503 was thirteen acres and a mill. Six acres and three rods were added later, and by the 1530s the income from this property was in excess of £6 10s. 0d. a year. It was transferred to the churchwardens in 1538 as the guild divested itself of property. See Farnhill, 'Religious Policy and Parish Conformity' (1997), pp. 220–9; Botelho, 'Provisions for the Elderly' (1995), p. 231.

[16] At parish expense, four poor boys were educated at the local school (see Notes 17 & 262). The cost was £2 a year. No records of the school itself survive, and its size and composition are unknown.

[17] The schoolhouse dated from the late 16th century and was located near the church, but was separate from the guildhall.

[18] In the annual accounts Shadow Pightle was often confused with Sallow Pightle: one was often crossed out and the other inserted (see Note 95). Note that in this entry and elsewhere, the ampersand was used for the word 'an'.

|  | £ | s. | d. |
|---|---|---|---|
| and in lewe of 7 eggs due with these aforesaid sumes for the towne land[19] |  |  | 1½ |
| laid out for the composecion[20] | 3 | 0 | 0 |
| laid out to M[r] [Gabriel] Eland for writinge of the bills indented |  | 2 | 0 |
| laid out to the Widow [Elizabeth] Brisingham att our reckoning day, for firewode and other nesesary thinges then and there had |  | 4 | 0 |
| Aprill the 27th, laid out att the generall att Yoxford for our horses standinge |  |  | 4 |
| laid out for Sara Cadyes house rent |  | 6 | 0 |
| laid out att Halleseworth[21] when we gave in the account for the poore, for our dinerrs |  | 4 | 2 |
| May the 10th, given to John Willson and his wife and cheildren who were travelling from St Thomas Hospitall in Lundon unto the towne of Riseing in Norfolke, as by ther surteficat did apare[22] |  |  | 3 |
| laid out at the pulveringe day[23] for our diners and beere | 1 | 8 | 0 |
| laid out to the Widow [Dorothy] Adams in the time of har sicknes |  | 2 | 0 |
| given to Cornelias Newman with his wife and sister and too cheildren who had a surteficat of a lose by sea of 6 hundred pound and were to goe to London |  | 1 | 0 |
| laid out to Sameull Miles for fetchinge the too doores from Fresingfeild, which stand betwene the church and chanccell[24] |  |  | 6 |
| laid out to the joyner for makeinge of the doores, and for bere he had |  | 13 | 0 |
| laid out too travellars with ther cheildren travelling from the hospitall to Norfolke |  |  | 6 |
| laid out when M[r] [Thomas] Bedingfeild tooke the names of the hired soulgers to Edmond Brudbanke, for beere |  |  | 6 |
| laid out to John Dennes and William Dennes who had a surtefficat of a great lose by sea and were to travell to London |  |  | 8 |
| laid out for 12 pints of wine for the cort |  | 4 | 0 |
| laid out to John Williams for one pound and a halfe of suger |  | 3 | 0 |
| paid to William Crose for the gimers for the chancell doores |  | 3 | 0 |
| laid out to Edmond Miles for 3 fines for the close he bought | 1 | 6 | 10 |
| laid out to John Miles for springe |  | 6 | 8 |
| laid out to William Warren for bricke and lime for the church, and for bringeing of it |  | 4 | 7 |
| given to James Miles he beinge then sicke |  | 5 | 0 |
| paid to Ruben Tallen for fetchinge of sand for the mason |  |  | 4 |

[19] A manorial rent, traditionally paid in eggs, was here commuted to money.

[20] 'Composition' seems to refer to purveyance, the obligation to support the royal household in money or in kind (see Notes 42, 57 & 85).

[21] Halesworth, Suffolk, 5 miles from Cratfield and the nearest market town.

[22] St Thomas's Hospital was a medieval foundation in London. Armed with an official pass or warrant, this family were on their way to Castle Rising, Norfolk.

[23] See Note 6, above.

[24] Two doors, made in the adjoining parish of Fressingfield, were installed in Cratfield church at the junction of nave and chancel where the rood-screen had stood before the Reformation. The purpose was presumably to divide off the chancel for the celebration of Holy Communion. Compare the two folding doors dated 1619 which still survive at Kedington, Suffolk.

|  | £ | s. | d. |
|---|---|---|---|
| paid the same day to James Miles to releve him in his sicknes |  | 2 | 0 |
| the sume is | 11 | 12 | 2 |
|  |  |  |  |
| The 4th of August, paid to James Miles in the time of his sicknes to releve him |  | 2 | 0 |
| laid out to Robart Meilles for strawe |  | 3 | 4 |
| laid out for too pound of splentyarne the same time |  |  | 8 |
| given to Mary Browne and Kattrin Browne and 3 small cheildren, Irish people who had sustained the lose of 4 hundred pound by the Turkes[25] |  | 1 | 0 |
| The 11th of August, given to James Miles to releve him in his sicknes |  | 2 | 0 |
| August the 27th, given to James Miles to releve him in his sicknes |  | 2 | 0 |
| September the 17, laid out to Edmond Miles, James Miles and Sameull Miles for makeing of clay and dabinge att Benclings[26] | 1 | 2 | 4 |
| September the 23th, laid out to a brefe for Josen Daniell and Elisabeth Sponer, the lose was 8 score and 10 pounds |  | 1 | 6 |
| laid out to Frances Aldus for 3 hookes for the doores att Benclings |  | 1 | 0 |
| laid out to Thomas Willobie with his wife and cheildren who had a surteficat of a lose by Turkish pirats of on thousand pound |  | 1 | 0 |
| laid out to Samuell Newson for strawe to make clay |  | 1 | 3 |
| laid out for digging and makeing of clay and dabinge of the towne hall[27] and the other houses there to be longinge |  | 14 | 5 |
| more laid out for nailes used there |  |  | 4 |
| laid out to Rubin Tallen for wier for the clock |  |  | 3 |
| laid out at Yoxford att the generall for wrigthing of our vardit and other charges laid out att the same time |  | 12 | 0 |
| paid unto Thomas Adams for worke about the church and scholhouse chemnye |  | 4 | 8 |
| September the 29, paid unto Mr [William] Aldus for teatching the 4 poore cheildren for half a yere | 1 | 0 | 0 |
| laid out to Francis Aldus for the composecion | 2 | 15 | 0 |
| given to John Stanton and Irish man who had sustained the lose of £300 by sea |  | 1 | 0 |
| October the 5th, laid out for Sary Cadyes house rent |  | 6 | 0 |

[25] Payments for the relief or redemption of Christians suffering at the hands of the Turks appear throughout these accounts (see Biographies, p. 128). The victims were generally seamen, travellers or merchants captured on the Barbary coast of North Africa. Suffolk was noted for the wide ranging activities of its mercantile and gentry families: for example, two brothers of Sir Thomas Barnardiston of Kedington were merchants in Turkey. See Everitt, *Suffolk and the Great Rebellion* (1961), p. 17.

[26] Benselyn's farm was given to the church in 1461 by John Fyn. By 1510 it consisted of 14 acres; by 1534 it had grown to 18 acres. Its name was variously spelt, e.g. Besnalles.

[27] The town hall (or town house) was the former guildhall, situated near the church. Its maintenance is frequently mentioned in the accounts. The hall was originally given to the guild of St Thomas the Martyr in 1502 by the priest John Rusale. Later, in 1538, it was transferred to the parish, allegedly in response to the dissolution of St Neots Priory which held both the advowson of the church and the manor of Cratfield. In its new role, it functioned as an almshouse and village bakery. In 1553 in was given to the parish. Cratfield TB, SROI, FC62/E1/3; Cratfield Deed, SROI FC62/L1/15; Farnhill, 'Religious Policy and Parish Conformity' (1997), p. 220; and Botelho, 'Provisions for the Elderly' (1995), pp. 231–6.

|                                                                                              | £  | s. | d.  |
|----------------------------------------------------------------------------------------------|----|----|-----|
| given to William Townesen ministar who was travelling from out of Garmine into Flege in Norfolke[28] |    |    | 6   |
| laid out to John Williams for 22 quartrs of pouder and for match                             |    | 12 | 0   |
| laid out to him allso for a sute of aparell for William Aldus                                | 1  | 0  | 0   |
| paid to him for nailes that were used at Frances Aldus is a sume that Rubin Tallen [sic]      |    | 2  | 0   |
| given to William Donegan with his wife and cheildren who had gret loses by fire and were travellinge unto there frinds att Yarmouth |    |    | 6   |
| October the 17, laid out to Edmund Miles first for the Towne Close                            |    |    | 7   |
| more for the towne land                                                                      |    | 3  | 6   |
| more for &[sic] aker in Shadow Pightle                                                       |    |    | 1½  |
| more for Crispes land lat Aldus is                                                           |    |    | 1   |
| more for the common fine                                                                     |    | 6  | 8   |
| more to him for a fre rent for the Towne Close                                               |    |    | 4   |
| paid to Edmond Brudbanke when he made the [?]booke for the traininge,[29] for beere          |    | 1  | 2   |
| the sume is                                                                                  | 9  | 19 | 2   |

[*separate sheet, unnumbered; with identical handwriting*]

|                                                                                              | £  | s. | d.  |
|----------------------------------------------------------------------------------------------|----|----|-----|
| laid out to William Aldus for sarveing in the towne armour[30]                               |    | 2  | 4   |
| paid to William Warren for careinge of the armour to Sippen Green[31]                        |    | 8  | 0   |
| paid to [Henry] Worlich his aprentice for gooeng to gett William Warren and his cart for the use aforesaid |    |    | 2   |
| laid out for too headpeeces for the towne                                                    |    | 12 | 0   |
| paid to James Miles for triminge of the towne hall doore and mendinge of the irons           |    |    | 8   |
| paid to John Miles for four combe of otes for composecion                                    | 1  | 0  | 0   |
| laid out for a bell roope                                                                    |    | 3  | 0   |
| given to William Roach and James Roach, too souldgers who had a surteficat to travell to ther frinds to Sumerlye in Kent[32] |    | 1  | 0   |
| laid out to William Crose for a plat of iron to lay over the ovens mouth at Frances Aldusis  |    | 1  | 8   |
| laid out to Robart Smith of Laxfeild for glasinge the church windos                          |    | 11 | 6   |
| laid out to Rubin Tallen for helpeing of the glaser                                          |    | 1  | 0   |
| laid out to Rubin Tallens wife in har sicknes                                                |    | 2  | 0   |
| laid out to too souldgers who had a surteficat of a lose by Turks                            |    | 1  | 0   |
| laid out to John Williams for paper                                                          |    |    | 1   |

---

[28] A Protestant minister travelling from Germany to the Flegg district of east Norfolk.

[29] This book was probably one of many then available on the subject of military training. For example: *The Military Discipline* (London, 1623), James Achesone, *The Military Garden. . .* (Edinburgh, 1629) and William Barriffe, *Military Discipline. . .* (London, 1635), which were reprinted frequently between 1640 and 1661.

[30] The armour belonging to the parish is frequently mentioned, both in general and as specified items (e.g. headpieces, corslets, musket, etc.).

[31] The parish's armour was carted to the site of an official muster at Sibton Green, about 5 miles south-east of Cratfield.

[32] Perhaps Somerley in West Sussex.

|  | £ | s. | d. |
|---|---|---|---|
| laid out to John Slea who had a surteficat of a lose by Turkish pirates of 1000 pound and upwards |  | 1 | 0 |
| laid out to a brefe be longing to Thomas Bridges, the lose where of was 200 pounds |  | 1 | 0 |
| laid out to a brefe belonging to the towne of Calne[33] the lose there of amounted to 3000 pounds and upwards |  | 2 | 0 |
| laid out to a brefe belonging to the towne of Stone in the county of Kent, the lose where of was 1000 and 50 pounds |  | ?1 | ? |
| laid out to a brefe belonging to the towne of Boxworth in Cambridge shere, the lose was 500 pounds |  | 1 | 0 |
| laid out to Elisabeth Smith and Margaret Wells and six cheildren, and to a poore seaferinge man which travelled by a surteficat |  | 1 | 0 |
| laid out to the Widow [Dorothy] Adams to releve har in har sicknes |  | 2 | 0 |
| laid out to John Williams for nailes for the glaser to repear the church windows with all |  |  | 1 |
| laid out to John Hovell in part of paiment for the bellframes[34] |  | 5 | 0 |
| laid out to Thomas Adams for bricke and worke done att Benclings |  | 1 | 8 |
| laid out to Edmond Brudbanke for mending the towne pightle gatt, and for a spur |  |  | 10 |
| laid out to Robart Smith for boord to mend the towne hall chamber |  | 3 | 0 |
| the sume is | 4 | 4 | 6 |

|  | £ | s. | d. |
|---|---|---|---|
| laid out for coleckcion for the poore for the fortnight begining the first day the 14th day of Aprill[35] |  | 8 | 2 |
| to the Widow [Ann] Spinke |  | 2 | 8 |
| to the Widow [Ann] Newson |  | 2 | 0 |
| to the Widow [Avice] Haiward |  | 1 | 0 |
| to William Browne |  | 2 | 0 |
| to Rose Browne |  |  | 6 |
| for five and twentye fortnights the sume is | 10 | 4 | 2 |

|  | £ | s. | d. |
|---|---|---|---|
| oweing to me from the towne at the last reconinge day | 8 | 15 | 2 |
| the sume is | 18 | 19 | 4 |

|  | £ | s. | d. |
|---|---|---|---|
| the sume totall | 44 | 15 | 2 |

|  | £ | s. | d. |
|---|---|---|---|
| received of Frances Aldus for rent for the town | 17 | 0 | 0 |
| received of Gregorie Rouse | 5 | 0 | 0 |
| received of John Williams | 5 | 0 | 0 |
| received of Edmond Brudbanke | 2 | 0 | 0 |

[33] Calne, Wiltshire.

[34] Major repairs of the church tower ('steeple') and its bellframe were clearly taking place between 1639 and 1641. Several different kinds of craftsmen are mentioned, also raw materials and quantities of beer.

[35] Churchwardens often list the recipients of poor-relief in these accounts. The 'collection' came from local ratepayers.

[177]

A true coppie of charges and layings out for the towne of Cratfield by mee Robert Smith junior, being churchwarden there, from my first coming on to that office [on] March the 23th 1639 untill the 22th of this instant March 1640 [for 1640–1]

| | £ | s. | d. |
|---|---|---|---|
| Inprimis laid out at Broadbanckes for the towne, March the 23th 1639 | | 12 | 0 |
| Item laid out more the same day to the Widdow [Elizabeth] Brisingham for fireing | | 4 | 0 |
| Item laid out at that time to Ruben Tallent for his attendance | | 1 | 0 |
| Item laid out to Mr [William] Fiske junior | 3 | 0 | 5 |
| Item laid out to the schoolmaster for teaching the 4 children | 1 | 0 | 0 |
| Item laid out to John Newson that was due to him from the towne, March the 28th | 8 | 0 | 0 |
| Item laid out more the same day for a bill of charges to Gregory Rowse | 1 | 11 | 10 |
| Item given to the Widdow Grimston for healing of [John] Stannard's sonne | | 15 | 0 |
| Item paid to a composition rate about that time to Mr [Thomas] Beddingfield | 3 | 0 | 0 |
| Item paid to Samuell Cady for felling of trees | | 5 | 0 |
| Item given to [Edmund] Broadbancke for beere and fire at the rate makinge | | 1 | 6 |
| Item given to maimed soldiers, Aprill the 9th | | 8 | 8 |
| Item laid out for the account giving in at Halsworth for the poore | | 6 | 5 |
| Item laid out at Beckles[36] for mansmeate, horsmeate and other charges, and for councell to plead the cause | | 13 | 8 |
| Item laid out at the generall court at Yoxford in charges, and in our owne expences there, Aprill the 20th | | 17 | 7 |
| Item given to a briefe to William Noble, Aprill the 10th | | 2 | 6 |
| Item laid out to Mr [Gabriel] Elond for writinge the billes indented | | 2 | 0 |
| Item paid to William Mingy for his father's wages | | 6 | 0 |
| Item laid \out/ at [Edmund] Broadbanckes on the pullering day for a rate makinge[37] and other expences, May the 7th | 2 | 5 | 0 |
| Item given \to/ three Irish people with a passe, May the 20th[38] | | | 10 |
| Item given about that time to two Irish people more | | | 6 |
| Item paid out to William Warne for carrying of the timber to the sawing pitt and to the church, and alsoe for beere at those times | 1 | 0 | 0 |
| Item laid out for wine and sugar for the court at Whitsontide | | 6 | 0 |
| Item given to maimed soldiers about that time | | 8 | 8 |
| Item paid to Cox for two paire of shooes for our soldiers | | 5 | 0 |
| Item given to [Edmund] Broadbancke for beere for the townsmen | | 1 | 6 |
| Item given to two gentlemen soldiers | | | 6 |
| Item given to two Irish soldiers, June the 7th | | | 6 |
| Item given to [Edmund] Broadbancke for keping our soldiers | 2 | 5 | 0 |

---

36 Beccles, Suffolk, a major town about 12 miles north-east of Cratfield. Also spelt 'Becells' in these accounts.

37 'Making a rate' denotes the setting of a rate to be levied in the parish, at so many pence to the pound (£).

38 The first of many references to Irish travellers and refugees (see Notes 82 & 210).

| | £ | s. | d. |
|---|---|---|---|
| Item given to those soldiers, June the 8th | | 10 | 0 |
| Item given to [Edmund] Broadbancke the same day for all our dinners | 1 | 1 | 6 |
| Item laid out for beere to Howell at the bellframes at sundry times and often | | 2 | 0 |
| Item given to John Bond for a briefe | | 2 | 6 |
| Item laid out more for beere for the workemen at the fram | | | 6 |
| Item paid to Mr [John] Goldsmith for writinge and for journies | 1 | 10 | 0 |
| Item laid out for a booke for the fast,[39] and for beere for the workemen | | 1 | 6 |
| Item laid out at Yoxford court for my expences and other things, July the 10th | | 3 | 8 |
| Item paid to the visitors for theire demission fees, July the 16th | | 3 | 0 |
| Item paid more the same day for all our dinners and other expences | 1 | 7 | 0 |
| Item paid to Thomas Legat about that time by the consent of the towne | 6 | 0 | 0 |
| Item paid for belleropes | | 9 | 8 |
| The summe of this side [of paper] is | 39 | 12 | 5 |
| | | | |
| Item laid out about that time for beere for the workmen | | 1 | 0 |
| Item laid out for lime and beere againe given to the workmen | | 6 | 0 |
| Item laid out to William Warne for carrying of lime and stones, and for beere that day to all the workmen | | 8 | 0 |
| Item given to [?James] Mills for makeing of a sawing pitt | | 1 | 6 |
| Item paid to the sawers for theire wages, August the 8th | | 9 | 0 |
| Item paid more the same day for beere for the sawers, carpenters, masons and carters | | 1 | 3 |
| Item paid for beere, August the 13th, which the workemen had in three dayes | | 2 | 0 |
| Item paid more about that time for beere to all the workmen | | 1 | 0 |
| Item laid out when the straw was carried for the schoolehouse, in meate and beere | | | 8 |
| Item laid out for beere which all the workmen had in ij dayes, August the 26th | | 1 | 4 |
| Item laid out more in beere ij dayes together to the workemen, and for mending theire tackling | | 3 | 0 |
| Item given to Irish people about that time | | | 6 |
| Item paid to the thatchers for theire worke, for bindings and swayes | 1 | 5 | 0 |
| Item paid to the schoolemaster about that time for teaching 4 boyes | 1 | 0 | 0 |
| Item paid to the masons for theire worke about the steeple | 1 | 12 | 0 |
| Item given to Irish people, September the 12th | | 1 | 0 |
| Item given more about that time to a boy for going on 2 severall errandes | | | 4 |
| Item laid out at the generall court at Yoxford for all charges, and for mine owne expences there, September the 18th | | 9 | 6 |
| Item laid out in beere for the workmen about that time | | 1 | 4 |
| Item laid out for the composition mony, October the 4th | 2 | 5 | 0 |
| Item given the same day to maimed soldiers | | 8 | 8 |
| Item paid about that time to Henry Richardson for board | | 12 | 0 |

[39] The parish acquired a book of special prayers for a public fast.

| | £ | s. | d. |
|---|---|---|---|
| Item paid to William Crosse for iron worke, October the 11th | 4 | 0 | 0 |
| Item laid out for the x commandementes writing, for the frame and for the bringinge[40] | 1 | 0 | 6 |
| Item paid out for beere for the workemen in 2 dayes | | 1 | 4 |
| Item paid for another bill of charges, to Gregory Rowse | 2 | 5 | 0 |
| Item paid to John Howell for his worke about the frame and the bells, October 28th | 6 | 18 | 2 |
| Item paid more the same day to [Ruben] Tallent for beere and worke | | 10 | 0 |
| Item given to the ringers for ringing, November the 5th [41] | | 5 | 0 |
| Item paid the same day to John Howell for his worke | 2 | 13 | 0 |
| Item paid to the baily for Rose Larkes | | 2 | 4 |
| Item paid about that time for oates for the Kinges Majesties houshold[42] | 1 | 4 | 0 |
| Item given to Mr [Gabriel] Elond, January the 2d | 3 | 0 | 0 |
| Item given alsoe to Mr [Nicholas] Kemp about that time for admission fee | | 1 | 6 |
| Item laid out at Halsworth about that time when I gave in my presentment to the Justices, and for my expences that day | | 2 | 0 |
| Item laid out this last Christmas to maimed souldiers | | 8 | 8 |
| Item given to Sara Cady | | 2 | 0 |
| Item given to Robert Broadbancke for looking to the towne corslet | | 1 | 0 |
| Item paid more to William Crosse for iron worke about the church | | 2 | 0 |
| Item given to [Nicholas] Kemp for keeping us from Yoxford court | | 2 | 0 |
| Item given to a glazer for mending the schoolehouse windowes | | 2 | 10 |
| The summe of this side is | 32 | 11 | 5 |
| | | | |
| Laid out in all | 72 | 3 | 10 |

[178]

The accoumpt of John Rous, one of the churchwardens of the towne of Cratfield, made and given up to the inhabitants[43] of the sayd towne the 22th of March Anno 1640 [for 1640–1]

| | £ | s. | d. |
|---|---|---|---|
| Receyptes | | | |
| Imprimus receyved of Frauncis Alldous for his rent or fearme of the towne land called Bessnalles | 17 | 0 | 0 |
| Item receyved of Richard Raydon for his yeares rent or fearme of the Towne Meadowe | 6 | 10 | 0 |

---

[40] The Ten Commandments were painted, mounted in a wooden frame, and installed in the church.

[41] Gun Powder Treason Day, a comparatively new and distinctly Protestant festival which was celebrated at Cratfield by bell-ringing. See Cressy, *Bonfires and Bells* (1989).

[42] A clear reference to 'purveyance', one of the crown's prerogatives. This involved the requisition and collection of provisions as a right; especially the right to purchase whatever was needed for the royal household at a fixed price. Charles I increasingly used his prerogatives to finance government, especially during the period of personal rule. Purveyance was generally resented, and was declared illegal in 1642.

[43] The inhabitants, also known as chief inhabitants, were the leading men and elected officers of the community, who oversaw the running of the parish (see Appendix 2, pp. 145–7).

|  | £ | s. | d. |
|---|---|---|---|
| Item receyved of John Willyames for his yeares rent or fearme of the towne land | 5 | 0 | 0 |
| Item receyved of Edmund Broadbancke and the Widdowe [Mary] Broadbanck for there yeares rent or fearme of the Towne Pyghtell | 1 | 0 | 0 |
| receyved of Robert Smyth in the Closse for part of his bargayne of tymber that he bought of Sir Thurstone Smyth and M$^r$ Robert Warner, and the rest of the townes men one the towne land | 10 | 0 | 0 |
| receyved of M$^r$ [Gabriel] Eland for the wood in the Scoolehouse Pyghtel that he bought of the townsemen | 1 | 0 | 0 |
| Item sould to Henery Doallinge one beell wheele |  | 5 | 0 |
| Sum' | 40 | 15 | 0 |

Cratfield
Disbursmentes for the towne in the yeare of Our Lord 1640

| | £ | s. | d. |
|---|---|---|---|
| Imprimus layd out for bread and wine for the Sacrament the 28$^{th}$ of March | | 4 | 10 |
| Item layd out to Ruben Tallen for his quarters wages | | 10 | 0 |
| Item layd out for bread and wine for the Sacrament the 4$^{th}$ of Aprill | | 4 | 2 |
| Item layd out for bread and wine for the Sacrament the 11$^{th}$ of Aprill | | 5 | 6 |
| Item layd out to James Smyth for broaches making | | 1 | 10 |
| Item layd out to Edmund Milles for the lordes rent of the towne land | | 4 | 0 |
| Item layd out for the rent of <Shaddow> Psallow Pightell to the said Edmund Milles | | | 6 |
| Item payd to him more for arerages of rent | | 1 | 6 |
| Item layd out to Kathering Travinian and her daughter, Ireshwomen that were goeing to Ireland the 6 of Maye | | 1 | 0 |
| Item given to 5 Iresh people | | | 6 |
| Item layd out for bread and wine for the Sacrament the 24$^{th}$ of Maye | | 3 | 0 |
| Item layd out to Willyam Crose for a payre of hookes and eyes for a gate at Bessnalles | | 1 | 6 |
| Item layd out to Robert Smyth in the Close for conductinge mony and souldgers paye and for other charges as by the warrant doe apeare the 6 of June[44] | 7 | 10 | 9 |
| Item layd out to Goodman [Nicholas] More for mending of the churchyard palles and 100 nayles | | 2 | 4 |
| Item given to the Widdow Pearse for laying of Danyell Monnes wife, the Ireshwoman, in chilldbeed the 11 of June | | 2 | 6 |
| Item given to Danyell Moone for his wife and thre chrildrens mayntenance in the tyme of hir childebeed[45] | | 10 | 0 |

[44] Robert Smyth 'in the Close', perhaps serving as constable, escorted money raised in the parish to an undisclosed location, perhaps Beccles or Halesworth. Part of the money was to pay soldiers.
[45] The economy of some poor households could not withstand the disruption of the mother's lying-in period, when she was unable to work. Parishes frequently stepped in and gave assistance at such moments, either in cash or kind. They also often covered the cost of caring for the mother.

|  | £ | s. | d. |
|---|---|---|---|
| Item given to the Goodwife Alldous for keeping of the Ireshwoman in childbeed[46] |  | 6 | 0 |
| Summ | 10 | 9 | 11 |

Disbursmentes

| | | | |
|---|---|---|---|
| Item given to John Alecorne, his wife and thre childrene that were travelleinge to Lemmingeton in Hampshire[47] |  |  | 6 |
| Item given to Goodman [Ruben] Tallinge for makeinge of the grave for the 2 Iresh children[48] |  |  | 6 |
| Item layd out to James Smyth for thatching at Bessnalles |  | 3 | 6 |
| Item layd out to the breefe of John Chriseules, a poore gentleman and Christian of Grece, for the losse of £4000 taken from him by the Turkes, and alsoe his wife and childrene and other frindes in bondage, untill 2000 ducketes more be payd for there redemtion |  | 6 | 8 |
| Item layd out to the breefe of Edward Boswell of Flitwick, in the countie of Bedford, for his lose of £250 by fire[49] |  | 2 | 0 |
| Item layd out to the breefe of Willyam Symmes, clarke of Harlington in Bedford, and divers others of the same towne for there lose of £1100 by fire |  | 2 | 6 |
| Item layd out to the brefe of John Thurketle of Dunston in Norffolk for his lose of £200 by fire |  | 2 | 6 |
| Item layd out to the breefe of Robert Smyth and divers others of the parish of Saint Olave of Southwarke, in the countie of Surry,[50] for the loose of £1776 14s. 4d. |  | 1 | 8 |
| Item layd out [to] the breefe of Thomas Dawson of Stanton in Suffolk for his loose of £400 by fire |  | 2 | 6 |
| Item layd out for bread and wine for the Sacrament the 6 of September |  | 4 | 6 |
| Item given to [?]Elion' Smyth and Margaret Smyth that travelled by certificate and had susstayned great loose |  |  | 6 |
| Summ | 1 | 7 | 4 |

Disbursments

| | | | |
|---|---|---|---|
| Item given to Willyam Alldous for servinge in the towne armes[51] the 15 of September and the [?]24th of September |  | 3 | 0 |
| Item given to Thomas Johnson for serving in the towne armes the <29th>\24th/ of September |  | 1 | 6 |
| Item layd out to Edmund Milles for the lordes rent of the towne landes |  | 10 | 11½ |
| Item for the rent of <Shaddow> \Psallow/ Pightell |  |  | 6 |

---

[46] At parish expense, a poor stranger was given nursing assistance during childbirth.

[47] Lymington, Hampshire.

[48] The cost of a pauper's burial was paid by the parish. Expenses included an entry in the parish register, the sexton's fee and the cost of a coffin or shroud .

[49] Cratfield's ability to assist other communities in need reflects its prosperous economic condition (see Introduction, pp. 4–9).

[50] Southwark, on the south bank of the River Thames, directly opposite the city of London.

[51] Alldous and other soldiers served under arms on behalf of the parish during the Second Bishops' War. The English were defeated in October 1640, and the war ended with the Treaty of Ripon. See Fissel, *The Bishops' Wars* (1994).

|  | £ | s. | d. |
|---|---|---|---|
| Item payd unto Ruben Talling for his quarters wages |  | 10 | 0 |
| Item payd unto Ruben Talling for grease for the belles and oyle and wire for the clocke |  |  | 10 |
| Item given to a poore Ireshwoman and thre children |  |  | 6 |
| Item payd unto Willyam Warne for carriing of the armor for the towne to two trayeninges[52] |  | 16 | 0 |
| Item given to two mayned soulgers that cam out of Jermynie[53] and wer travalinge into Kent |  |  | 6 |
| Item layd out for one of the towne coslets, cullering and nayelinge[54] |  | 16 | 0 |
| Item layd out to Robert Smyth [in the Close] for planck and board | 1 | 4 | 0 |
| Item layd out to Thomas Johnson and Willyam Alldous for servinge in the towne armes the 13 of November |  | 3 | 0 |
| Item layd out to the breefe of Metrophanes Attebeg who haveinge sustayned imprissonment 5 yeares and lose of £2000 |  | 3 | 0 |
| Item layd out to the breefe of thre Inglishmen who had susstayned the lose of £600 by fire |  | 2 | 0 |
| Item layd out for the towne coslet makeinge | 1 | 6 | 8 |
| Item layd out for bread and wine for the Sacrament on the Nativitie of Christ[55] |  | 4 | 3 |
| Item layd out to Ruben Tallinge for his quarters wages |  | 10 | 0 |
| Summ | 6 | 12 | 8 |

[179]
A true coppie of charges and layings out for the towne of Cratfield by mee Robert Smith junior, being churchwarden there from the 22th day of March last past in the yeere 1640 untill the 21th day of this instant March (1641) [*for 1641–2*]

|  | £ | s. | d. |
|---|---|---|---|
| Inprimis laid out on our reckoning day which was the 22th of March 1640, for fyring and wine and othere expences that day |  | 12 | 0 |
| Item more at that time to my brother Alldis for his bill of charges | 2 | 9 | 5 |
| Item laid out to the schoolemaster for teaching the 4 poore children the 25th of March | 1 | 0 | 0 |
| Item given to 2 gentlemen souldiers the 28th of March |  |  | 6 |
| Item paid to my selfe a debt due from the towne | 14 | 9 | 0 |
| Item given to a gentleman travailer with a passe which had great losse |  |  | 6 |
| Item more for riding to the jusstices and my expences and my horsemeat 3 times rideing \about Finet Adams/[56] |  | 3 | 0 |
| Item given to [Nicolas] Kempe |  | 2 | 0 |

---

[52] Trainings were official musters when local troops were drilled and trained on some suitable open space, usually a green or common such as Sibton Green or Bulcamp Heath (see Notes 31 & 103).
[53] Germany.
[54] At this time, the parish spent money on the making and repair of corslets. Here, nailing and 'colouring' seem to be involved.
[55] Christmas, 25 December.
[56] Robert Smith, junior, made three trips to Justices of the Peace while pursuing the case of Finet Adams, probably in connection with her illegitimate child born in 1640.

| | £ | s. | d. |
|---|---|---|---|
| Item the 25th of Aprill for the composition warrant[57] | 3 | 0 | 0 |
| more the same day for Maimed Souldiers | | 8 | 8 |
| Item the 2th day of May to Samuell Cady for stowing of wood for the poore and bratlyng of that wood[58] | | 10 | 0 |
| more about that time given to [Samuel] Cady towards the burying [of] the Widdow [Ann] Spinke | | 5 | 0 |
| Item the 6th day of May laid out for charges in the court and our expences and horsemeat at Yoxford[59] | | 9 | 0 |
| more at that time to Mr [Gabriel] Eland for writing the billes indented | | 2 | 0 |
| Item given to Thomas Adams for worke about his trade \for the church/ | | 2 | 0 |
| Item given to Mr [Thomas] Bedingfield at Barnaby court[60] for Maimed Souldiers | | 8 | 8 |
| Item laid out for 2 subsidies[61] at Whitsontid court for the towne | 4 | 16 | 0 |
| more laid out that same day for wine and sugar and beere at the court | | 7 | 8 |
| Item given to Ruben Tallowing for his attendance at the reckoning day and worke about the church yard | | 1 | 6 |
| Item given to 3 gentlemen souldiers with Sir Thomas Glemhams hand to theire passe[62] | | | 6 |
| Item laid out at Yoxford court for charges and & [sic] for my expences the 9th of July | | 4 | 1 |
| Item for many travailars the 10th day of July sent by Sir Thurston Smith | | | 8 |
| Item the 12th day of August to other poore people with a passe | | | 6 |
| Item the 29th day of September to the schoolemaster for teaching the 4 poore boyes | 1 | 0 | 0 |
| more the same day to Thomas Legat for Maimed Souldiers | | 8 | 8 |
| The whole summe of this side is | 31 | 1 | 4 |
| | | | |
| Item about that time to travaillars | | | 4 |
| Item laid out to my brother [John] Aldis for pullering mony for diners[63] | | 12 | 0 |
| Item the 10th day of October to Goodman [John] Ebes for Composition Mony | 2 | 10 | 0 |
| more the same time to the Widdow [Frances] Rouse for straw and thatching | 1 | 4 | 0 |
| Item the same day to Gregorie Rouse for carriing the poore folkes woode, 13 lodes | 1 | 6 | 0 |
| Item at that time for worke about the barn dores and brickes for the oven | | | 10 |

---

[57] The composition warrant constituted an order to levy purveyance (see Notes 42 & 85).

[58] A recurrent item in the accounts is wood as fuel for the poor, and the costs of felling, cutting, carrying, etc. Samuel Cady was usually involved.

[59] See Note 8.

[60] Barnaby court, an unknown location.

[61] These are the parliamentary subsidies voted in 1641 to defray the costs of war in the previous year. Cratfield paid at Whitsun and in November.

[62] Colonel Sir Thomas Glemham, leader of Charles I's Fourth Regiment (see Biographies, p. 134). When the parish honoured his pass, and earlier cooperated with the king's purveyor, it demonstrated that parliament's authority was not complete at the start of hostilities.

[63] Pulvering money was spent on feeding the town's men on the day of reckoning, or Pulvering Day (see Note 6, and Glossary).

|  | £ | s. | d. |
|---|---|---|---|
| Item the 3th day of November given to the baly for Rose Larkes for rent |  | 2 | 4 |
| more the same day given to 6 poore people sent by Mr [Gabriel] Eland |  |  | 6 |
| Item the 20th day of November given to 2 Irish gentlewomen supper and lodging and breakfast and mony, with a certificate from Ireland and a passe from the balyes of Yarmouth,[64] theire losse was 8 hundred pounds |  | 1 | 0 |
| Item the 27th day of November for one subsidie for the towne | 2 | 8 | 0 |
| Item more the same day for oates for the King[65] | 1 | 5 | 4 |
| Item the 6th day of December to travailers |  |  | 6 |
| Item the same time to Thomas Adams for bricke and worke for the schoolhowse, and ashes and clay for morter for the stocke,[66] and more harthes and stockes at the poore folkes howses |  | 9 | 0 |
| Item given to Mr [Gabriel] Eland on New Yeere day | 3 | 0 | 0 |
| more at that time to Mr [Thomas] Bedingfield for Maimed Souldiers |  | 8 | \8/ |
| Item given to 2 seafaring men travailing in to Norffolk |  |  | 4 |
| Item given to 7 seafaring men |  |  | 6 |
| Item at Yoxford the 25th day of February for all our expences with Mr [Gabriel] Eland |  | 5 | 0 |
| Item given to 2 seafaring men |  |  | 4 |
| Item given to Mr Banckes the minister |  | 6 | 0 |
| The whole summe of this side is | 14 | 0 | 8 |
| The summe totul is | 45 | 2 | 0 |
| received of the Widdow [Frances] Rouse for hir whole yeers rent, 1641 | 45 | 0 | 0 |

[180]

The accoumpt of John Rous, one of the churchwardens of the towne of Cratfield, made and given up to Sir Thurston Smyth and Mr Robert Warner and diverse other inhabitantes of the towne March 21th Anno 1641 [for 1641–2]

Receyptes for the towne

|  | £ | s. | d. |
|---|---|---|---|
| receyved of Richard Raydon for his rent or fearme of the Towne Meadowes for one yeare |  | 6 | 10 | 0 |
| receyved of Frauncis Alldous for his rent or fearme of Besnalles for one yeare | 17 | 0 | 0 |
| receyved of John Willyams for his rent or fearme of the townes mens land for one yere | 5 | 0 | 0 |
| receyved of the Widdow [Mary] Broadbanck for her rent or fearme of the Towne Pyghtell | 1 | 0 | 0 |
| Summ | 29 | 10 | 0 |

---

[64] Great Yarmouth, a major port in east Norfolk.
[65] Again, purveyance for the royal household (see Note 42).
[66] Ash and clay were common ingredients in the making of mortar. In this entry, the word 'stock' may have been used in two different senses (see Glossary).

|  | £ | s. | d. |
|---|---|---|---|
| Disbursmentes for the towne in the yeare Anno 1641, March 25th |  |  |  |
| Imprimis ther is oweinge to me uppon my accoumpt to the towne for the yeare last past | 3 | 9 | 7 |
| Item layd out to Edmund Milles for the lordes rent of the towne land |  | 4 | 6 |
| Item layd out to Robert Smyth in the Close, the collectors deputie, for 2 subsidies the 13 day of Aprill | 4 | 16 | 0 |
| Item layd out to John Newson for the use of his monye the towne hath of his[67] |  | 12 | 0 |
| Item layd out to Ruben Tallinge for his quarters wages |  | 10 | 0 |
| Item layd out the 18th of Aprill for bread and wine for the Sacrament |  | 5 | 2 |
| Item layd out to Henery Doallinge for mendinge of the beel stoopes |  | 3 | 0 |
| Item layd out the 25 of Aprill for bread and wine for the Sacrament |  | 5 | 6 |
| Item layd out for our exspence at Hallsworth when we gave our accoumpt to the Justice[68] |  | 2 | 6 |
| Item layd out for a warant to destrayne[69] |  |  | 6 |
| Item layd out the second daye of May for bread and wine for the Sacrament |  | 5 | 6 |
| Summ | 10 | 14 | 3 |

|  | £ | s. | d. |
|---|---|---|---|
| Disbursmentes |  |  |  |
| Item layd out to a poore souldier |  |  | 4 |
| Item layd out to a breefe of diverse men who had susstayned lose to the vallue of £2000 by fire |  | 4 | 0 |
| Item layd out for bread and wine for the Sacrament one Whitsundaye |  | 4 | 6 |
| Item layd out <for> \to/ the vissiters[70] for there fee |  | 1 | 6 |
| Item layd out for Robert Smyth his exspence and mine owne at Bliborrowgh[71] at our giveinge in of men names for the Pole Monye[72] |  | 2 | 10 |
| Item given to a poore souldier |  |  | 3 |
| Item layd out to Ruben Tallion for his quarterage |  | 10 | 0 |
| Item layd out to two brefes |  | 3 | 6 |
| Item given to a poore souldier |  |  | 6 |
| Item given to John Lee who travaled by certificate and had susstained great lose by fire in Ireland |  | 1 | 0 |
| Item given to a poore woman that traveled by certificate |  |  | 6 |
| Item layd out to Edmund Milles for the lordes rent of the towne land, \and for the common fine/ |  | 16 | 11½ |

---

[67] This is an interest payment on money that John Newson loaned to the town. Because usury, the act of lending money at interest, especially charging excessive or illegal rates of interest on loans, was considered contrary to Christian behaviour, many interest payments were recorded in this fashion to avoid the suggestion of usury. By this date, however, attitudes were changing. See also the town's £20 interest payment for three-quarters of a year in 1651–2.

[68] An unnamed Justice of the Peace.

[69] Distraint of knighthood. In 1631, Charles appointed commissioners in every county to locate and fine gentlemen who failed to sue for knighthood upon his accession. It was one of the Royal Prerogatives attacked by Parliament in January, 1641.

[70] Ecclesiastical visitors were regularly paid fees (see Note 12).

[71] Blythburgh, a small inland port about 9 miles east of Cratfield.

[72] The Poll Tax was granted by Parliament in the summer of 1641. Tax evasion was particularly high and it netted only £169,000.

|  | £ | s. | d. |
|---|---|---|---|
| Item for the lordes rent of \<shad\> Psallow Pightell |  |  | 6 |
| Item layd out for 3 yardes of diaper for a cloath for the communion table |  | 17 | 0 |
| Item layd out to Ruben Tallion for his quarterage |  | 10 | 0 |
| Item layd out unto John Milles for his exspence and charges \<and\> when he was constable, as by his bill apere | 1 | 17 | 10 |
| Item layd out unto Mr [Thomas] Beddingefield for one subsidie of the towne landes, the 27 of November | 2 | 8 | 0 |
| Item layd out unto Mr [Thomas] Beddingefield for arrerages of the compossition the same daye | 1 | 0 | 0 |
| Item layd out to James Smyth for thachinge at Besnalles |  | 4 | 4 |
| Item layd out to Frauncis Alldous for strawe |  | 6 | 0 |
| Item layd out unto Simon Warne for mendinge of a stoole in the church wheare the pulpit stood[73] |  | 1 | 6 |
| Summ | 9 | 5 | 10½ |

|  | £ | s. | d. |
|---|---|---|---|
| Item layd out to Symon Warne for mendinge of the gate into Coopers Close |  |  | 6 |
| Item layd out to Edmund Milles for the lordes rent |  |  | 4 |
| Item layd out for bread and wine for the Sacrament one the Nativitie of our Savioure[74] |  | 4 | 10 |
| Item layd out to a breefe for the repayre of the church of Winchelsie in the countie of Sussex[75] |  | 2 | 6 |
| Item layd out to the breefe of Thomas Youngman of Blackeny in the countie of Norffolk[76] |  | 2 | 0 |
| Item layd out to a poore saylor |  |  | 6 |
| Item layd out unto Ruben Tallion for his quarters wages |  | 10 | 0 |
| Item layd out to the breefe of John Man of Bradfield in Norffolk who had great lose by fyre |  | 2 | 0 |
| Item layd out for a glaseinge of the church windowes and three iron bares |  | 7 | 7 |
| Summ | 1 | 10 | 3 |

Disbursmentes unto the poore

|  | Monthly | Yearely |  |  |
|---|---|---|---|---|
| Ann Newson, widdow | 4s. | 2 | 12 | 0 |
| Avice Hayward, widdow | 2s. | 1 | 6 | 0 |
| Joan Mingaye | 2s. | 1 | 6 | 0 |
| Rose Browne | 1s. |  | 13 | 0 |
| Finit Adames | 2s. | 1 | 3 | 0 |
| Ann Spinke, widdow | 2s. 8d for 2 wekes and died |  | 2 | 8 |

[73] The pulpit may have been moved to a more prominent position in the nave, thus necessitating repairs to the adjacent pews. On the other hand, this could be a reference to a stool of penance, used to shame sinners publicly and to warn the assembled parish of the consequences of sin: see J. H. Baker, 'Criminal Courts and Procedure at Common Law, 1550–1800' (1977), p. 32.

[74] Christmas, 25 December.

[75] Winchelsea, Sussex.

[76] Blakeney, in north Norfolk.

|  | £ | s. | d. |
|---|---|---|---|
| Item given unto the Widdow [Ann] Spinke in her siknese, the 28 of March |  | 5 | 0 |
| Item given unto Sarye Cady in her nessesitie |  | 7 | 6 |
| Item laid out unto the Widdow [Ann] Newson the 14th of May in the tyme of sikenese |  | 4 | 0 |
| Summ | 7 | 19 | 2 |
| Summa totalis | 29 | 9 | 6½ |

[181]

The acoumpt' of Robert Smyth senier, one of the churchwardings of the towne of Crattfeilld for the yeare 1642: *vidillicet per me*, Robert Smyth [*for 1642–3*]

|  | £ | s. | d. |
|---|---|---|---|
| Item the disburcments |  |  |  |
| Inprimis to Robert Smyth de Colltshawe, one of the precedent churchwardings, for that yeare then past, that the towne ought unto him then as dide apeere upon his acoumpt |  | 2 | 0 |
| Item to the Widowe [Ann] Haywarde upon the reconing daye for hir fireing and fitting the roome[77] |  | 2 | 0 |
| Item to Rubine Talline for his attendence that daye |  | 1 | 6 |
| Item that for wine |  | 6 | 0 |
| Item to Mr [Thomas] Bedingfeilld for the composistione for the whole year as apeare by warants | 5 | 10 | 0 |
| Item to Mr [Thomas] Bedingfeilld for fouer quarters for the Mayned Solldiers and Marshallseas, being viijs. viijd. a quarter as apeare by his warants | 1 | 14 | 8 |
| Item to Mr [Thomas] Crosbye for one whole \yeare/ lecture ended the 28 of Februarij 1642[78] | 20 | 0 | 0 |
| Item given to Mr Banks, the first of May, who dide [?]preched upon that Lords daye twice |  | 10 | 0 |
| Item to Wyllyam Neuson for housfearme for his mother for one yeare and a half at Mykilltide 1642[79] | 1 | 0 | 0 |
| Item at Hallsworth for 4 men and there horses that were sumened thither by warant for making of the rate inacted by Parlement for [?]leaving moneys[80] |  | 5 | 4 |
| Item given the Widowe [Mary] Broadbanke when the rate was made, for a roome and fireing |  | 1 | 0 |
| Item to Goodwife [Mary] Tallin the 7 of June in hir sicknes |  | 5 | 0 |

---

[77] Widow Hayward hosted the reckoning day and her expenses were reimbursed by the parish.

[78] The first mention of an annual 'lecture' at Cratfield. This was a series of sermons given at regular intervals, probably, because of the high cost, supported by an endowment. (For Thomas Crosby, see Biographies, p. 132.)

[79] Michaeltide or Michaelmas, 29 September.

[80] Individual tax assessments were determined for an unidentified parliamentary levy.

The account of Robert Smyth senior one of the
churchwardings of the towne of cratffield for the
yeare - 1642: [bidillet] - pme Robt Smyth

Item the disburcments                                £ - s - d

Imprimis to Robert Smyth se collt shave one of
the precedent churchwardings for that yeare       00-02-00
then past that the towne ought unto him than
as did apeere upon his acountt

Item to the widowe hayward upon the crowing       00-02-00
dayes for hir firing and fitting the roome

Item to Dubins callins for his attendance that day 00-01-06

Item that for wind _____            00-06-00

Item to mr Bodingsfield for the composstion       05-10-00
for the whole yeare as apeare by warantis

Item to mr Bodingsfield for foure quarters for
the mayned souldies and marshallseas being        01-14-08
[bin]_[blind] a quarter as apeare by his warants

Item to mr crosbye for one whole lecture ouded     20-00-00
the - 28 of februarij 1642

Item given to mr Banks the first of may whose side 00-10-00
preched upon that londs dayes twice

Item to wylliam nunn for housfearme for his        01-00-00
mother for one yeare at a half at mykiltide 1642

Item at hallsworth for 4 men and there horses that
were sumoned thither by warant for making of       00-05-04
the rate inacted by ye loment for bausing maisis

Item given the widowe Broadbanke when the rate     00-01-00
was made for a roome and firing

Item to Goodwife callin that 7 of june in hir siknes - 00-05-00

Item to Edd Smyth by the advise of the constmen
to search the offices for and concerning felons    00-13-06
goods that he layd out of his purse and his paynes

Item to goodwife callin for mr clarke for phisicke 00-05-00

Item to John Browne with 4 others taken h. to t.

2. Extract from the account of Robert Smyth, senior, churchwarden of Cratfield,
for the year 1642–3 (SROI, FC62/A6/181).

|  | £ | s. | d. |
|---|---|---|---|
| Item to Edd' Smyth, by the advise of the townsmen, to search the offices for, and concerning, fellons goods that he layd out of his purse and his paynes | | 13 | 6 |
| Item to Goodwife [Mary] Tallin for M[r] Clarke for phisicke | | 5 | 0 |
| Item to John Browne with 4 others taken by the the Turkes, the 29 of June as apeared by a certifficate | | 2 | 0 |
| Item to M[r] [Thomas] Bedingfeilld that he layd out of purse for the gitting of a solldier [*that*] was put upon our towne, as apeard by warant and his paynes[81] | | 10 | 0 |
| Item to Robert Carye and John Carye who were taken by the rebells, and there father misarblye used and then slaine in Ireland, being a capteyn, as did apeare by the minsters hande the 7 of Jullii[82] | | 2 | 0 |
| Item to Goodwife [Mary] Tallin the 17 of Jullij in hir sicknes | | 5 | 0 |
| Item to John Hirbirt, his wife and sister and chilldren, the 21 of Jullij, driven out of Ireland, and Capteyn Herbirt there father, by the rebells babarously slaine | | 1 | 0 |
| Item to Henerye Carye who lost by the rebells, as did apeare by a certifficate, two thousand pounds | | 2 | 0 |
| Item to Thomas Bennit whose house was burnte at Thorpe[83] and lost £200 as apeeard by certificat' | | | 6 |
| Item to Kathrine Retoricke an Ireshe woeman | | | 6 |
| Item to M[r] [John] Fyske for our townsmens lands acording to the rate and Acte of Parlement as apeare by that rate | 2 | 0 | 0 |
| Item to him that it came unto, above vjd. in the pound | | 14 | 9 |
| Item to Robert Lotham, his wife and 9 chilldreen who hade his house burned as apeared by a certificat | | 1 | 0 |
| Item for caryeing the armes to Yoxford 20 of October | | 7 | 0 |
| Item at Yoxford for 4 mens dinners and there horse, when theye payde in the money and plate lent to the Parlement upon the Propistions[84] | | 4 | 0 |
| Summe | 35 | 5 | 9 |

---

[81] Probably the cost of billeting. Both sides in the Civil War forced civilians to provide free accommodation, food and horses to the armed forces. Constables were required to keep a record of these costs, but except in case of extreme hardship, they were seldom repaid. See Coward, *The Stuart Age*, p. 186.

[82] Irish travellers are mentioned earlier in these accounts, but this is the first specific reference to the Irish rebellion, 1641–3, when many Protestants were massacred or driven from their homes (see Note 210 and Introduction, p. 19, n. 100).

[83] Probably Thorpe, near Aldeburgh, Suffolk.

[84] The Propositions for Money and Plate, August 1642, became the basis of the Parliamentarian war effort and of a national army, but were initially passed to pay for the army under Essex. Parliament requested the loan of money and plate, plus offers to support horsemen and their horses, with the promise of repayment with 8 per cent interest. Some were sceptical of the chances of repayment, and those who did not contribute were threatened with fines. As Anthony Fletcher notes, 'in the long run, of course, the Propositions were a vital element in Parliament's war machine and even tiny villages in some districts contributed impressively'. He uses a village in East Suffolk as an example before continuing: 'but this was because Propositions money came to be spent mainly on local defence'. In fact, some areas refused to contribute until they could be assured that the money would be used in defence of their own county. See Fletcher, *The Outbreak of the English Civil War* (1981), pp. 336–9.

|  | £ | s. | d. |
|---|---|---|---|
| Item to Wyllyam Crose as apeare by a bill left to be payd by the olld churchwardings | | 8 | 2 |
| Item to Wyllyam Crose as apeare by a bill to yeare | | 10 | 10 |
| Item to Thomas Leggitt that he layd out when he was counstable as apeare by his bill | | 8 | 9 |
| Item to John Ebbs that he layde out when he was counstable as apeare by his bill | | 7 | 2 |
| Item to the Widowe [Mary] Broadbanke that morning the trayned solldiers went first to Yoxford, for the 2 towne solldiers breakfast and a horse for one of them and getting the armes together | | 3 | 6 |
| Item for compostistion oates as apear by warant[85] | | 18 | 0 |
| Item for two naggs and a mare lent the Parlement upon the Propostions | 11 | 0 | 0 |
| Item for three saddlles and bridlles upon the same | | 18 | 0 |
| Item to Thomas Leggitt for his and the 3 solldiers dyett at Ipswiche as apeare by his bill | | 11 | 0 |
| Item to Wyllyam Wills, 22 of November, taken by the Turks | | | 6 |
| Item to Katherin Fouller and hir sister and 4 chilldren whose husbands were slayne by the rebels, 23 November[86] | | 1 | 0 |
| Item for a planke \to/ Francis Alldus in the towne house[87] to laye before the fire | | 3 | 4 |
| Item the 12 of September to John Hartly in his sicknes | | 5 | 0 |
| Item the 10 of December to Thomas Joanes whose house was burnte at Bungay,[88] and his lose £50 | | 1 | 0 |
| Item to John Smyth a solldier | | | 2 |
| Item for caryeing the armes to Blyborowe[89] | | 8 | 0 |
| Item for stoweing and brattlling the wodd for poore follks | | 12 | 0 |
| Item for caryeing 17 loades of wodd to the poore | 1 | 10 | 0 |
| Item to Gregorye Rouse for a muskett resst | | 2 | 0 |
| Item for a locke of the dore in the halle at Richard Reidons that the Widowe [Frances] Rouse left there | | | 8 |
| Item the 15 of Januarij to Goodwife [Mary] Tallin in hir sicknes | | 2 | 6 |
| Item to Wyllyam Taylor the 26 of Januarij who hade his house burned in Garbidg Thorpe in Norfollk[90] | | | 6 |
| Item the 6 of Februarij to John [?]Harpes, Robert Lawde and Wyllyam Goodwin whose shipp was cast awaye within 3 leags \of Yermouth/,[91] as apeared upon certifficate | | 1 | 0 |
| Item to Wyllyam Kinge the 12 of Februarij, a minister who was driven out of Irland frome his benifice by the rebells | | 2 | 0 |

[85] Here is clear proof that purveyance or 'composition' involved the issuing of royal warrants (see Notes 42 & 57).

[86] These may be the Irish rebels with whom Charles was negotiating, and with whom he signed the Cessation Treaty in September 1643.

[87] The town house is the same as the town hall (see Note 27).

[88] Bungay, Suffolk, a town about 9 miles north-east of Cratfield.

[89] Blythburgh, Suffolk.

[90] Probably Garboldisham, Norfolk.

[91] Great Yarmouth, Norfolk.

|  | £ | s. | d. |
|---|---|---|---|
| Item to John Edwards whose whose [sic] house and goods were burned in Jermynnye[92] as apeard upon certificat, the 3 of March |  | 1 | 0 |
| Item to Francis Garrett the 4 of March, a solldier |  |  | 6 |
| Item to Goodwife [Mary] Tallin the 8 of March to bye hir meat |  | 2 | 6 |
| Item to Finite Adams the 15 of March towards the buringe of hir childe |  | 2 | 0 |
| Item to M^r [John] Stebbing for the townsmens lands, beinge the second payment acording to the act of Parlement[93] | 3 | 8 | 2 |
| Item for oyle and wyare for the clocke |  |  | 6 |
| Sum of this side | 22 | 9 | 9 |
| The totall of bothe sides | 57 | 15 | 6 |

|  | £ | s. | d. |
|---|---|---|---|
| Item receivd of my sister [Frances] Rouse for rent for the towne | 45 | 0 | 0 |
| Item of Ricard Reiden for rent for the town | 5 | 0 | 0 |
| Item of M^r [Thomas] Bedingfeilld that he payd backe of money in his hand | 1 | 4 | 0 |
| The totall receivd by me, Robert Smyth | 51 | 4 | 0 |

[182]

The account of William Aldus, one of the churchwardens of Cratfeild, for the yeere of Our Lord 1642 [for 1642–3]

|  | £ | s. | d. |
|---|---|---|---|
| Inprimus laid out to John Williams for raisons and for amons and figges and suger |  | 11 | 6 |
| laid out to Ruben Tallowinge for his quarters wages due att Our Lady[94] |  | 10 | 0 |
| laid out to John Newson his mony due to him from the towne since he was churchwarden | 9 | 7 | 2 |
| laid out to Jeremy Baldry for his cunstabels bill |  | 10 | 4 |
| laid out to six brefes which I recived of the other churchwardens |  | 13 | 4 |
| given to Edmond Miles his wife to releve har with all |  | 5 | 0 |
| laid out to Edmond Miles for rent for the towne <land> for the towne land [sic] 3s. 2d. and vij egges, for the Towne Close 7d., for the Shadow Pittell, 1½d., for Sallow Pitells 6d.[95] |  | 4 | 6 |
| laid out to John Stanard of Laxfeild[96] for bread and wine for the three communions att Easter |  | 16 | 0 |
| laid out to John Gouldsmith for writeng and other things he did for the towne | 1 | 0 | 0 |
| laid out to the Widow [Mary] Brudbanke att the pullvaringe day for our diners | 1 | 7 | 0 |
| given to Ruben Tallowings wife in har sicknes |  | 5 | 0 |
| laid out to Rose Browne for keepinge Ruben Tallowins wife |  | 1 | 8 |

---

[92] Germany.

[93] The act of £400,000 (1642) was another attempt to raise money after the failure of the Poll Tax of the same year. This act proposed to raise money, ironically, on Charles I's much resented Ship Money principle of fixed assessments on each county.

[94] Lady Day, 25 March.

[95] This entry proves that Shadow and Sallow Pightles were two distinct pieces of land (see Note 18).

[96] Laxfield, a parish adjacent to Cratfield.

|  | £ | s. | d. |
|---|---|---|---|
| laid out when thay gave in the acount to the Justes, for there dinners and a warrent |  | 3 | 0 |
| laid out to John Stanards wife for keepeing of Rubens wife |  | 2 | 6 |
| laid out to John Stanard of Laxfeild for thirtenne pints of wine for the coorte |  | 4 | 0 |
| laid out to William Aldus for fetchinge of the wine |  |  | 4 |
| laid out to eight Irish peopell which came with a surteficat to travell to there freindes |  | 1 | 0 |
| laid out to Robart Smith for his cunstables bill | 1 | 10 | 9 |
| laid out to M[r] [?William] Aldus for teatching the fouer poore cheildren for the yeere | 2 | 0 | 0 |
| given to Ruben Tallowings wife beinge still sicke |  | 5 | 0 |
| laid out to Ruben Tallowinge for his quarters wages due att Midsumer |  | 10 | 0 |
| laid out to John Stanard of Laxfeild for bread and wine for the cumemunion[sic] on the fast day[97] |  | 1 | 6 |
| laid out to Heniry Dallinge for too dayes worke in the stepell |  | 4 | 0 |
| laid out to a brefe for the repareinge of a church att St Edmonds in Norich[98] |  | 2 | 6 |
| laid out to James Smith to releve him with all |  | 5 | 0 |
| laid out to Ruben Tallowinge for his quarters wages due att St Michell |  | 10 | 0 |
| laid out to Edmund Miles for a free rent for the maner of Cratfeild Rose[99] |  |  | 4 |
| laid out to Thomas Johnson and William Aldus for sarveinge in the towne armes att Yoxford |  | 3 | 0 |
| laid out to Ruben Tallowinges wife being still sicke |  | 5 | 0 |
| given to Edmond Miles is[100] wife to releve har with all |  | 5 | 0 |
| laid out att Frances Aldus is for a dich[101] and a paier of staires makeinge | 0 | 0 | 0 [sic] |
| laid out to Edmond Miles for rent for the towne land and for the common fine |  | 11 | 4 |
| The sume of this side is | 22 | 15 | 9 |
| given to Sary Cary to releve har with all |  | 1 | 0 |
| given to six Irish people which came with a surteficat to travell to ther freindes to Gallstone[102] |  | 1 | 0 |
| given to Edmond Miles his wife to releve har with all |  | 5 | 0 |
| laid out to Frances Aldus for a ditch and staires which he made |  | 11 | 0 |
| laid out to the Widow [Mary] Brudbanke for a pike and a sword for the towne |  | 13 | 0 |

[97] At its first meeting, the Long Parliament ordered that certain days were to be set aside as fast days. Starting on 23 February 1642, fasts were held in Parliament on the last Wednesday of the month, with a sermon in the morning and another in the afternoon. See Coward, *The Stuart Age*, p. 202, fn. 5.
[98] St Edmund's church in the major city of Norwich in Norfolk.
[99] The manor of Cratfield Roos: see Copinger, *Manors of Suffolk*, II (1908), 52–3.
[100] This and the next entry show the use of 'is' (or 'his') as a separate word, implying the possessive or genitive case.
[101] Making a ditch, as is revealed five entries later.
[102] Probably Gorleston, opposite Gt Yarmouth, Norfolk.

|  | £ | s. | d. |
|---|---|---|---|
| laid out when wee trained att Bullcum Heath,[103] to Thomas Johnson and William Aldus |  | 3 | 6 |
| laid out to Richard Piet of Laxfeild for too newe bell ropes |  | 8 | 0 |
| laid out to John Stanard for bread and wine for the cummunion att Cristmas |  | 5 | 2 |
| laid out to John Hartly att sundry times to releve him in his sicknes |  | 15 | 0 |
| laid out to Robart Lithum, &[sic] Irish man, with his wife and 9 cheildren, which had a surteficat |  | 1 | 0 |
| laid out to the Widow [Mary] Brudbanke for beere and fireinge when thay made the rate |  | 2 | 8 |
| laid out to Ruben Tallowinge for his quarters wages due att Cristmas |  | 10 | 0 |
| laid out to the too towne souldgers for fouer dayes traininge att Peasenall[104] |  | 12 | 0 |
| laid out to Hinry Dallinge for mending a bell whelle |  | 6 | 0 |
| laid out to Edmond Miles is wife to releve har |  | 5 | 0 |
| laid out to Edmond Wattlinge for the towne shipe of Cratfeild for the maner of Cratfeild Rose |  | 2 | 4 |
| laid out att Frances Aldus is for dichinge and springe |  | 19 | 0 |
| laid out for five dayes worke of a carpendar |  | 6 | 8 |
| laid out for nailes and hookes and eyes for a gatte |  | 2 | 0 |
| laid out for a paier of bar postes, to Gregory Smith |  |  | 10 |
| laid out to the towne souldgers for traineinge at Wallpoolle[105] |  | 3 | 0 |
| laid out to five brefes, to James Grauner |  | 8 | 4 |
| laid out to John Williams for nailes and salet oyle and wire [that] Ruben [Tallant] had |  | 1 | 0 |
| laid out for Mr William Smith of Laxfeild whech he was over ratted in your last ratte |  | 1 | 4½ |
| more laid out for my cuson John Rouse |  | 1 | 11 |
| more laid out for James Frier |  | 2 | 0 |
| laid out to John Williams for match for the <illeg.> watchers[106] |  | 1 | 6 |
|  |  |  |  |
| laid out for colection for the poore weekely, three shillinges a weeke |  |  |  |
| to the Widow [Ann] Newson |  | 1 | 0 |
| to the Widow [Ann] Haiward |  |  | 6 |
| to the Widow [Elizabeth] Brisingham |  |  | 6 |
| to Finett Adams |  |  | 6 |
| and to Sary Cary and Rose Browne |  |  | 6 |
| mounthly twelve shillings a mounth, for thirtenne mounthes | 7 | 16 | 0 |
| more laid out to Jonne Mingy for tenne weekes colection, 6d. a weeke |  | 5 | 0 |

---

[103] Bulcamp Heath, near Blythburgh, another area of common land used for training the militia (see Note 52). Musters were also held in the same year at Peasenhall and Walpole.

[104] Peasenhall, a parish about 4 miles south-east of Cratfield.

[105] Walpole, a parish about 3 miles east of Cratfield.

[106] These were sentries who were posted to watch against approaching enemies. They are probably related to the 'alarms' paid for by public rate in 1646–7 (see Note 166).

|  | £ | s. | d. |
|---|---|---|---|
| laid out to John Williams for pouder and bulletes and match which every musketter was to have: too lbs pouder, 2 lbs bullets and a lb. of match | 2 | 7 | 7 |
| laid out to John Williams for pouder and match which the souldgers have had to carry to to [*sic*] the traininges with them, evry on a quarter of pouder and sume match | 1 | 2 | 1 |
| The sume of this side is | 18 | 19 | 11½ |
| Totalis | 41 | 15 | 8½ |

|  | £ | s. | d. |
|---|---|---|---|
| Resived of John Rouse, on of the presedent churchwardens, which remained in his hand |  |  | 5½ |
| resived of Frances Aldus for his wholle yeers rent | 17 | 0 | 0 |
| resived of Richard Raidon for the Towne Medows which Mr [John] Fiske had | 6 | 10 | 0 |
| resived of John Williams for the land in his occupasion | 5 | 0 | 0 |
| resived of Mary Brudbanke, widow, for the Towne Pightle | 1 | 0 | 0 |
| The totall is | 29 | 10 | 5½ |

[183]
The 23 of March 1643
Suffollk
The acoumpt of Robert Smyth seneor, one of the churchwardinges of Cratfeilld, for the yeare 1643 as followeth [*for 1643–4*]

|  | £ | s. | d. |
|---|---|---|---|
| Item ther remayns to me upon the last acoumpt | 6 | 11 | 6 |
| Item layd out upon the reconing day for fire |  | 4 | 0 |
| Item for beating the drume for vollunteers[107] |  | 1 | 6 |
| Item to Barnabas Allyott a minister driven out of Ireland |  | 1 | 0 |
| Item to John White who hade his house burned in Ireland |  | 1 | 0 |
| Item to Ellin Osborne and hir sister driven out of Ireland |  | 1 | 0 |
| Item to Wyllyam Neuson for his mothers house fearme[108] |  | 13 | 4 |
| Item to the Widowe [Mary] Brodbank, at the makeing of a rate |  | 2 | 0 |
| Item at Bliborowe when we rodd to receive instrustions for makeing rates for the weekly paye acording to [?]ordinance[109] |  | 3 | 6 |
| Item to Edmond Mells for ditching at the Town Meades |  | 10 | 0 |
| Item to the Goodwife [Mary] Tallin in hir time of sicknes | 1 | 8 | 6 |
| Item at Bliborowe for the solldiers and townsmen |  | 6 | 0 |
| Item for worke about the Towne Pitlle for puting downe to posts for the great gate and riveing pale |  | 6 | 9 |

---

[107] A call for volunteer soldiers.
[108] The churchwarden reimbursed William for paying his aged mother's rent.
[109] This is probably the Weekly Assessment Ordinance of 1643 which ordered the collection and distribution of a weekly assessment drawn from the five counties of the Eastern Association (Norfolk, Suffolk, Essex, Cambridgeshire and Hertfordshire). The Assessment was organised by a central committee based in Cambridge and under the control of the Earl of Manchester. See Coward, *The Stuart Age*, pp. 180–1.

|  | £ | s. | d. |
|---|---|---|---|
| Item to M^r [William] Alldus for teaching foure poore chilldren | 2 | 0 | 0 |
| Item for a newe pike, sword, and bellt |  | 18 | 6 |
| Item to Barbara Browne hir husband being slaine |  | 1 | 6 |
| Item to John Allyson who was plundered at Reeding[110] |  | 1 | 0 |
| Item for stoweing and bratlling the wodd for the poore |  | 12 | 0 |
| Item to Wyllyam Nunn a mayned solldier in the Parlements [?]service |  | 1 | 0 |
| Item to M^r [Thomas] Crosby for the year lectur' ended the 28 Januarij 1643 | 20 | 0 | 0 |
| Item to Richard and John Coyner, ther lose £900 |  | 1 | 6 |
| Item to Wyllyam Purdin his lose a £1000 in Ireland |  | 1 | 0 |
| Item to Henery Potts lost a £1000 in Yorkshire |  | 1 | 0 |
| Item to Larans Carter, a docter in divinity, beaten from his house in Ireland, his sonn slayne, his lose £350 *per annum* and £4000 in stocke, as by testimonye at large aperd |  | 3 | 4 |
| Item to Rubeen Tallin for ringing the lecture bell for the first year at 4d. a day |  | 17 | 4 |
| Item to Robert Grant a solldier mayned in the Parlements [?]service |  |  | 6 |
| Item to Robert Davis his house and estate burnt by the rebels |  | 1 | 0 |
| Item for caryeing the volluntary armes[111] to Hallsworthe |  | 5 | 0 |
| Item for caryeing the armes to Cyppin Greene |  | 6 | 0 |
| Item to Katherin Graye and hir sister who had ther house burned and husbands slayne as apeared |  | 1 | 0 |
| Item to Joan Morfeilld hir husband slayne and hir lose <lose> £1500 as apeared at large by a certicate |  | 1 | 6 |
| Item to Richard Smyth taken by the Dunkards |  | 1 | 0 |
| Item to John Browne, a cryplle, and 12 mor with him |  | 1 | 0 |
| Item to Margery Bellymyn and Jane Neuton ther lose in Ireland £500, and ther husbands slayne |  | 1 | 6 |
| Item to John Johnson taken by the Dunkards, lose £200 |  | 1 | 6 |
| Item to James Sickellmer undone by the rebels in Ireland |  | 1 | 0 |
| Item to Ellin Obert and hir sister undone by the rebels |  | 1 | 0 |
| Item to Wyllyam Winckfeilld, gent', his lose £1700 |  | 2 | 0 |
| Item to the Widowe [Mary] Brodbank upon the making a rate |  | 1 | 6 |
| Item to two widowes ther husbands slayn at Banbury[112] |  | 1 | 0 |
| Item to Edward Davis undon by malignants in [?]Lincoln[113] |  | 1 | 0 |

110 Reading, Berkshire. The Parliamentarian Earl of Essex captured Reading in April 1643 after a siege. Essex was unable to maintain discipline over his troops and after his victory they pillaged for days. It is unclear from this entry whether John Allyson was plundered by Royalists during the siege, or by Parliamentarians after it.

111 In August 1643 a Parliamentary ordinance legalised conscription, and another ordinance authorised the Earl of Manchester to raise an Eastern Association army by conscription. These arms may be in addition to those authorised by Parliament and were probably those who responded to the 'beating of the drume for vollunteers'. The arms were carried to Halesworth and also, as before, to Sibton Green (see next entry and Notes 31 & 52).

112 Banbury, Oxfordshire.

113 'Malignants' were the worst sort of royalists (as against 'delinquents', the softer sort). Here the meaning is, 'undone by the malice of royalist sympathisers in Lincoln'. Hitherto, Lincoln and area had strongly supported the parliamentarian cause but from January 1643 the royalists gained in strength. On 24 March the king's supporters took Grantham and then moved on to threaten the walls of Lincoln.

| | £ | s. | d. |
|---|---|---|---|
| Item to James Withers being plundered lost £200 | | 1 | 0 |
| Item to a solldier [who] lost his hand in the Parlements service | | | 6 |
| Item to the Widowe [Mary] Brodbank at 5 severall times, for provision for the solldiers and ther kepers[114] | 6 | 1 | 6 |
| Item for a horse for an impresed \sollder/[115] to ride to Becells | | 1 | 6 |
| Item for recruting dragoneers as apeare by warant[116] | 2 | 15 | 0 |
| Item for coats and prese money as apear by warant | 1 | 12 | 0 |
| Item for Capteyn [William] Po[e] as apear by warrant[117] | 1 | 10 | 0 |
| Item for fouer ablle loads of straw and carying it ine | 2 | 0 | 0 |
| Item to Wyllyam Neuson for goeing to Flixton[118] and Becells, being sent by the cunstablles | | 2 | 6 |
| The sume of this side is | 50 | 19 | 9 |
| | | | |
| Item to the Widowe [Mary] Brodbank upon the makeing a rate | | 2 | 0 |
| Item for a booke to be read in the church | | | 6 |
| Item for a load of bricke and bringing of it ine | | 14 | 8 |
| Item layd out amoungst the trayned solldiers that morning theye advanced for Bury[119] | | 2 | 0 |
| Item to John Baxter and Wyllyam \Baxter/ solldiers | | | 6 |
| Item to Wyllyame Tayllor his wife and 5 chilldren | | 1 | 0 |
| Item for thatching at the towen hall [illeg.] and the other houses | | 8 | 6 |
| Item to Robert Grene his wife and chilldren | | | 6 |
| Item to John Clarke a Linn solldier[120] | | | 4 |
| Item for carying 17 loads of wood to the poore folks | 1 | 14 | 0 |
| Item to John Cook and John Butler plunderd at Reeding | | 1 | 0 |
| Item to John Ellott a Linn solldier | | | 6 |
| Item to Christopher Cook, Georg Gunson and Richard Grene, solldiers that came frome Germynye as apeared | | 1 | 0 |
| Item to Margeret Myller and Ann Harison ther husbands slayne at Woodstock in Derbyshire[121] as apeared | | 1 | 0 |

Eventually the parliamentary forces regained the initiative, partly because the royalists did not press home their advantage in July-August when King's Lynn also declared for the king. See Holmes, *Seventeenth-Century Lincolnshire* (1980), pp. 161–5.

[114] It appears that Widow Broadbank's public house was also used to treat injured soldiers, or to house captive prisoners and their guards.

[115] Parliament passed the Impressment Ordinance in 1643 authorising the raising of troops by conscription.

[116] Originally, dragoons were to be raised in Essex from volunteers, but the cost of their maintenance was to be divided amongst all five counties of the Association. Volunteers quickly proved inadequate and dragoons were impressed. See Holmes, *The Eastern Association*, p. 169. (See Glossary *sub* 'dragoneers'.)

[117] The financial condition of the Association was grim. Money intended for the Army's war chest, such as that collected by the Propositions, was frequently kept and used locally instead. It was also a system that 'invited corruption'. Horses, in particular, were seized and put to personal use on the flimsiest of pretexts (recusancy, Royalism) and with little regard for the truth. Captain William Poe was one of the most 'notorious' in Suffolk, where 'extreame complaints of . . . miscarriages and oppressions' were levelled against him. See Holmes, *Seventeenth-Century Lincolnshire*, p. 81 and Biographies, p. 139.

[118] Probably Flixton near Bungay, Suffolk.

[119] Bury St Edmunds, Suffolk.

[120] A soldier who had served at the seige of King's Lynn, Norfolk, in 1642. Another is mentioned three entries later.

[121] This probably refers to Woodstock in Oxfordshire.

|  | £ | s. | d. |
|---|---|---|---|
| Item to Thomas Collverton [?]driven frome house and home |  | 1 | 0 |
| Item for a knapp sacke for one of the impresed soldiers[122] |  | 1 | 6 |
| Item to the two towne solldiers when they went to Bury, mor then was alowed backe for paye |  | 16 | 4 |
| Item to Henery Oweing and Francis Byrde mayned soldiers |  |  | 6 |
| Item to the Widowe [Mary] Mells to burye hir husband |  | 8 | 0 |
| Item to Wyllyam Cooper for his cunstable byll as apear |  | 17 | 1 |
| Item to Edmond Mells for diching in the Crose Meadow | 1 | 1 | 8 |
| Item to [Raynold] Rackam the carpenter for paleing in the yards at Rose Larks and making a coatt[123], with other worke | 1 | 0 | 0 |
| Item for glaseing the windowes at Rose Larkes |  | 16 | 0 |
| Item for thatching and broaches at Rose Larks as doe apear by bill as allso the other particullers | 1 | 8 | 8 |
| Item for paper to make rates, and for a book to enter the Covenant, and the covenanters names[124] |  |  | 6 |
| Item at Becells for my self and my horse when I tooke the Covenant, being required thither by warrant |  | 2 | 0 |
| Item for cloathes for Wyllyam Myngye his daughter by the consent of the townesmen | 1 | 1 | 0 |
| Item to M<sup>r</sup> Robert Warner that he hathe bene out of above two yeares for pouder | 2 | 12 | 0 |
| Item to a poore widowe driven out of Ireland in great want |  |  | 8 |
| Item for the first three mounths weekly paye for all the feofees lands | 4 | 13 | 0 |
| Item for the fourthe part of the great rate for the feofees lands | 1 | 5 | 5 |
| Item to a rate of £31 9s. for setting forth a horse and paye[125] | 1 | 12 | 7½ |
| Item for a rate for eight weeks pay for the feofees lands | 3 | 0 | 10 |
| Item to a rate for fouer weeks pay for the feofees lands | 1 | 11 | 11¼ |
| Item to a rate for eight weeks pay for the feofees lands | 2 | 19 | 4½ |
| Item to a rate for syxe weeks pay for the feofees lands | 1 | 16 | 3 |
| Item to rate for fouer weeks being as much as syxe weeks for the feofees lands | 1 | 16 | 3 |
| Item to Robert Tredeskin in part for his cunstables bill | 7 | 4 | 6 |

[122] A conscripted soldier of the Eastern Association. The summer of 1643 was a desperate time for the Parliamentary armies in eastern England and by July Newcastle's army was threatening the heart of the Eastern Association.

[123] Probably a 'cote' or animal shelter (see Note 146).

[124] This refers to Pym's Vow and Covenant of June 1643, and not to the Solemn League and Covenant of August 1643. Pym's covenant bound its signatories to support Parliament's forces against the king's army, 'so long as the Papists now in open war against the Parliament shall by the force of arms be protected from the Justice thereof'. On 9 June, sixteen peers in the House took the oath, and six days later a public fast was observed. This covenant was extremely popular in the city, and leading men wrote pamphlets in its support. Ultimately this document was ignored by Parliament, although Hexter suggests that it set the stage for the passing of the Solemn League and Covenant later that year. The main thrust of that was to reform the church according to 'the example of the best reformed churches'. Religious reformation was to be in exchange for Anglo-Scottish military cooperation against the king. A copy of the Solemn Vow and Covenant survived in the parish chest of Cratfield (p. 17, above). See Gardiner, *History of the Great Civil War* (1893 & 1965), vol. 1, p. 149; Hexter, *The Reign of King Pym* (1941), p. 30; SROI, FC62/A3/1.

[125] A rate to provide a horse and probably to contribute towards the pay of a Parliamentary soldier.

|  | £ | s. | d. |
|---|---|---|---|
| Item to Henery Worledg in part for his cunstables bill | 1 | 10 | 0 |
| The sume of this side is | 41 | 4 | 7¼ |
|  |  |  |  |
| The sume tottal is | 92 | 4 | 4¼ |
|  |  |  |  |
| Received in part of this above sayd sume of Richard Royden | 56 | 0 | 0 |
| Soe remayns unto Robert Smyth, senior, upon this acoumpt | 36 | 4 | 4¼ |
| Item ther due unto Robert Tredeskin for his cunstables bill | 5 | 19 | 4 |
| And to Henery Worledg for his cunstables bill | 8 | 1 | 1 |
| Besides that I payd unto them as apear above | 8 | 14 | 6 |

September 14th, 1644
The abstract of the accompts of the towne of Crattfeild

|  | £ | s. | d. |
|---|---|---|---|
| Expended by Robert Smyth, senior, as in this accompt appeereth | 92 | 4 | 4¼ |
| Received by him in part | 56 | 0 | 0 |
| Sum' due to him | 36 | 4 | 4¼ |
|  |  |  |  |
| Expended by William Aldus | 45 | 5 | 3½ |
| Received by him | 29 | 10 | 0 |
| Rest due to him | 15 | 15 | 3½ |
|  |  |  |  |
| The totall sum' due to both the churchwardens abovesaid | 51 | 19 | 7¾ |
| Wherof received since the accompt was made for tymber | 40 | 0 | 0 |
| Item received more out of a rate dated the 25th of March 1644 | 6 | 0 | 0 |
| So due to the church wardens abovesaid to be paid by the churchwardens of the said town | 5 | 19 | 7¾ |

[184]
Cratfeild
March the 23
The account of William Aldus, one of the churchwardens of the towne aforesaid, for the yeere of Our Lord 1643 as followeth [for 1643–4]

| Imprimis | £ | s. | d. |
|---|---|---|---|
| Is due to me from the towne since the last account day | 12 | 5 | 3 |
| laid out att the reckininge day to the Widow [Mary] Brudbanke for beere |  | 8 | 0 |
| laid out to Edmond Melles for rent for the towne lands |  | 4 | 6 |
| laid out to Edmond Wattlinge the bally for rent for the towneshipe of Cratfeild |  | 2 | 4 |
| laid out to John Stanard of Laxfeild for bread and wine for the three comunions att Easter |  | 18 | 0 |
| laid out when we gave in the account to the Justes |  | 2 | 8 |
| laid out to John Stanard of Laxfeild for wine for the cort and for fetchinge of it |  | 5 | 0 |
| laid out to the Widow [Mary] Brudbanke att the poulveringe day for our diners |  | 17 | 0 |

|  | £ | s. | d. |
|---|---|---|---|
| laid out to a brefe, the lose was £20,000 |  | 5 | 0 |
| laid out to Thomas Johnson and William Aldus when thay were called to goe to Beckells[126] |  | 1 | 6 |
| laid out to John Fiske, senior, as dooe apeere by warent | 3 | 13 | 8 |
| laid out to Robart Smyth the glaser and to Ruben Tallowing for helpinge of him[127] | 1 | 0 | 0 |
| laid out to John Williams for his cunstabels bill | 1 | 0 | 5 |
| laid out to Edmond Melles for rent for the towne land |  | 4 | 9½ |
| more for comons fine |  | 6 | 8 |
| more for a fre rent |  |  | 4 |
| laid out to John Williams for pouder and match and other theinges as doe apeere by his bill[128] | 3 | 10 | 6 |
| laid out to Thomas Johnson and William Aldus for sarveinge in the towne armes for thirtenne dayes | 1 | 19 | 0 |
| laid out to Ruben Tallowinge for his holle yeeres wages | 2 | 0 | 0 |
| laid out for takeinge up of the pavements and throwinge downe of the stepes in the chancell[129] |  | 3 | 0 |
| laid out when we went to Beckells to take the Covenant |  | 2 | 0 |
| laid out to John Gouldsmith for his charges when he went to give in a ratte to the Justes |  | 6 | 8 |
| laid out to Edmond Melles to releve his wife with, att severall times | 1 | 0 | 0 |
| laid out to John Hartly to releve him in his sicknes |  | 8 | 0 |
| given to James Smith to releve him withall |  | 10 | 0 |
| laid out to Finett Adames for 12 weekes colection |  | 6 | 0 |
| laid out to Ruben Tallowinge since his wife died for colection | 1 | 12 | 0 |
| given to James Melles in the time of his sicknes | 1 | 18 | 0 |
| The sume of this side is | ? | 10 | 3½ |

| laid out for colection to the poore for the fortnight seven shillings and six pence |  |  |  |
|---|---|---|---|
| To John Hartly |  | 2 | 0 |
| To the Widow [Ann] Haiward |  | 1 | 0 |
| To the Widow [Ann] Newson |  | 2 | 0 |
| To the Widow [Elizabeth] Breisingham |  | 1 | 0 |
| To Rose Browne |  |  | 6 |
| To Sary Cary |  | 1 | 0 |
| for a month fivetenne shillings, [so] for thirtenne monthes | 9 | 15 | 0 |

| The sume totall is | 45 | 5 | 3½ |
|---|---|---|---|

| Recived of Frances Aldus for his rent for one holle yeere | 17 | 0 | 0 |
|---|---|---|---|
| recived of Richard Raidon for the Towne Medowes he doe occupie | 6 | 10 | 0 |

126 The town's two trained soldiers were sent to Beccles, about 12 miles north-east of Cratfield.
127 Stained glass with offensive 'popish' imagery was being replaced with white glass (see Notes 131 & 142). This is probably the first trace of the destructive work of William Dowsing, appointed Parliamentary Visitor of churches in 1643, and of his deputies. See Evelyn White (ed.), *The Journal of William Dowsing* (1885).
128 Military provisions for the town's soldiers.
129 The chancel steps had been removed as idolatrous by Dowsing or his agents.

|  | £ | s. | d. |
|---|---|---|---|

recived of John Williams for the whole yeers rent of the land he
have in occupacion — 5 0 0

resived of Mary Brudbanke, widow, for rent for the Towne Pightle — 1 0 0

The sume received in all — 29 10 0

soe remayne unto William Aldus upon this acoumpt — 15 15 3

We doe elect for the year 1644 John Wyllyams and John Smyth de Worllots
churchwardings

[unnumbered, ?185]
Cratfeild
The accoumpt of John Williams, being one of the churchwardens, for the yeere
1644, March the 24th [for 1644–5]

Inprimis — £ s. d.

Item layd out uppon the reckoning day for beere and other provition,
the soome of — 16 2

Item layd out the same day to Ruben Tallen for fyer and the losse of
his time, and to the Widow [Ann] Hayward — 3 0

Item layd out to the 2 towne souldiers when they went to Burry, the
28th of March 1644 — 1 5 4

Item layd out for 2 knapsacks for the 2 towne souldiers — 3 0

Item payd for 2 horses for them — 6 0

Item payd to Mr [William] Alldus scoolemaster for teaching the poore
chilldrin for one whole yeere — 2 0 0

Item paid to William Crosse for worke about the clock and church
as appreth by his bill, the soome of — 18 5

Item layd out to 3 poore weemen which lost above £400, and there
husbandes slayne in the warres, as apreth by there sirtificate,
the soome of — 1 0

Item paid to Henery Worlich to make upp the weekly rate, the
17th of Apriell for 2 monthes — 14 11

Item layd out to 4 men and 2 wemen which lost above £600 as appreth
by there sirtificat from the Parlement — 2 0

Item layd out to 3 wemen and 7 small chilldrin for there releife — 2 0

Item paid to [Ruben] Tallen for ringing of the bell uppon our lectur day
for one whole yeere — 17 4

Item payd to Henery Worlich the constabell for charges for impressing
and carying in of souldiers for the Parlementes service — 7 18 10

Item paid to Edmond Mills for rent for the towne grownd — 4 6

Item paid to Morphew for ryding to Broome Hall[130] for
John Gowldsmyth, the soome of — 1 0

---

[130] The case of John Goldsmith necessitated a visit to Brome Hall, 10 miles west of Cratfield, which was
the home of Sir Frederick Cornwallis, bart.

|  | £ | s. | d. |
|---|---|---|---|
| Item paid to Robert Smyth the glasser for glassing of the church windowes, in part, the soome of[131] | 3 | 15 | 1 |
| Item paid to Mr [Thomas] Bedingfeild according unto a warrant for mayned souldiers and poore widowes, the soome of | 1 | 10 | 0 |
| Item to 2 poore widowes whose husbandes wer slaine in the warrs as appreth by there sirtificate | | 1 | 0 |
| Item to an owld man which was 4 score yeeres owld and had lost £400 and uppward as appreth by his sirtificat | | 2 | 0 |
| Item paid to Simond Warne for taking downe the crosses of the church and stepell[132] | | 3 | 0 |
| Item paid to Tredeskin Coushall for charges for impressing souldiers and carying them in for the Parlementes service | 4 | 2 | 5 |
| Item paid to Mr [Thomas] Bedingfeild the 16th of June for Marshell[sic] and Mayned Souldiers according unto a warrant \for arrearres/ | 3 | 0 | 8 |
| Item laid out for wine and sewgr att the court and for fetching it | | 6 | 4 |
| Item paid to William Fisk and James Fryer to make upp the rate for the weekly sessement, for 2 monthes | | 17 | 6 |
| Item laid out to 18 poore pepell which lost all they had by fyre in Lynkonshir as appreth by there sirtificat from Parlement | | 3 | 10 |
| Item laid out to the 2 towne souldiers when they went to Bury | | 18 | 8 |
| Item layd out to Henery Worlich for charges which John Fisk layd out in the time that he was constabell | 1 | 0 | 4 |
| [sum of page] | 31 | 13 | 6 |
| | | | |
| Item paid for 2 horses for the trayned souldiers being gon 5 days | | 8 | 0 |
| Item layd out to 6 poore pepell which wer driven from all they had by the rebbels in Yreland, as appreth by ther sirtificat | | 1 | 0 |
| Item paid to Samewell Cady for himselfe and his horse to Burry with the trayned souldiers, \to bring back there horses/ | | 9 | 0 |
| Item paid to William Cooper for his marre to Beckls with the souldiers | | 1 | 6 |
| Item paid to [Ruben] Tallen for wire for the clock and for nayles [that] he had | | 1 | 6 |
| Item paid to Simond Warne for a frame for the ordinance of Parlement for the observation of the Sabboth day[133] | | 1 | 0 |
| Item layd out to 9 poore pepell which lost ther whole estate in Yreland by the rebells | | 1 | 10 |
| Item paid to John Mills to make upp the weekly rate for 2 monthes | | 19 | 0 |
| Item for pouder and match for the trayned soulders and for the awxilleryes | 2 | 4 | 2 |

---

131 This item for glazing, and a similar one in the next account, constitute the major cost of substituting clear glass for 'superstitious' stained glass (see Notes 127, 137 & 142).

132 Crosses were proscribed by ordinance, and were particularly objectionable to the hotter sort of Protestant. They were associated with the locally unpopular Laudian reforms, as well as with Roman Catholicism more generally.

133 In January 1645, Parliament approved the Westminster Assembly's recommendation that the Book of Common Prayer be replaced by the Presbyterian Directory of Public Worship, giving Parliament the final voice in Church affairs. A Parliamentary ordinance establishing a national Presbyterian Church was passed in August.

|  | £ | s. | d. |
|---|---|---|---|
| Item paid to Robert Smyth senior, the owld church warden, which was due to him | 5 | 19 | 7¾ |
| Item paid to Goodman [Thomas] Turner to make upp the rate for the horses | 1 | 2 | 1½ |
| Item paid to Enock Gyrling for a sute fine[134] for the towne |  |  | 6 |
| Item paid to Samewell Cady for a horse to Bury |  | 3 | 0 |
| Item layd out to [Edmond] Watlin for rent for Rosse Larkes |  | 2 | 4 |
| Item paid to Lawne for 3 new bell ropes |  | 11 | 0 |
| Item layd out to Mr Harbot and divers others which lost £40,000 in Brimingam in Wawickshir[135] |  | 4 | 0 |
| Item paid to Simond Warne for putting a gudgin into the litell bell, and for mending the third bell |  | 2 | 0 |
| Item paid to Richard Royden which he laid out to the weekely sessement and other charges as appreth by his bill | 18 | 6 | 1½ |
| Item paid to [Robert] Smyth the glasser for mending of a window which the wind blewe downe |  | 3 | 0 |
| Item layd out by the apointment of the towne to the blynd man which preached here, which Mr [Gabriel] Eland procured |  | 4 | 0 |
| Item layd out by the apointment of the towne to a boye which was prest out of this towne |  | 3 | 0 |
| Item payd att the Widow [Mary] Brodbanks 4 severall times when the towne mett to make rattes |  | 2 | 8 |
| Item paid to my cusson John Rouse for his charges to Burry for the towne, for the Scotts advance[136] |  | 4 | 0 |
| Item layd out to [Edmond] Wattlin the bally for the shreiffes turne |  | 1 | 0 |
| Item layd out to John Hall which lost £500, for his releife |  |  | 4 |
| Item paid to the 2 towne souldiers for 2 dayes trayning |  | 6 | 0 |
| Item payd to Robert Smyth the glasser for 8 pounds sooder[137] and for his worke, and for [Ruben] Tallens, to mend the leads |  | 9 | 0 |
| Item paid to Mr [Thomas] Bedingfeild for forrtifiing of Newpoort Panell[138] according unto warrant received | 2 | 7 | 0 |
| [Sum of page] | 34 | 17 | 8¾ |
| Item paid to William Newson, senior, for one musket and rest and bandelears and sword, the soome of[139] | 1 | 4 | 0 |
| Item paid for a newe skabbard for the sword and scowring it |  | 1 | 8 |
| Item paid to William Crosse for triming the 2 muskets |  | 1 | 0 |

---

[134] A due paid in lieu of attendance at a manorial court.

[135] Birmingham, Warwickshire.

[136] In 1645, Charles I surrendered to the Scots. Over the years Cratfield contributed a great deal of money to assist the Scots (see Introduction, p. 19).

[137] More glazing expenses involving Robert Smyth.

[138] Newport Pagnell, Buckinghamshire. This town was captured by royalists under Sir Lewis Dyve on 16 October 1644, severing Parliament's lines of communication between London and the north, and threatening the heart of the Eastern Association. The next day the Cambridge Committee called up its trained-bands and by 28 October the town had been retaken by the Earl of Essex. Subsequent references in account no. 186 mention a rate levied specifically for Newport Pagnell.

[139] This constitutes part of the arms required for a dragoon.

|  | £ | s. | d. |
|---|---|---|---|
| Item layd out to the ringers for there laboures for ringing uppon the 5th day of November 1644 | | 2 | 0 |
| Item payd to Henery Worlich, constabell, and William Yonges and Thomas Johnson and Samewell Cady and William Newson and other poore men for ther charges concerning the Parlementes cause | 3 | 8 | 0 |
| Item paid to Mr Crossby for his labbours for preaching uppon our lectur day for one whole yeere ending the 28th of Jannewari 1644 | 20 | 0 | 0 |
| Item paid to [Ruben] Tallen for ringing of the bell uppon our lectur day for one whole yeere ending the 28th of Jannewari 1644 | | 17 | 4 |
| Item layd out to John Alldus wife for there releife in the time of there sicknes | | 7 | 0 |
| Item payd to Thomas Turner, constabell, for charges which he have layd out for the towne as appreth by his bill | 1 | 2 | 0 |
| Item layd out to John Newson, constabell, for charges which he have layd out for the towne as appreth by his bill | | 8 | 0 |
| Item paid to William Crosse for his worke about the clock and the barrs of the glasse windowes as appreth by his bill | | 12 | 4 |
| Item payd to Simond Warne for mending the wheles of the bells and other work about the church as appreth by his bill | | 8 | 2 |
| Item payd to Robert Keabell, junior, for for [sic] trayning 7 dayes and moony layd out for drume and collours, the soome of[140] | | 12 | 0 |
| It laid out to Robert Smyth de Coulshall and Robert Smyth, senior, to make upp the rate for the wekly sessement for 2 monthes | | 7 | 0 |
| It laid out to John Smyth de Stubbards[141] and Jeorg Balldry to make upp the rate for the weekly sessement for 2 monthes | | 3 | 9 |
| [Sum of page] | 29 | 14 | 3 |

|  | £ | s. | d. |
|---|---|---|---|
| Sume Totallis | 96 | 5 | 5¾ |

|  | £ | s. | d. |
|---|---|---|---|
| Received of Richard Royden for one yeeres rent ending att Mychalltid 1644 the soome of fifty sixx poundes, soe I say received | 56 | 0 | 0 |

|  | £ | s. | d. |
|---|---|---|---|
| Soe there is due unto John Williams from the towne the soome of forty poundes, five shillings, five pence, halpeny, farthing, soe I say the soome of | 40 | 5 | 5¾ |

[?185 cont.]
The account of John <Williams> \Smyth/ of Norwood [*written in a different, later hand*] [*for 1644–5*]

|  | £ | s. | d. |
|---|---|---|---|
| Item payd to [Ruben] Tallen for his wages for on hole yer | 2 | 0 | 0 |
| Item payd to Edmund Mells for on yere | 1 | 4 | 0 |

---

140 This is the parish's contribution to the troop's emblem and drum.
141 'De Stubbards' was attached to this name to help differentiate between several John Smiths then living in Cratfield.

|  | £ | s. | d. |
|---|---|---|---|
| Item payd to Wilam Nausun for fearme for his mother |  | 6 | 8 |
| Item payd to [William] Minggi for 4 dayes trainning |  | 6 | 0 |
| Item payd moore to Minggi for cullurs |  |  | 6 |
| Item payd more to Minggi for 2 dayes training and cullurs |  | 4 | 0 |
| Item payd to the glasier[142] | 3 | 10 | 0 |
| Item payd for 6 peints of win and 2 breades |  | 4 | 2 |
| Item more for 8 peints of wien and 2 breades |  | 5 | 6 |
| Item moore for 8 peints of wein and 2 breades |  | 5 | 6 |
| Item moore for bread and wein |  | 1 | 1 |
| Item payd for [?]stouing the poore folkes oud[143] |  | 12 | 0 |
| Item laid ought at Blibro for our seilves and our horsses and a warant |  | 2 | 8 |
| Item payd to Mr [Francis] Varden for his fe[144] |  | 6 | 8 |
| Item payd for Marsheles and Mained Soulgers |  | 8 | 8 |
| Item payd for lordes rent and rent for Cratfild Rose |  | 11 | 2½ |
| Item paid for the pulvering denner | 1 | 4 | 0 |
| Item for 2 leders for the church |  | 7 | 0 |
| Item payd at Holsworth for the 2 toun soulgers |  |  | 6 |
| Item payd to [John] Hartlet heis wife in the tim of seknes |  | 1 | 0 |
| Item for one musket with the nesisares to it |  | 19 | 6 |
| Item paid to a reat for the touene |  | 6 | 5 |
| Item more for a reate |  | 3 | 9 |
| Item paid to [Ruben] Tallen for helping the gleasur |  | 6 | 0 |
| Item paid moore to [Ruben] Tallen for helping the wedous to remove[145] |  | 1 | 0 |
| The sum of this beil com to | 13 | 16 | 9½ |

A note of the monthli colecion

| Item paid for 13 monthes and 2 weckes at £1 5s. the month, com to £16 17s. 6d. | 16 | 17 | 6 |
|---|---|---|---|
| Item geven to a por man that had a pas |  |  | 6 |
| Item mor to por Erish peopel |  |  | 6 |
| Item mor to a por man |  |  | 6 |
| Item mor to 4 por peopel |  |  | 4 |
| Item mor to por peopel that wear lame |  |  | 6 |
| Item mor to another mane |  |  | 4 |
| Item more to 4 travlers |  |  | 6 |
| Item more to a man which had a bref |  |  | 6 |
| Item more to a mane which had a bref |  |  | 8 |
| Item more to a mane |  |  | 4 |
| Item more t[o] 2 mean |  |  | 6 |
| Item more to other meane |  |  | 4 |
| Item more to 2 wemane |  | 3 | 0 |

---

[142] Another payment to a glazier, presumably Robert Smyth (see Note 127). Later in the same account, Ruben Tallen is paid for assisting the glazier.

[143] Once again, 'stowing [cutting] the poor folks' wood'.

[144] Francis Verdon of Linstead Magna, Dowsing's deputy for Dunwich Deanery.

[145] To remove poor widows to the town house. See also Botelho, 'Accommodation for the Aged Poor' (1995), 19–31.

|  | £ | s. | d. |
|---|---|---|---|
| Item more to a woman |  | 1 | 6 |
| Item mor to travlers |  |  | 4 |
| The sum of this bel com to |  | 10 | 4 |

Aprill the 22 \for the weekly sessement of Benclins/

|  | £ | s. | d. |
|---|---|---|---|
| Item for one month |  | 6 | 11¾ |
| Item for one month |  | 6 | 11¾ |
| Item payd to [Henry] Worleg |  | 4 | 3 |
| Item for one month |  | 6 | 11¾ |
| Item for one month |  | 6 | 11¾ |
| Item laid ought for dragoners |  | 4 | 7¾ |
| Item for 2 month |  | 13 | 11½ |
| Item for thaching the hogs cot and strawe[146] |  | 1 | 6 |

|  | £ | s. | d. |
|---|---|---|---|
| September the 29 for one month |  | 7 | 1 |
| Item paid to the constabels reat |  | 2 | 1½ |
| Item payd for on month |  | 7 | 1 |
| Item payd for on month |  | 7 | 1 |
| Item payd for [Gabriel] Eyerland on reat |  | 5 | 1 |
| Francis Alldous his laiinges ought for on yeere com | 4 | 7 | ?9¼ |
| Item layd out for the towne land in thoccupation[*sic*] of John Willyams for weekly assesment for a yeere | 1 | 6 | 1 |

|  | £ | s. | d. |
|---|---|---|---|
| A not of what mauni I have resaived |  |  |  |
| Inprimus reseaived of Richard Raiden | 6 | 10 | 0 |
| resaived of John Willyams | 5 | 0 | 0 |
| resaived of Francis Alldous | 17 | 0 | 0 |
| resaived of the Wedou Bredbank | 1 | 0 | 0 |
| resaived in all | 29 | 10 | 0 |
| The total sum of all my beles com [*to*] | 36 | 18 | 3¾ |
| Memorandum ther is owing unto me upon this accoumpt from the towne | 7 | 8 | 5¾ |

[186]
[*heading damaged*] [. . . . .] de Norward Grene 1645 [. . . . .] of what moony I have laid out [. . . . .] rates for the grownd which I have of the townes since Our Lady Day [*account of John Smyth of Norwood Green, ?for 1645–6*]

|  | £ | s. | d. |
|---|---|---|---|
| Inprimis |  |  |  |
| Item paid to John Rousse for the weekly asessement for 2 monthes |  | 4 | 0 |
| Item paid to [Thomas] Turner for the rate for Newport Panell |  |  | 10 |
| Item paid to him for the rate for the Scotts advanc |  | 1 | 0 |
| Item paid to John Smyth, junior, for 2 monthes asessement |  | 4 | 0 |

---

146 Thatching a pigsty.

| | £ | s. | d. |
|---|---|---|---|
| Item paid to William Newson for the Scotts advance | | 1 | 0 |
| Item paid to Gregory Rousse for 2 monthes asessement | | 4 | 0 |
| Item paid to him for the British army rate[147] | | 1 | 4 |
| Item paid to Richard Royden for the rate for Newwork[148] | | | 8 |
| Item paid to Richard Royden for Newport Panell | | | 10 |
| Item paid to Richard Royden for the 5 garrison rate[149] | | 1 | 4 |
| Item paid to William Alldus for 2 monthes asessement | | 4 | 0 |
| Item paid to Francis Barow for 4 monthes for the Scottes \being in arearre/ | | 2 | 0 |
| Item paid by my selfe for the 2 last monthes of the [?]10, October and November | | 4 | 0 |
| Item 1 quart of sallet oyle | | | 3 |
| Item di' a 100, 8d., and di' a 100, 6d. nayles[150] | | | 7 |
| Item more for 8d. nayles and 6d. nayles | | | 4 |
| Item paid Richard Royden for the rate for Newport Panell, being in areare | | | 6 |
| Item paid Siprian Samson for 2 monthes, December and Januarye £1 14s. 8d. | | 4 | 0 |
| Item laid out att Halsworth for wine and bread for the comunion £1 19s. 10d. | | 5 | 2 |
| | | | |
| Item John Williams is to pay to make upp his rent with this bell | 2 | 0 | 2 |

[187]
Cratfeild
March the 22th 1645
The acoumpt of John Williams of what moonyes he have disbursed for the towne, being one of the churchwardens for the yeere of Our Lord 1645 [for 1645–6]

| Inprimis | £ | s. | d. |
|---|---|---|---|
| Item there was due unto him the last reckoning daye being the 23th of March 1644, the sume of | 40 | 5 | 5¾ |
| Item laid out the same day to the Widow [Mary] Brodbank for beere and bread | | 6 | 8 |
| Item layd out to Ruben Tallen for his attendance | | | 6 |
| Item laid out to Goodman [Thomas] Turner to make upp the rate for Newport Panell | | 6 | 9 |
| Item laid out to Goodman [Thomas] Turner to mak upp the rate for the Scotts | | 4 | 7 |
| Item laid out to John Rousse to make upp the rate for the weekley asessement for 2 monthes | | 18 | 0 |

---

147 The modern-sounding phrase, 'the British army', refers to the Anglo-Scottish force serving in Ireland.
148 Newark, Nottinghamshire. This strategic town was besieged by the Earl of Manchester and the Parliamentarian cavalry a number of times, beginning in 1643.
149 The five garrisons represented the five counties of the Eastern Association: Norfolk, Suffolk, Essex, Cambridgeshire and Hertfordshire.
150 Nails of two sizes, costed by the hundred, were here bought by the half-hundred (dimidium, Latin for 'a half'). In the next entry, smaller quantities were clearly bought.

|  | £ | s. | d. |
|---|---|---|---|

Item laid out to 3 poore pepell which loast all there estattes in
Northamthonshire, [*loss of*] £300[151] — 6

Item laid out att the maaking of the accoumptes and for delivering them
to the Justeses of the Peace — 2 6

Item laid out to Gregory Rousse to mak upp the rate for the weekely
asessement — 5 4

Item laid out to William Newson, senior, to make upp the rate for the
Scotts, our well afected bretherin,[152] the sume of — 2 2

Item laid out to 6 poore widows and 7 small chilldrin whose fathers wer
killed in the warres — 1 0

Item laid out to John Fisk, junior, to make upp the rate for the weekely
asessement — 1 10

Item laid out to Richard Royden to make upp the rate for
Newport \Panell/ — 5 11

Item laid out to Richard Royden to make upp the rate for the
British armye — 2 2½

Item laid out to a poore widow and 6 small chilldren which lost all by
fyer in Hamshire — 1 0

Item laid out to [Edmond] Watlin, the ballye, for rent for Rosse Larkes — 2 4

Item laid out to Edmund Melles for rent for the towne grownd — 4 9½

Item laid out to Edmund Melles for the \comon/ fine \for 2 yeeres/ — 13 4

Item laid out to John Newson and Thomas Turner to make upp there rate
for ther constables charges for the Parlementes service — 11 ½

Item laid out to John Bulletout by the apointment of the towne, he being
prest from this towne and came hither for releife[153] — 3 4

Item laid out to a poore widow and 4 small children which loast all there
estattes in Northampthonshire, [*loss of*] £300 — 6

Item laid out to the 2 trained souldiers for the towne — 13 4

Item laid out to a poore man and 7 small chilldrin, [*loss of*] £500 — 8

Item laid out att the making of the book for the accoumptes of the whole
towne[154] and carying \them/ in to the comissioners, and we wer
constrained to lye out all nyght — 10 0

Item paid to William Alldus, junior, to make upp the rate for the weekely
asessement — 1 10

Item for pouder and match and bullets for the townsmen, and for the
trained souldiers and awxilleryes — 4 12 4

---

151 In this account, sums of money written in the left-hand margin give the losses of individuals who were assisted by the parish.

152 The alliance with the Scots is enthusiastically endorsed by Cratfield.

153 Many constables seized and impressed strangers and those travelling through their towns, rather than making the difficult selection from friends, family and neighbours. Significantly, both John Bulletout and the parish felt that Cratfield was obliged to provide some relief as a result.

154 The commissioners are those from the county sub-committee of the Committee for Taking Accounts of the Kingdom (created February 1644) that was sitting in Cornhill, London. The commissioners were charged with auditing and verifying parochial accounts of taxation, free quarter and similar matters. The order from Cornhill was precise, including an insistence on clean and fairly written account books. Northamptonshire took this last directive very seriously, sending back the accounts of one parish because 'the said book is not perfect but full of blots and queries'. For the fullest discussion of this work, see Pennington, 'The Accounts of the Kingdom' (1961), esp. p. 194.

|  | £ | s. | d. |
|---|---|---|---|
| Item laid out to Richard Royden to mak upp the rate for Newwork |  | 3 | 6 |
| [*Sum of page*] | 50 | 11 | 4¾ |

|  | £ | s. | d. |
|---|---|---|---|
| Item paid unto Mr Crossbye for his labouers uppon our lectuer day untill Mychelltid 1645, the sume of | 5 | 10 | 0 |
| Item paid unto Richard Royden which he laid \out/ for the townes mens land for weekely asessement and other charges as appereth by his bill, the sume of | 14 | 17 | 8 |
| Item paid to Robert Keabell, junior, for training for the towne in the awxilleres[155] and moonyes he laid out for collers |  | 13 | 4 |
| Item laid out to Symond Warren for 4 dayes work att the scoolehowse and in the church |  | 6 | 0 |
| Item for palles and 1 post and other peces of tymber for the scoole howse and for plank he used in the church |  | 8 | 0 |
| Item laid out to Lawne, the knacker, for one newe rope for the great bell |  | 5 | 0 |
| Item laid out to 21 poore pepell whose howses wer burnt in the borders of Walles by the Cavellers[156] |  | 1 | 0 |
| Item laid out to John Fisk, junior, for strawe for the scollehowse |  | 8 | 0 |
| Item laid out to the Widow [Elizabeth] Stanard for her releife in the tyme of her great want and extreame nesessety att severall tymes, the sume of | 1 | 4 | 8 |
| Item paid to Mr [Thomas] Bedingfeild for 2 quarters for Marshells and Mayned Souldiers the sume of |  | 17 | 4 |
| Item laid out to my brother [Francis] Barrow to make upp the rate for our good bretherin of Scotland |  | 4 | 9½ |
| Item laid out to make upp the rate for the weekely asessement for 2 monthes which John Williams colected |  | 1 | 8 |
| Item laid out to 11 poore pepell which lost all being fyred by the enemey in Hampshire, [*loss of*] £600 |  | 1 | 0 |
| Item laid out to [Edmond] Wattlin, the ballye, for a fine for not doing service att the shreifes turne |  | 1 | 0 |
| Item given to 2 poore wemen and 6 small chilldren which had a sirtificate to have gathered in all churches |  | 1 | 0 |
| Item laid out to William Newson, senior, for strawe for the scollehowse |  | 6 | 0 |
| It laid out to the sawers for sawing of timber to repayer Benslings as appreth by there bill |  | 16 | 4 |
| Item paid to Mr [Thomas] Bedingfeild for the Directory[157] |  | 1 | 3 |
| Item layd out to a poore man and 8 small chilldrin which had lost all all [*sic*] there estatte, [*loss of*] £250 |  |  | 6 |
| Item paid to Symond Warren for 3 dayes worke about the tymber to repayer Beanselyns |  | 4 | 6 |

---

[155] Auxiliary troops were frequently used for local defence while the main army was away on campaign.
[156] Relief was given to victims of Royalist troops in the Welsh Marches.
[157] The Presbyterian *Directory of Worship* which replaced the *Book of Common Prayer*.

|  | £ | s. | d. |
|---|---|---|---|
| Item paid to William Crosse for tryming of the towne pyke and for makink[*sic*] of soome spikens for the scollehowse |  | 1 | 0 |
| [*Sum of page*] | 26 | 10 | 0½ |

Cratfeild[158]

A note of what moonyes I have received for the towne in the yeere of Our Lord 1645

|  | £ | s. | d. |
|---|---|---|---|
| Inprimis |  |  |  |
| Received of Richard Royden for his halfe yeeres rent due att Our Ladye 1645 | 27 | 0 | 0 |
| Item more received by Rotten Ashes [*sic*][159] | 20 | 0 | 0 |
| Item received more by Richard Royden for his halfe yeeres rent due att Mychalltid 1645 | 27 | 0 | 0 |
| Item received more of Thomas Turner for the halfe yeeres rent of the scoolehowse due att Mychalltid 1645 the sume of | 1 | 0 | 0 |
| Sume totallis | 75 | 0 | 0 |
| The totall sume of my receiptes is | 75 | 0 | 0 |
| The totall sume of my disbursmentes is | 77 | 1 | 5¼ |
| Soe there remane due unto John Williams the sume of | 2 | 1 | 5¼ |

[188]

A note of what moony was owing unto me from the towne att the reckoning daye 1646 and allso what monny I have laide out for the towne since the last reckoning day, *per me* John Williams [*for 1645–6*]

|  | £ | s. | d. |
|---|---|---|---|
| Inprimis |  |  |  |
| Item there was due unto John Williams from the towne uppon the reckoning day the sume of | 2 | 1 | 5½ |
| Item paid to Goodman [Robert] Smyth de Coulshall for the weekely asessment for Feberewaii and March |  | 4 | 0 |
| Item paid to William Fisk for the rate for the 5 garrisons |  | 1 | 4 |
| Item laid out for bread and wine for the comunion the 5th of Apriell, and for fetching of it |  | 6 | 0 |
| Item 1 lb. of doubell [?]refine sewger had att the court |  | 2 | 0 |
| Item paid to William Yonges for the weekly asessment for Apriell and May |  | 4 | 0 |
| Item paid to the rate for the moonyes lent upon the allarams,[160] and other publique charges |  | 2 | 0 |

---

[158] These receipts are written separately on the back of the account, but are placed here in order to precede the final calculations.

[159] This could be the name of lands belonging to the parish, or may refer to the sale of timber.

[160] These were warnings, alarms, of potential attack from Royalist troops.

|                                                                                                           | £ | s. | d. |
|-----------------------------------------------------------------------------------------------------------|---|----|----|
| Item laid out att the making of the accoumptes and for delivering of them in to the Justices of the Peace |   | 2  | 6  |
| Item paid to Gregory Rousse for the weekely rate for June and July                                        |   | 4  | 0  |
| Item paid to the rate for Ireland for 7 monthes                                                           |   | 1  | 7  |
| Item paid to the rate for Ireland for 6 monthes                                                           |   | 1  | 4  |
| Item paid to Henery Worlich for the weekly rate for August and September                                  |   | 4  | 0  |
| Item for 5 quarters of pouder and match for, delivered to the awxilleris the 4th of Apriell 1646          |   | 2  | 1  |
| Item for wire and nayles [Ruben] Tallen had                                                               |   | 1  | 6  |
| Item for 2 quarters of oyle he had                                                                        |   |    | 6  |
| Item for di' a 100 6d. nayles he had                                                                      |   |    | 3  |
| Item paid to [Edmond] Watlin, the ballye, for rent for Rosse Larkes                                       |   | 2  | 4  |
| [Sum of page]                                                                                             | 4 | 0  | 10½ |

[foot of document damaged]

[189]
The second day of Aprill 1646
The accoumpt of John Smyth of Norward, one of the church wardens of the towne of Cratfeld, for one whole yeere last past of all his <illeg.> receiptes and disbursmentes for the same yere in manner following (videlicet) [for 1645–6]

| his receiptes                                                               | £  | s. | d. |
|----------------------------------------------------------------------------|----|----|----|
| Inprimis received of Francis Aldous for his yeres rent in monyes           | 11 | 0  | 6  |
| and in bills of charges                                                    | 5  | 19 | 6  |
| Item received of Richard Reydon for his yeeres rent                        | 6  | 10 | 0  |
| Item received of Mary Broadbancke, widow,[161] for hir yeres rent          | 1  | 0  | 0  |
| Sum' received in moneys                                                    | 18 | 10 | 6  |
| and in bills                                                               | 5  | 19 | 6  |

| his disbursmentes                                                                                         | £  | s. | d.  |
|-----------------------------------------------------------------------------------------------------------|----|----|-----|
| Inprimis paid to the poore of the said towne from the sixt of Aprill 1645 untill the two and twentith of March then next following | 16 | 5  | 0   |
| Item paid to Edmund Mills for releive for his wife                                                        | 1  | 4  | 0   |
| Item paid to Reuben Tallent for his yeres wages                                                           | 2  | 0  | 0   |
| Item paid to Edmund Mills for rent and egges                                                              |    | 4  | 6½  |
| Item paid more to Edmund Mills for rent due to the mannor of Cratfeld Roos                                |    |    | 4   |
| Item paid to Reuben Tallent for 12 dayes serveing the thatcher                                            |    | 12 | 0   |
| Item paid to Captaine [John] Browning[162] for <colur> culours                                            |    | 1  | 6   |
| Item paid for a bushell and halfe of lyme                                                                 |    |    | 9   |

---

161 Here and elsewhere in these accounts, the Latin word *vidua* is used, often shortened to *vid'*. In this transcript it has always been converted into its English equivalent of 'widow'.

162 Captain John Browne or Browning. Originally from London, he became a captain in Cromwell's regiment in early 1644. See Holmes, *Seventeenth-Century Lincolnshire*, p. 176.

|  | £ | s. | d. |
|---|---|---|---|
| Item paid to M<sup>r</sup> [Thomas] Beddingfeld for the Maymed Soldiers and Marciallseas |  | 17 | 4 |
| Item paid for felling, heweing, and sawing of a peece of tymber |  | 2 | 6 |
| Item paid for fiftene hundred broatches |  | 3 | 9 |
| Item paid to Thomas Barmby for twelve dayes worke of thatching |  | 18 | 0 |
| Item paid for stoughing of the wood for the poore |  | 12 | 0 |
| Item paid for two loads of strawe |  | 13 | 4 |
| Item paid for six pynts of wyne and two breads |  | 4 | 2 |
| Item paid for fower pynts of wyne and two breads |  | 2 | 10 |
| Item paid for seaven pynts of wyne and two breads |  | 4 | 10 |
| Item paid to William Myngay for one dayes exercise |  | 1 | 6 |
| Item paid to Beinamyn Raokham for 3 day exercise |  | 3 | 0 |
| Item paid to the Widdow [Mary] Broadbancke for their dynners when they went a pullering<sup>163</sup> |  | 17 | 6 |
| Item paid to Samuell Mills |  | 5 | 0 |
|  |  |  |  |
| Item paid for two knapsacks for the towne |  | 3 | 0 |
| Item paid to make up a rate short rated |  | 1 | 1½ |
| Item paid to the ringers |  | 1 | 0 |
| Item paid for byndeings |  | 1 | 0 |
| Item paid to divers severall poore soldiers and passengers |  | 13 | 1 |
| Sum' disbursed | 26 | 13 | 1 |

[190]
Cratfeild
The accoumpt of William Fisk, senior, one of the churchwardens for the yeere 1646
[*for 1646–7*]

|  | £ | s. | d. |
|---|---|---|---|
| Inprimis |  |  |  |
| Item paid to Ruben Tallen for his quarters wages due att Our Lady 1646 the sume of |  | 10 | 0 |
| Item laid out to Edmund Mills for one whole yeere | 1 | 4 | 0 |
| Item laid out to Edmund Mills for lords rent due att Our Lady 1646 the sume of |  | 4 | 6 |
| Item laid out for wine for the court |  | 3 | 10 |
| Item laid out to make upp the rate for the 5 garrisons |  |  | 8 |
| Item laid out for nayles |  |  | 2 |
| Item laid out to William Yonges to make upp the weekly rate |  | 3 | 2½ |
| Item laid out to 3 poore peopell for ther releife |  |  | 6 |
| Item laid out for wine and bread for the comunion<sup>164</sup> |  | 1 | 11 |
| Item laid out for 2 breffes |  | 2 | 0 |

---

163 Another version of 'poulvering' (see Glossary).
164 In 1646 Parliament banned the celebration of the three great traditional feasts of Easter, Whitsun and Christmas. In response, Cratfield changed from a quarterly pattern to a single Holy Communion each year; this continued until 1650 when the number of communions was increased (see Introduction, pp. 14–15).

|  | £ | s. | d. |
|---|---|---|---|
| Item laid out to Ruben Tallen for his quarters wages due att Midsomer the sume of | | 10 | 0 |
| Item laid out to Samewell Mills by the appoinment of the towne the sume of | | 5 | 0 |
| Item laid out \to/ Robert Keabell for exercising in the towne armes and for mending of his musket | | 3 | 0 |
| Item laid out to divers poore pepell att severall times | | 2 | 4 |
| Item laid out to the constabls for Mayned Souldiers for 2 quarters | | 17 | 4 |
| Item laid out to the 2 towne souldiers | | 3 | 0 |
| Item laid out to William Crosse for mending of the boult of the bell | | | 4 |
| Item laid out to 10 poore pepell | | 1 | 0 |
| Item laid out to Edmund Mills for lords rent and commens fine, the sume of | | 11 | 5½ |
| Item laid out to the constable for the repayring of bridges | 1 | 6 | 0 |
| Item laid out to 5 poore pepell att 2 severall tymes | | 2 | 0 |
| Item laid out to Edmund Mills for rent | | | 4 |
| Item given to 4 poore pepell | | | 7 |
| Item laid out to the Widow [Ann] Newson and the Widow [Elizabeth] Brissingam and John Hearcles wife in the tyme of there sicknes | | 6 | 0 |
| Item laid out to the Widow [Elizabeth] Stanard for the releife of her chilldren | | 2 | 0 |
| Item laid out to divers poore pepell att severall times | | 1 | 6 |
| Item paid to Ruben Tallen for 2 quarters wages | 1 | 0 | 0 |
| Item laid out to divers poore pepell | | 1 | 7 |
| Item laid out to Widow [Ann] Newson and the Widow [Elizabeth] Brissingam in the tyme of there sicknes | | 1 | 10 |
| Item laid out to 18 poore pepell | | 2 | 0 |
| Item laid out to Rosse Browne for looking to the Widow [Ann] Newson in the tyme of her sicknes | | 2 | 0 |
| | 8 | 10 | 1 |
| Item layd out unto John Smyth of Norwood | | 10 | 0 |
| Item laid out to the Widow [Mary] Brodbank for beere and other provition att the pullvering day, as appereth by her bill | | 11 | 4 |
| Item laid out to the poore for collection for thirten months at fower and twenty the month, comes to | 15 | 12 | 0 |
| Item laid out to John Williams as apeeres by bill of particulers, the some of | 4 | 0 | 10½ |
| Item laid out to Frauncis Aldus as apeeres by his bill of partickculers, the some of | 6 | 12 | 1 |
| [total of page] | 27 | 6 | 3½ |
| Sum' total' | 35 | 16 | 4½ |
| received of Frauncis Aldus for his yeeres rent ending the 29th of September 1646, the some of | 18 | 0 | 0 |

|  | £ | s. | d. |
|---|---|---|---|

received of Richard Roydon for his rente for the Towne Medoes for one holl yeere — 6 10 0

received of John Williams for one holl yeere for his rent ending the 29th of September 1646 — 4 0 0

received of Samuell Haward for his rent for one holl yeers rent ending the 29th September 1646 — 2 0 0

received of Widow [Mary] Brudbancke for rent — 10 0

[total of receipts] — 31 10 0

[191]

The accompt of John Newsone, junior, one of the churchwardens [of] Cratfeild, given in the <the 10th Aprill 1646> for the yeere 164[6] [for 1646–7]

|  | £ | s. | d. |
|---|---|---|---|

laid out for constabls charges to Richard Roydon — 16 5 0

laid out to Richard Roydon for the wekly assesmentes and other charges — 25 8 7½

paid to Henry Worlich to make up the rate for the wekly assesment for August and September — 3 2½

paid William Aldus to make up the rate for the releefe of Irland for 6 monthes — 2 5½

paid Mr [Thomas] Crosby, 13th October 1646[165] — 15 7 9

laid out to make up a rate for the alaromes[166] — 1 11½

layd out for 3 bell rops — 10 6

layd out to severall companies of poore people — 3 0

laid for a stocke for the third bell — 5 0

layd for stocking the same bell — 10 0

laid out to [?]Widow [Mary] Crosse for a collor for hir — 1 6

laid out for beere when they stoked the bell — 2 0

laid out for glasinge the steeple wendoe — 2 9

laid out for seting the steeple wendoe <faste> peller[167] faste — 6

laid out for heare[168] and lime and one Iron wege to sete the peller faste — 8

laid out to a rate for the demollishing of the garisones[169] — 7 9

laid out to William Wieth at his going to Bury assises — 2 0 0

laid out for stoweng, bratling, and caring of the poore folks wod — 3 2 0

[total of account] — 64 14 8

Received of Richard Roydon for his holl yeers rent ending at Mycallmes last 1646, the some of — 54 0 0

---

165 For preaching (see Note 78).

166 Alarms and sentries, such as those paid for by the parish in 1642–3, are evidence of the general state of preparedness. They were also the product of a realistic fear of uprisings, as demonstrated by the events of 1648 (see Note 106).

167 The 'pillar' or mullion of a window in the church tower was being replaced.

168 In the making of morter, hair was mixed into the lime as a binding agent.

169 At the end of the first Civil War in 1646, certain 'garrisons' or defensive works were systematically destroyed.

[192]

1647

An acompt of the desbursments of John Newsone, junior, one of the churchwardens of Cratfeild, upon the 27th of March 1648 for one whole yeare [*for 1647–8*]

| | £ | s. | d. |
|---|---|---|---|
| Imprimis | | | |
| dew unto me at the laste reconyng day from the towne | 10 | 14 | 8 |
| paid to the towns men which was lent by them | 5 | 0 | 0 |
| paid Mr [Thomas] Crosby for one half yeare[170] | 7 | 13 | 10½ |
| laid out for a diner uppon the pullerin day | | 10 | 0 |
| paid Symon Waren for trinyng[*sic*] the bells | | 1 | 0 |
| payd William Crosse for a scrue boult for the bell wheele | | | 6 |
| paid for glazing the steeple wendoe | | 4 | 0 |
| paid to Mr [Thomas] Crosby for one half yeare | 7 | 13 | 10½ |
| paid to the ringers 5th of November 1647 | | 5 | 0 |
| paid to William Yonges for making of Edmond Mylles indenture[171] | | 2 | 6 |
| paid to William Fiske churchwarden | 2 | 0 | 0 |
| paid out for constables charges | | 11 | 8½ |
| layd out to soulgers and other poore pasingers | | 2 | 1 |
| laid out for glazing of 4 wendoes at the towne house | | 11 | 4 |
| paid William Wieth at his going to Bury assis' | 1 | 2 | 0 |
| paid John Smyth de Norwod 10th October 1647 by Mr [Robert] Warners assigment and others of the inhabitane[*sic*] | 6 | 10 | 0 |
| paid James Frier for constabes charges | 3 | 4 | 0 |
| paid to Mr [Robert] Warner and others of the inhabitanc' which they lent William Wieth at his goinge to Bury assises | 4 | 17 | 0 |
| paid for stowing, bratling, and caring of the poore folks woode | 2 | 10 | 0 |
| [*Sum of page*] | 53 | 13 | 6½ |

<Received of Richard Roydon 16th October 1647 for half yeeres rent>

| | | | |
|---|---|---|---|
| Received the 10th of October 1647 of Richard Roydon for his whole yeeres rent of the towne fearme ending at Mycalmes last the some of fiftie fower pounds, I say | 54 | 0 | 0 |

| | | | |
|---|---|---|---|
| <Received for the towne for this yeere 1647 the sume of> | <54 | 0 | 0> |
| Disburssed for the towne this yeere 1647 the sume of | 53 | 17 | 6½ |

| | | | |
|---|---|---|---|
| Soe there remaine due unto the towne from John Newson, junior, being one of the churchwardens the sume of | | 6 | 5½ |

---

[170] He was again paid for giving the parish lecture (see Note 78). In this account Thomas Crosby was paid twice, and the total sum was less than in 1642–3.
[171] The drawing up of his apprenticeship indenture (see Note 173).

[*unnumbered*]
Cratfeild
The accoumpt of William Fisk, senior, of what moonyes he have disbursed for the towne, being one of the churchwardens for the yeere of Our Lord 1647 [*for 1647–8*]

| | £ | s. | d. |
|---|---|---|---|
| Inprimis | | | |
| Item there was due unto William Fisk, senior, from the towne uppon the last reckoning daye the sume of | 4 | 6 | 4½ |
| Item paid to William Wyith for charges for the towne the sume of | 2 | 0 | 0 |
| Item paid to the Widow [Ann] Hayward for her fyer for the townesmen uppon the reckoning daye the sume of | | 2 | 6 |
| Item paid to the Widow [Mary] Brodbank for beere for the townsmen uppon the reckoning daye the sume of | | 6 | 3 |
| Item paid to Edmund Milles for lordes rent due att Our Lady 1647 | | 4 | 6 |
| Item laide out for bread and wine for the comunion | | 1 | 0 |
| Item paid to the Widow [Mary] Brodbank for making of a newe stille in the Towne Pitell[172] the sume of | | 1 | 6 |
| Item paid to Goodman Wyith for the Mayned Soulders for halfe a yeere, the 22th of Apriell 1647, the sume of | | 17 | 4 |
| Item paid to the Widow [Mary] Brodbank for beere and bread and meate for the ringers the 5th of November 1646[*sic*], the sume of | | 4 | 10 |
| Item paid to Robert Carter for stowing of a litell wood for [John] Herclyes wife | | | 6 |
| Item paid to John Newson, senior, for bynding forth of the Widow [Mary] Millses boy[173] | | 10 | 0 |
| Item laid out to Edmund Milles for one whole yeere which the towne aloweth him for the releife of his wife, the sume of | 1 | 4 | 0 |
| Item given to Edmund Millses wife att severall tymes for her releife in the tyme of her sicknes, the sume of | | 10 | 0 |
| Item paid to Ruben Tallen for his yeeres wages the sume of | 2 | 0 | 0 |
| Item laid out to Symond Waren the 30th of October 1647 for trymig[*sic*] of the bells | | 5 | 0 |
| Item laid out to Edmund Milles for lordes rent the 8th of November 1647 | | 11 | 5½ |
| Item laid out to Ruben Tallen for weeding of the stones att the porch doore | | 1 | 6 |
| Item laid out to Ruben Tallen for washing of the comunion cloath and napkins | | | 3 |
| Item laid out to the Widow [Elizabeth] Stanard att severall tymes for the releife of her small chilldren the sume of | | 9 | 6 |
| Item paid to Edmund Milles for the whitt rent | | | 4 |
| Item paid to John Williams for moonyes he have laid out for the towne as appreth by his bill, the sume of | | 18 | 11 |

---

172 A new stile was made to give entry to the pightle.
173 An apprentice was bound out, at parish expense. John Newsone mentioned this apprenticeship in his account for the same year.

|  | £ | s. | d. |
|---|---|---|---|
| Item laid out att severall tymes to 153 poore pepell [*sic*] as appreth in my note, the sume of |  | 13 | 11 |
| Item laid out to Goodman [William] Wyith, the constabell, the sume of |  | 2 | 0 |
| Item paid to the poore for 52 weekes colection as appreth by my note, the sume of | 17 | 12 | 0 |

| Sume totall of the disbursmentes for the towne this yeere 1647 is just | 33 | 3 | 8 |
|---|---|---|---|

| Soe there remaine due unto the towne from William Fisk the sume of |  | 6 | 4 |
|---|---|---|---|

Cratfeild

The accoumpt of William Fisk, senior, being one of the churchwardens, of what moonyes he have received for the towne in the yeere of Our Lord 1647 [*for 1647–8*]

| Inprimis | £ | s. | d. |
|---|---|---|---|
| received of Richard Royden for his yeeres rent for the Towne Mydowes due att Mychallmas 1647, the sume of | 6 | 10 | 0 |
| received of Francis Alldus for his yeeres rent for Benclins due att Mychallmas 1647, the sume of | 18 | 0 | 0 |
| received of John Williams for his yeeres rent for the Towne Closse and the mydow due att Mychallmas 1647, the sume of | 4 | 0 | 0 |
| received of Samewell Hayward for his yeeres rent for the scoolehowse and the scoolehowse pitell due att Mychallmas 1647, the sume of | 2 | 0 | 0 |
| received of the Widow [Mary] Brodbank for her yeeres rent for the Towne Pitell due att Mychallmas 1647, the sume of | 1 | 0 | 0 |
| received of John Newson, junior, my partener, the 19th of March 1647, the sume of | 2 | 0 | 0 |

| Sume totall of the receiptes for this yeere 1647 is just | 33 | 10 | 0 |
|---|---|---|---|

[193]

Cratfeild

March the 26th 1648

The accoumpt of John Fisk, being one of the churchwardins for the yeere abovsaid, of what moonyes he have disbursed for the towne as followeth [*for 1648–9*]

| Inprimis | £ | s. | d. |
|---|---|---|---|
| Item laid out att seaverall tymes to 24 poore peepell the sume of |  | 5 | 6 |
| Item paid to Gregory Rousse for part of the Widow [Abre] Smythes howsse fearme the sume of |  | 7 | 6 |
| Item paid to Edmund Milles for the Lady quarter the sume of |  | 6 | 0 |
| Item paid to Ruben Tallen for beere for the townsmen uppon the reckoning day the sume of |  | 5 | 4 |
| Item paid to Symond Warren for mending of the gyld hall doore |  | 1 | 4 |
| Item paid to the Widow [Ann] Hayward for her fyer uppon the reckoning day |  | 2 | 6 |

|  | £ | s. | d. |
|---|---|---|---|
| Item paid to William Crosse the 18th of January 1648 the sume of |  | 9 | 0 |
| Item paid to Ruben Tallen for weeding of the stones before the porch doore[174] |  | 1 | 0 |
| Item paid to Ruben Tallen for ringing of the bell uppon the leckter day the sume of \for the whole yeere 1648/ |  | 5 | 0 |
| Item paid to Robert Brodbank one of the towne sowldiers for 2 dayes to Peassnall and 4 dayes to Duncish[175] the sume of |  | 13 | 6 |
| Item for a horrse for him |  | 5 | 0 |
| Item paid to Ruben Tallen for his yeeres wages the sume of | 2 | 0 | 0 |
| Item laid out to a man that should have gathered in the church the sume of |  | 5 | 0 |
| Item laid out to Samewell Milles for the releife of his chilldren |  | 5 | 0 |
| Item laid out to the Widow [Elizabeth] Stanard att seaverall tymes for the releife of her chilldren the sume of |  | 12 | 0 |
| Item laid out to Doll Adams att severall tymes for the releife of the owld woomen the sume of |  | 5 | 0 |
| Item laid out to the Widow [Ann] Newson for her releife the sume of |  | 2 | 0 |
| Item laid out to Widow [Elizabeth] Brissingam for her releife the sume of |  | 2 | 0 |
| Item laid out for one whole yeere for the colection for the poore the sume of | 19 | 6 | 0 |
| Item laid out to Symond Warne as appreth by his bill the sume of |  | 8 | 4 |
| Item laid out to Francis Alldus for moonyes he have disbursed for the towne the sume of | 5 | 7 | 6½ |
| Item laid out to Samewell Hayward for making of a newe floore in the scoolehowse the sume of |  | 4 | 0 |
| Item paid to the Widow [Mary] Brodbank as appreth by her bill the sume of \for the pullers dinners/[176] |  | 18 | 0 |
| Item paid to John Williams as appreth by his bill the sume of | 6 | 7 | 1 |
| Item paid unto William Crosse for looking to repayer the clock for the yeere 1648 the sume of |  | 6 | 8 |
| Sume totall of the disbursmentes this yeere 1648 is | 39 | 10 | 3½ |

A note of what moony John Fisk, being one of the church wardens, have received for the towne in the yeere 1648

|  | £ | s. | d. |
|---|---|---|---|
| Inprimis |  |  |  |
| received in moony from William Fisk, being one of the former churchwardens, the sume of |  | 6 | 4 |
| received of Francis Alldus for his yeeres rent due att Mychallmas 1648 the sume of | 18 | 0 | 0 |
| received of Richard Royden for his yeeres rent for the Towne Mydowes due att Mychallmas 1648 |  | 6 10 | 0 |

---

[174] Routine weeding of the cobbles in the church porch and path approaching it. This was necessary because grass and moss would make the approach slippery.
[175] Dunwich, Suffolk.
[176] 'Pullers' or 'pulverers', meaning those who took part in 'pulvering day' (see Note 6).

|  | £ | s. | d. |
|---|---|---|---|
| received of John Williams for his yeeres rent due att Mychallmas 1648, the sume of | 4 | 0 | 0 |
| received of Mary Brodbank, widow, for her yeeres rent for the Towne Pitell due att Mychallmas 1648 | 1 | 0 | 0 |
| received of Samewell Hayward for his yeeres rent for the scoolehowse the sume of | 2 | 0 | 0 |
| Sume totall of the receiptes this yeere 1648 is | 31 | 16 | 4 |
| Soe there is due unto John Fisk from the towne the sume of | 7 | 13 | 11½ |

[197]
Cratfeild
March the 26th 1649
The accoumpt of John Fisk of what monyes he have disbursed in the behalfe of the towne, being one of the churchwardens, for the yeere abovesaid [*for 1649–50*][177]

|  | £ | s. | d. |
|---|---|---|---|
| Inprimis |  |  |  |
| Item theire was owing unto John Fisk from the towne the last reckoning daye the sume of | 7 | 13 | 11½ |
| Item laid out for bread and wine for the communion |  | 3 | 4 |
| Item laid out towardes a breife that should have bin gatherd in the church the 25th of March 1649 |  | 3 | 4 |
| Item laid out at severall tymes to poore travellers |  | 5 | 0 |
| Item paid to Ruben Tallowing for his beere upon the reckoning daye the sume of |  | 6 | 0 |
| Item paid to the Widow [Ann] Hayward the 11th of Maye 1649 for her fyer upon the reckoning daye the sume of |  | 2 | 6 |
| Item paid to Ruben Tallowing the 13th of Maye for his Ladye quarter wages the sume of |  | 10 | 0 |
| Item paid to Ruben Tallowing for Mydsomer quarter wages the 29th of Julye the sume of |  | 10 | 0 |
| Item paid to the Widow [Mary] Brodbank the 16th of August 1649 the sume of |  | 10 | 0 |
| Item paid to William Crosse for making of a latch |  |  | 4 |
| Item paid to William Brodbank the 28th of August for goeing to Beckells for the cronyer[178] the sume of |  | 3 | 0 |
| Item paid to Ruben Tallowing the 8th daye of October for his Mychallmas quarter wages, the sume of |  | 10 | 0 |
| Item paid him for ringing the bell for the lecktor, and for weding the stones before the porch doore |  | 6 | 0 |

---

[177] During the year 1649 (new style), momentous national events were happening. Charles I was beheaded on 30 January; the monarchy was abolished on 17 March; and England was declared a 'Commonwealth and Free State' on 19 May, governed thereafter by the 'Rump' of the Long Parliament with a Council of State consisting of forty-one members.
[178] The coroner, a royal official.

|  | £ | s. | d. |
|---|---|---|---|

Item given to the Widow [Elizabeth] Stanard the 8th of October for the releife of her poore chilldren the sume of — 5 0

Item given to the Widow [Ann] Newson in tyme of her necessitye the sume of — 4 8

Item laid out for a peck of wheat for her — 2 2

Item paid to the Widow [Mary] Brodbanke for the ringers upon the fift daye of November the sume of — 6 0

Item laid out for 2 loades of wood carryeing in for the poore, the some of — 2 0

Item paid to John Williams for monyes he laid out as appereth by his bill the sume of — 1 14 3

Item paid to the poore for 42 weekes collection the sume of — 17 17 0

Item more paid to the Widow [Elizabeth] Brissingam for one monthes collection — 3 0

£31 19s. 6½d.

Item paid to the Widow [Abre] Smyth for one moonthes collection — 2 0

The sume of this syde is — 31 19 6½

[damaged] paid to the Widow [?Mary] Milles for one monthes collection — 2 0

[damaged] paid to John Hearclye for 6 weekes collection — 6 0

[damaged] paid to Francis Alldus which he laid out for the towne for the weekely asessment and other charges as appereth by his bill, the sume of — 3 8 11½

Item given to the Widow [?]Savard for the releife of her chilldren — 7 0

Item paid to John Hearcly for one monthes colection — 4 0

Item paid to Sara Cady in part for 10 weekes colection — 2 6

4 10 5½

Sume totall of my disbursmentes this yeere 1649 is just — 36 10 0

Cratfield
March the 26th 1649
A note of what moonyes John Fiske have received in the behalfe of the towne, being churchwarden for the yeere abovesaid

Inprimis £ s. d.

received of Richard Roydon for his yeeres rent for the Towne Myddowes due at Mychallmas last past the some of — 6 10 0

received of Francis Alldus for his yeeres rent due att Mychallmas last for Benclens the some of — 18 0 0

received of Mr [Robert] Warner in mooney which he lent to the towne the first of Julye 1649 the summe of — 5 0 0

received of John Williams for his yeeres rent for the Towne Closse and Mowlings Myddowe due att Mychallmas last the sume of — 4 0 0

received of Samewell Hayward for his yeeres rent for the scoolehowse due att Mychallmas last past the sume of — 2 0 0

|  | £ | s. | d. |
|---|---|---|---|
| received of the Widow [Mary] Brodbank for her yeeres rent for the Towne Pitell due at Mychallmas last past the somme of | 1 | 0 | 0 |
| Sume totall of my receiptes this yeere 1649 for the towne is just | 36 | 10 | 0 |

[200]

A note of the charges which have bine laid out by me Robert Smith de Coulshall, being one of the churchwardens for the said towne, begining the 23 of March 1649 and untill the 1th of Maij (1651) [for 1650–1]

|  | £ | s. | d. |
|---|---|---|---|
| Inprimis laid out to Stephen Adams for a bill of charges |  | 16 | 6 |
| Item more for bere and fiering the same day |  | 8 | 0 |
| Item more the same time laid out to Mr [Thomas] Bedingfield for a warrant for Bliborow brige |  | 15 | 0 |
| Item laid out to Mr [Thomas] Crosbe the 25th of March (1650) | 7 | 15 | 0 |
| Item laid out to Mr [Thomas] Bedingfield about that time for Mained Souldiers |  | 17 | 4 |
| Item laid out for stowing and bratling the pore folkes wood, and laying it of heapes | 1 | 3 | 0 |
| Item laid out at Beackles and at home fore our charges the 18th of May |  | 5 | 5 |
| Item laid out fore worke about the buttes[179] and for loking to the towne armes and for bread for the Widdowe [Elizabeth] Stanards children when she was gone |  | 6 | 0 |
| Item laid out for towne rent and a marsement |  | 4 | 10 |
| Item laid out to Mr Gooding for his charges being counstable as apeere by his bill | 2 | 13 | 4 |
| Item laid out to Edward Carsy for his charges as apeere by his bill |  | 13 | 2 |
| Item laid out to John Smith of Norwod Greene |  | 2 | 0 |
| Item laid out for beere fore the 4 constables and others at the cort |  | 1 | 0 |
| Item laid out to Mr [Gabriel] Eland for bokes binding |  | 10 | 0 |
| Item laid out at the bocke makeing for the armes in the towne,[180] for expences for 9 or 10 [men] |  | 3 | 6 |
| Item to John Newson that I did borrow for hime | 5 | 0 | 0 |
| Item laid out about the church |  | 12 | 4 |
| Item more fore iorn worke and othere things |  | 18 | 0 |
| more to [Nick] Becker | 1 | 17 | 6 |
| Item more to [Nick] Becker | 1 | 10 | 0 |
| Item laid out for a rope fore the great bell |  | 5 | 10 |
| Item laid out the 8th of October for beere for the ringers, being a day of thankes giveing |  | 2 | 0 |
| Item for souldieren |  | 2 | 2 |
| Item to William Alldis and Gregory Rowse for wod |  | 3 | 0 |
| Item laid out to Mr [Henry] Meene for 3 monthes assesment | 1 | 6 | 9 |
| This sid is iust | 28 | 11 | 4 |

[179] Parishes had been responsible for the good repair of the local butts since 'An Acte for Mayntenance of Artyllarie and Debarringe of Unlawful Games' (1541–2).
[180] A muster-roll or 'book' was drawn up listing the arms and armour of the parish (see Notes 30 & 52).

|  | £ | s. | d. |
|---|---|---|---|
| Item to M^r [Thomas] Crosbe the 6^th of October | 7 | 15 | 0 |
| more at that time to Ruben [Tallant] for 9 dayes worke and fiering for the glaasers to plum and soder |  | 10 | 9 |
| Item to William Brodbancke for thrashing and faning | 1 | 3 | 9 |
| more for expences about the towne bessenes |  | 12 | 6 |
| Item out to John Rouse for careing of the wood for the pore | 2 | 12 | 0 |
| Item for glassing and othere thinges about the scoolhouse |  | 8 | 2 |
| Item laid out to the poore man and othare things about the stable |  | 2 | 8 |
| Item laid out to Finit Adams for keping of the poore woman |  | 5 | 5 |
| Item to John Newson, my partnor, for rent for the Towne Middows | 3 | 5 | 0 |
| Item laid out at my jorny to Blyborow the 25^th of November for horse hyre and my expences and a warrant fore [Robert] Koable and to 6 saylors |  | 3 | 6 |
| Item laid out for a locke, 2 staples, and a hasp |  | 1 | 8 |
| more fore carring of the warrant to [Robert] Koable |  |  | 6 |
| Item paid at Michalmis for towne rent |  | 11 | 6 |
| more at the same time for Mained Souldiers |  | 17 | 4 |
| Item paid for [?]euse for £10 for the towne |  | 6 | 8 |
| Item given to Joseph Smith in his truble |  | 10 | 0 |
| Item laid out for my expences about the ingoagment[181] |  | 1 | 5 |
| more given to Joseph Smith in his truble |  | 5 | 0 |
| Item given to the Widdow [Elizabeth] Stanard |  | 4 | 0 |
| Item laid out to Mother Grimston for Joseph Smith | 1 | 5 | 0 |
| Item paid to John Williams at Chrismis for his bill | 8 | 4 | 4 |
| Item to Thomis Turner for a bill of charges |  | 10 | 0 |
| Item given to 4 sailors taken at sea |  |  | 3 |
| Item paid to M^r [Thomas] Crosbe for Chrismis quarter | 4 | 5 | 0 |
| Item laid out to [Thomas] Johnson for souldierin at Bliboro |  | 3 | 0 |
| more to [Robert] Pace at the same time |  | 2 | 6 |
| Item more laid out about the towne armes and a belt for the sword and to pore people |  | 4 | 0 |
| Item to the bally for rent for Rose Larkes |  | 8 | 2 |
| Item to [Robert] Keable for charges |  | 5 | 6 |
| Item to [William] Crose for looking to the clock |  | 6 | 8 |
| Item for mortring about the church and other things |  | 6 | 10 |
| Item for Mained Souldiers March 25^th (1651) |  | 17 | 4 |
| Item laid out about the sawars |  | 1 | 8 |
| [Sum of page] | 37 | 7 | 1 |
| Item to Thomas Keamar for the Ladday[182] rent     [damaged] |  | 4 | ? |

---

[181] The Engagement was ordered by the Rump Parliament on 2 January 1650 and required of all males over eighteen years of age. It required obedience to 'the commonwealth, as it is now established, without a King or House of Lords'. Apparently, there was little ideological commitment to it, but rather it was an act by a desperate Parliament. It was one of the first acts to be abolished by the Protector, Oliver Cromwell. See Coward, *The Stuart Age*, pp. 212, 226.

[182] Lady Day, 25 March.

|                                                             |            | £ | s. | d. |
|-------------------------------------------------------------|------------|---|----|----|
| moeor to John Godball for his bill of charges               | [damaged]  | 1 | 10 | ?  |
| [Sum of receipts]                                           |            | 1 | 15 | 4  |

|                                                             | £ | s. | d. |
|-------------------------------------------------------------|----|----|----|
| The wholle summe is iust                                    | 67 | 13 | 9  |

[201]
What mony as have bine receyved by me, Robert Smith of Coulshall, from the 23th
of March 16[4]9 untill the 1th of Maij (1651) [for 1650–1]

|                                                                              | £ | s. | d. |
|------------------------------------------------------------------------------|----|----|-----|
| Inprimis of Richard Raydon                                                   | 1 | 3 | 7 |
| Item of Goodman [John] Rouse                                                 |   | 3 | 1 |
| Item receyved of Richard Raydon for part of the rent at Our Lady            |   |   |   |
|    (1650)                                                                     | 14 | 9 | 5½ |
| and the rest laid out as apere by his bill                                   | [blank] |  |  |
| Item receyved of Richard [Raydon] for part of his rent at Michellmis         | 1 | 10 | 0 |
| receyved <of> more of Richard Raydon for his rent, and for the               |   |   |   |
|    Towne Middowes for Michellmis rent 1650                                    | 25 | 16 | 0 |
| and the rest laid out as apere by his bill                                   | [blank] |  |  |
|    This summ is                                                               | 43 | 2 | 1½ |

[203]
March the 26th 1650
A note of what moonyes John Newson, senior, being one of the churchwardens,
doe laye oute in the behalfe of the towne in the yeere abovesaid [for 1650–1]

|                                                                                      | £ | s. | d. |
|--------------------------------------------------------------------------------------|----|----|----|
| Inprimis                                                                             |   |   |   |
| Item paid to Rubben Tallen for his quarter wages due att Our Lady                    |   |   |   |
|    1650, the sume of                                                                  |   | 10 | 0 |
| Item paid to the poore which taketh colection which John Fisk, the                    |   |   |   |
|    former churchwarden, left to pay, the sume of                                      | 3 | 18 | 8 |
| Item paid for [?]w'tt paper                                                           |   |   | 1 |
| Item paid to Ruben Tallen the 4th of Apriell for ringing of the bell for             |   |   |   |
|    the lector                                                                          |   | 5 | 0 |
| Item lent with the consent of the towne to Samuell Milles                            |   | 13 | 0 |
| Item paid to William Crosse for kepeing of the clock in time                         |   | 6 | 8 |
| Item laid out for 3 pintes of sack and bread for the communion[183]                   |   | 2 | 5 |
| Item laid oute for fetching of it, to Ruben Tallowing                                |   |   | 3 |
| Item laid out to Ruben Tallowing for his quarter wages due att                        |   |   |   |
|    Midsomer 1650, the some of                                                         |   | 10 | 0 |
| Item paid to Ruben Tallin for weeding the stones twice att the porch                  |   |   |   |
|    doore, the somme of                                                                |   | 1 | 0 |

---

[183] For the only time in these accounts, the communion wine is specified as 'sack', a dry wine from Spain
and the Canary Islands. Different wine was sometimes served to different social groups, for example 'rich
sweet wine such as Malmsey or Muscadine [being given] to the "better sort" and a cheaper Claret to the
rest'. See Craig, 'Co-operation and Initiatives' (1993), p. 376.

|  | £ | s. | d. |
|---|---|---|---|
| Item given to Sarah Cadye in tyme of sicknesse |  | 1 | 0 |
| Item paid to Thomas Johnsons wiffe for nursing of the poore child, and for the weare of her lining |  | 16 | 0 |
| Item paid to Ruben Tallowing for his quarter wages due att Michallmas 1650, the some of |  | 10 | 0 |
| Item laid out for bread and wine for the communion[184] |  | 1 | 10 |
| Item paid to Ruben Tallen for fetching of the bread and wine |  |  | 4 |
| Item paid to Ruben Tallen for his quarter wages due att Christed[185] 1650, the some of |  | 10 | 0 |
| Item paid the Widow [?Mary] Milles for kepeing of the pore child one daye |  |  | 6 |
| Item laid out to a breife the 23th Febbruary 1650 |  | 1 | 0 |
| Item paid to Joseph Smyth for mending the towne skabard |  |  | 2 |
| Item given more to Sarah Cadie in tyme of want |  | 1 | 0 |
| Item laid out for bread and wine for the communion |  | 2 | 0 |
| Item paid to Ruben Tallowing for fetching of it |  |  | 6 |
| Item paid to John Clerke for stowing of wood for the poore in the gyld hall, the somme of |  | 1 | 2 |
| Item paid to Samewell Haywood which he layd out for the towne as appreth by his bill, the sume of |  | 2 | 6 |
| Item paid to John Williams which he laid out for the towne for the weekely asessment and other charges as appreth by his bill, the sume of | 2 | 0 | 0 |
| Item paid to Francis Alldus which he laid out for the towne to the weekly asessment and other charges as by his bill appreth, the sume of | 1 | 13 | 4½ |

A note of what moonyes John Newson, senior, have disburssed in the behalfe of the towne in the yeere 1650

|  | £ | s. | d. |
|---|---|---|---|
| Item paid to the poore for 52 weekes colection ending the 7th daye of Apriell 1651, the sume of | 23 | 4 | 8 |
| Item paid to the Widow [Mary] Brodbank for the poulverers dinners and other charges as appreth by her bill, the sume of | 1 | 7 | 6 |

| Sume totall of my disbursmentes this yeere 1650 is just | 37 | 0 | 7½ |
|---|---|---|---|

| Soe there remaine due unto John Newson from the towne the sume of |  | 10 | 7½ |
|---|---|---|---|

A note of what moonyes John Newson, senior, being one of the churchwardens, have received in the behalfe of the towne in the yeere 1650

|  | £ | s. | d. |
|---|---|---|---|
| received of John Williams for his yeeres rent due att Michallmas 1650 for the Towne Closse and Mowlinges Mydowe, the sume of | 4 | 0 | 0 |

---

184 This appears to be a Christmas communion, and a revival of earlier practice. From 1644 to 1660 Parliament banned Easter, Whitsun and Christmas communions, but from 1650 onwards Cratfield celebrated communion at Easter, and in this case probably at Christmas (see Introduction, pp. 14–15).
185 Christ-tide or Christmas, 25 December.

|  | £ | s. | d. |
|---|---|---|---|
| received of Richard Royden for his yeeres rent for the Town Mydowes due att Mychallmas 1650 | 6 | 10 | 0 |
| received of Francis Alldus for his yeeres rent for Benslins due att Mychallmas 1650, the sume of | 18 | 0 | 0 |
| received of Samewell Hayward for his yeeres rent for the scoolehowse due att Mychallmas 1650 | 2 | 0 | 0 |
| received of the Widow [Mary] Brodbank for her yeeres rent for the Towne Pitell ending att Mychallmas 1650 | 1 | 0 | 0 |
| received of my partner Robert Smyth the sume of | 5 | 0 | 0 |
| Sume totall of my receiptes is | 36 | 10 | 0 |

[204]

Robert Smyth de Coulshall, churchwarden for the yeere 1650 [*for 1650–1*]
A note of what moonyes I ame to receive of him for the towne as foloweth[186]

|  | £ | s. | d. |
|---|---|---|---|
| Inprimis |  |  |  |
| Item laid out att the Widow [Mary] Brodbanks for bread and beere for the man which cam to bring word of the woman which left the child in our church porch[187] |  |  | 10 |
| Item more laid out att Metfield and Flixon[188] |  |  | 8 |
| Item laid out att Bnegay[189] for beere and for our suppers and breckfastes and for my horsmeat, the sume of |  | 6 | 0 |
| Item for victualls for the woman and her chilldren |  | 1 | 0 |
| Item laid out to Mr [John] Gooch for a warrant |  |  | 6 |
| Item laid out to Bottres for his paynes to seek after the woman and to find her | 1 | 0 | 0 |
| Item laid out to William Brodbank for his charges 18s., and for a horse for him 4s., in all the sume of | 1 | 2 | 0 |
| Item for my owne paynes and for my horse and for victualls for the woman and her chilldrin att my howse | 1 | 0 | 0 |
| Item paid to Mr [Henry] Meene for 3 monthes asessment ending att Christmas 1650, for the grownd which I have of the towne |  | 2 | 4 |
| Item for halfe a sheet of parchment John Rous had for the ingagement |  |  | 6 |
| Item for 6 quarters of pouder and 6 yards of match |  | 2 | 6 |
| Item to receive of the towne for Thomas Leggat of Wrentham[190] the sume of | 4 | 4 | 0 |
| Sume totalis | 8 | 0 | 4 |

|  | £ | s. | d. |
|---|---|---|---|
| received of Robert Smyth de Coulshall the 20th of December 1650, the sume of | 7 | 10 | 0 |
| remaine due |  | 14 | 4 |

---

[186] The writer is John Williams (see the end of this account).
[187] See the following entries, and Introduction, p. 7.
[188] Metfield and Flixton, Suffolk.
[189] Bungay, Suffolk.
[190] Wrentham, Suffolk.

|  | £ | s. | d. |
|---|---|---|---|

received of Robert Smyth de Coulshall the 28th of December 1650 in
full discarge of this bill the sume of 14s. 4d., soe I say received
in all the sume of
*Per me* John Williams

| | 8 | 4 | 4 |

[*unnumbered*]
The accoumpts of Robert Smyth de Coulshall and John Newson, senior [*written on back of account*]

Cratfield
A note of what mony John Newson, senior, being one of the churchwardens, have dissbursed in the behalfe of the towne from Our Ladye 1651 until Our Ladye 1652 as followeth [*for 1651–2*]

| | £ | s. | d. |
|---|---|---|---|
| Inprimis | | | |
| Item paid to Ruben Tallen for his whole yeeres wages | 2 | 0 | 0 |
| Item paid for beere on the pullvering daye | | 1 | 0 |
| Item to the Widow [Ann] Newson at severall tymes of her sicknesse | | 2 | 0 |
| Item to Sarah Cadye after the end of the yeere 1650 and before her death, she being out of the collection bill this yeere | | 4 | 10 |
| Item for the dinners of those that went a pulvering this yeere | 1 | 4 | 0 |
| Item paid to Rose Browne for keping the Widow [Ann] Newson in tyme of her sicknesse | | 1 | 0 |
| Item paid to Robert Pacye for stowing and bratling of the towne wood | | 15 | 0 |
| Item to Thomas Johnson for his journy to Yarmoth and service there as a soldier sixtene dayes | 1 | 0 | 0 |
| Item for bread and wine for 2 conmunions | | 3 | 6 |
| Item to Ruben Tallen for fetching of the bread and wine | | | 4 |
| Item for carrying of 20 loades of wood for the poore | 1 | 13 | 4 |
| Item to eightene poore people coming from Lincolnsheire | | 1 | 0 |
| Item paid to William [?]Broadbank for stowing and carying of the Widow [Ann] Newsons wood | | 1 | 0 |
| Item paid to Symond Warne for repayring of the towne barne | | 8 | 0 |
| Item paid to William Crosse for nayles and yrones used about the said reparacions | | 2 | 3 |
| Item paid to the poore for one whole yeres collection wanting twoe weekes the some of | 19 | 7 | 4 |
| It paid to Francis Alldus as apereth by his bill | 6 | 4 | 9½ |
| Item paid to John Williams as apereth by his bill | 3 | 18 | 2 |
| Item paid to Samuel Hayward as apereth by his bill | | 3 | 0 |
| Item there was due to John Newson at the last reckoning daye the somme of | | 10 | 7½ |
| Summe totall of the dissbursments this yeere is just | 38 | 1 | 2 |

Cratfield
A note of what mony John Newson, senior, being one of the churchwardens, have

received in the behalfe of the towne from Our Ladye 1651 untill Our Ladye 1652, as followeth

| | £ | s. | d. |
|---|---|---|---|
| Inprimis | | | |
| Received of John Williams for his whole yeeres rent ending at Michallmas 1651 the somme of | 12 | 0 | 0 |
| received of Francis Alldus for his whole yeres rent ending at Michallmas 1651 the somme of | 20 | 0 | 0 |
| received of Samuel Hayward for his whole yeres rent ending at Michallmas 1651 the somme of | 2 | 0 | 0 |
| received of William Carsy in part for his halfe yeeres rent due at Our Ladye 1652 for Bencelines | 2 | 0 | 0 |
| received more from the states for the towne soldier going to Yarmoth and being there 16 dayes | | 16 | 0 |
| received more of William Carse in in [sic] part for his halfe yeeres rent due att Our Lady 1652 the sume of | | 10 | 0 |
| received of Samewell Hayward for his halfe yeeres rent for the scollhowse due att Our Lady 1652 the sume of | 1 | 0 | 0 |
| Summe totall of the receipts this yeere is just | 38 | 6 | 0 |

Soe there remayneth due unto the towne from John Newson, senior, the some of

|  |  |
|---|---|
| | 4 10 |

[210]
A note of what mony Francis Alldus have laid out for the towne in the yeere of Our Lord 1651 [for 1651–2][191]

| | £ | s. | d. |
|---|---|---|---|
| Item paid to Mr [Henry] Meene for 2 monthes asessment | | 9 | 9½ |
| Item paid to Robert Milles for 2 monthes assessment | | 13 | 0 |
| Item paid to William Carsy for 2 monthes asessment | | 13 | 0 |
| Item paid to Goodman [John] Ebbes for 2 monthes asessment | | 13 | 0 |
| Item paid to Goodman [Thomas] Turner for 2 monthes asessment | | 13 | 0 |
| Item paid more to Thomas Turner for 2 monthes asessment | | 13 | 0 |
| Item to set of [sic] for the shope and the wall the somme of | 2 | 10 | 0 |
| Somme is | 6 | 4 | 9½ |

A note of what mony John Williams have laid out for the towne from the 21th of January 1650 [1651]

| | £ | s. | d. |
|---|---|---|---|
| Item paid to Thomas Turner for 2 monthes asessment begining the 25th of December | | 3 | 0 |
| Item 6 quarters powder and 6 yardes of match | | 2 | 6 |
| Item paid to Thomas Turner for 2 monthes asessment, March and Apriell, just | | 3 | 0 |

---

[191] This account and the next was pinned to the churchwardens' accounts. It was possible that Francis Alldus and John Williams were not actual churchwardens, but that their accounts were merely deposited with them.

|  | £ | s. | d. |
|---|---|---|---|
| Item 10 pounds raisons, 10 pounds figes[192] |  | 8 | 4 |
| Item 2 ounces Spanish tabacco, 1 dozen pipes |  | 2 | 3 |
| Item for making of the accoumpts for the pore and delivering them to the Justices of the Peace, and for a warrant |  | 5 | 0 |
| Item paid to Robert Milles for 2 monthes asessment begining the 25th of March 1651 |  | 3 | 0 |
| Item paid to John Lowe for 2 monthes asessment, June and July |  | 3 | 0 |
| Item paid to John Ebbes for 2 monthes asessment, August and September |  | 3 | 0 |
| Item half a hundred 8d. nayles, 1 quart sallet oyle |  |  | 7 |
| Item 6 quarters powder, 6 yards of match, and bullets |  | 4 | 0 |
| Item to receive of John Newson by the apoyntment of the towne, in part for my writing this 8 or 9 yeres[193] | 2 | 0 | 0 |
| Item 100 3d. nayles, j dozen 8d. nayles |  |  | 4 |
| Item for 6d. nayles Samuel Hayward had |  |  | 2 |
| Summe is | 3 | 18 | 2 |

[211]
Cratfield
A note of the charges which have bine laid out by me, Robart Smith de Coulshall, beinge one of the churchwardens from the 1th of Maij 1651 untill the [blank] of March 1652

|  | £ | s. | d. |
|---|---|---|---|
| Inprimis to Mr [Robert] Warnar for 14 yeeres rent for Rose Larkes |  | 4 | 8 |
| Item for fiering and beere, and to the pore on the reckening day |  | 9 | 10 |
| Item for careing of timber and othere thinges |  | 4 | 8 |
| Item for 2 lodes of straw to Goodman [Richard] Raydon |  | 11 | 0 |
| Item for worke about the towne mussket |  | 3 | 2 |
| Item to [Thomas] Johnsone and [Robert] Pace for soulgren[194] |  | 5 | 0 |
| Item mor about that time to Phinelias Smithes wife for dressing of hir fathareinlaws sore |  | 2 | 6 |
| Item for pore poople in destres,[195] \very many/ |  | 8 | 10 |
| Item laid out to William Brodbanck for keping of the towne armes, and for othere things about the churchyard |  | 5 | 6 |
| Item for a gatt post and for a new gatt and for palling and mending of another gatt, and for iorne worke and nailes and other things about the churchyard |  | 5 | 0 |
| Item more about weding of wheat |  | 6 | 6 |
| Item about the constables, laid out |  | 2 | 0 |
| Item laid out to Goodman [Richard] Raidone for the close of wheat | 13 | 0 | 0 |
| Item more for [John] Hartlates boye for clothes when he went to prentiz | 1 | 0 | 0 |

---

192 These luxuries, and the tobacco which follows, were consumed on the reckoning day.
193 The parish caught up with back payments for writing the accounts. The recipient was probably John Williams.
194 'Soldiering', a word which is spelt in several ways (see Glossary).
195 Distress.

|  | £ | s. | d. |
|---|---|---|---|
| Item for stoping in of the wheat |  | 1 | 0 |
| Item at a rate makeing and for worke about the steple, and iorns |  | 7 | 10 |
| Item laid out to Goodman Cempe for his constabls bill | 1 | 18 | 4 |
| Item laid out to for bell ropes and othere thinges about the belles, and pamments to mend the church |  | 13 | 0 |
| Item for new iornes and mending of oweld, and for sessond timber and carpenders worke and for mending of the peneckle | 1 | 3 | 10 |
| more to Edmond Milles |  | 1 | 0 |
| Item laid out for lokeing to the wheat, and powder and shott to kill varmen |  | 4 | 10 |
| Item given to the pore Widdow [Elizabeth] Stanard in hir need |  | 5 | 0 |
| Item laid out for moving of the wheat headlons, and making and carring of the hay, and weding and sharing of the wheat and caring it into the barne | 2 | 0 | 0 |
| Item laid out to Dallen for work about the belles |  | 1 | 8 |
| Item given to [Thomas] Johnson for soulgren at Beackles |  | 4 | 0 |
| more at that time for caring of the corslet |  | 1 | 0 |
| Sume | 25 | 0 | 2 |
|  |  |  |  |
| Item laid out for soulgren and to pore people |  | 4 | 11 |
| Item laid out to [Robert] Pace for soulgren at Yarmouth and to horse him |  | 17 | 0 |
| Item laid out to the Widdow [Margaret] Addames that was due to hire as apeare by hir billes | 15 | 15 | 0 |
| Item given to [Robert] Paces wife in the time of soulgren |  | 3 | 0 |
| Item given to poore saylors cast away at seae |  |  | 4 |
| Item laid out for 2 loodes of straw and carrying to the gilld halle and to the pore |  | 18 | 0 |
| Item laid out to Mr [Thomas] Bedingfield at Michelmise[196] |  | 17 | 4 |
| Item given to 3 poore dest[r]esed men with a passe |  |  | 8 |
| Item ther wasse dewe to me the last reckening day being the first of Maij last past | 24 | 11 | 7½ |
| Item laid out for staken of straw, and swayes and broches and bindings, and a new ladder |  | 8 | 3 |
| Item for more swayes and mending of ladders and legares and naylles and evfes bordes[197] |  | 3 | 0 |
| Item laid out for thachers wages and to Ruben [Tallant] for wages and for beere for the workmen |  | 18 | 10 |
| Item for putting up of [?]spaires and other worke and more nailles and spekens and laths |  | 13 | 4 |
| Item at Michellmas last laid out to Thomis Turner for the towne rent |  | 11 | 6 |
| Item given for routing of Brisingham[198] out of the town |  | 2 | 2 |

[196] This is probably the quarterly payment for Marshalsea and Maimed Soldiers, or two instalments for Maimed Soldiers only as in 1652–3.
[197] Boards fixed on the eaves of a building, probably the guildhall.
[198] One Brissingham, perhaps the elderly widow, was forcibly driven from town for unknown reasons.

|  | £ | s. | d. |
|---|---|---|---|
| Item given to pore [Robert] Pacie in the time of great siknes[199] |  | 10 | 0 |
| more at the same time to Joseph Smith in the time of great extremity |  | 10 | 0 |
| Item given to 9 saylors cast away at seae |  |  | 6 |
| more sent by M[r] [Gabriel] Elend coming from Wossester[200] and in great want |  |  | 5 |
| Item more given to a Greation[201] for a brefe not garthered |  | 2 | 0 |
| Item more about the belles and iorne worke and nayels |  | 2 | 0 |
| Item laid \out/ fore beare and tobackoe and fiering when the townsmen mett for Joseph Smith |  | 2 | 10 |
| more at that time lent to Joseph Smith |  | 10 | 0 |
| Item laid out againe about Joseph Smith |  | 2 | 6 |
| more to trauilars that ware undone |  |  | 6 |
| Item laid out to Robert Adames for takeing of Samuel Mills boy aprentize | 2 | ?0 | 6 |
| Item laid out to William Brodbanck for threshing and faning |  | 18 | 0 |
| Item laid out to Richard Raydon for wood and rayels and a calves cribe that he left | 2 | 0 | 0 |
| Item given to the Widdow [Elizabeth] Stanard towards this Lady rent |  | 5 | 0 |
| Sume is | 53 | 9 | 2½ |

|  | £ | s. | d. |
|---|---|---|---|
| Item laid out to [William] Crose for keping of the clock and othere worke about the belles |  | 8 | 6 |
| Item fore enterrest for £20 for 3 quarters | 1 | 0 | 0 |
| Item fore some glassen worke and new iorns, and ould iorns mending, and lime and morter |  | 5 | 0 |
| more for glassene worke and morter and lime and and [sic] iornes mending and newe iorns | 1 | 8 | 8 |
| more to the glassers for sodering and new leading |  | 14 | 0 |
| Item given to Ruben [Tallant] for tendance and fiering for the glassars |  | 1 | 4 |
| more at that time to many criples |  |  | 3 |
| Item about that time to 2 men and there wiffes and 10 chrildren with a certificate with handes and seals to passe |  |  | 10 |
| Item laid out to M[r] [Thomas] Bedingfield for 2 bridges upon his war[rant] |  | 6 | 6 |
| Item laid out for pamments and pamintine of the church, and brickes for the gilld hall <and a newe [?]oven for Hartles house> |  | 5 | 6 |
| Item laid out to M[r] [Gabriel] Elnd for clothing of the deske[202] and fringeing of it, and for a new iorne frame and for a pewter basone[203] | 1 | 0 | 0 |
| Item laid out to Simond Warne for worke about the bearne and to [William] Crosse for mending of the church dore key and other things |  | 3 | 4 |

---

[199] In 1651 the 'great sickness' may have been smallpox, which was reported to be 'very sore and heavy' at Halstead in Essex. In 1652, however, smallpox, fever and measles together created what the Essex clergyman, Ralph Josselin, described as a 'wonderful sickly time'. See Dobson, *A Chronology of Epidemic Disease and Mortality* (1990), p. 51.

[200] The battle of Worcester took place on 3 Sept. 1651.

[201] A Grecian or Greek.

[202] This is the reading desk in the church.

[203] Pewter basins were used for the baptism of infants and carried associations of reformed Protestantism (see Introduction, p. 12).

|  | £ | s. | d. |
|---|---|---|---|
| Item for swayes and beere for the thachers |  | 3 | 4 |
| Item given to a poore Irish woman with a brefe and 2 chrildren |  |  | 4 |
| Item given to 4 sailors and 4 poore cretuers |  |  | 4 |
| Item laid out to the Widdow [Margaret] Adames for charges as apeere |  |  |  |
|     by hir bill | 8 | 19 | 10 |
|     Sume is | 14 | 17 | 9 |
|  |  |  |  |
| Sume totallis | 93 | 7 | 1½ |

A note of the monyes which I have receved for the towne since the first of Maij (1651) untill the 26th of March (1652)

|  | £ | s. | d. |
|---|---|---|---|
| Inprimis of John Fiske for 14 yeeres \rent/ due \to/ the towne out of |  |  |  |
|     Mr [John] Lanyes land, \endyng att Mychallmas 1650/ |  | 4 | 8 |
| Item of the Widdow [Margaret] Adames for one whole yeeres rent |  |  |  |
|     ending at Michellmis (1651) | 53 | 0 | 0 |
| Item more of the Widdow Adames for the hay and the <of the> |  |  |  |
|     feede of the wheat headlons | 1 | 10 | 0 |
| Item for not laying of a lode of straw |  | 3 | 0 |
| Item more of my sonne for brick |  | 8 | 0 |
| Item more fore a 11 <cob> combe and one bushell of the best wheat | 10 | 2 | 6 |
| Item mor for fore course wheat and drosse |  | 6 | 6 |
| Item receyved more of souldgrene mony that was returned from Yarmouth |  | 16 | 0 |
| Item more for the halfe yeeres rent due this Lady \1652/ | 29 | 0 | 0 |
|     Sume totall of the reciptes this yeere is | 95 | 10 | 8 |

|  | £ | s. | d. |
|---|---|---|---|
| Soe there is due unto the towne from Robert Smyth de Coulshall the |  |  |  |
|     sume of | 2 | 3 | 6½ |

[214]
Suffolk
7º die Augustij Anno Domini 1652
The receiptes of William Fiske, gent', being one of the churchwardens chosen for the yeere 1652 for the towne of Cratfeld, as followeth

|  | £ | s. | d. |
|---|---|---|---|
| Inprimis received of Robert Smyth of Coltshall, one of the |  |  |  |
|     churchwardens there for the yeere 1651, the some of | 2 | 3 | 6 |
| Item received more of Margaret Addams, widdowe, the 24th day of |  |  |  |
|     July in part of hir halfe yeere due att Midsummer last | 16 | 0 | 0 |
|     Somme total | 18 | 3 | 6 |

Suffolk
The disbursementes of William Fiske, gent', being one of the churchwardens for the towne of Cratfeld for the yeere 1652, as followeth [for 1652–3]

|  | £ | s. | d. |
|---|---|---|---|
| Inprimis laid out for the charges exspended att the reckoning day last |  |  |  |
|     being the 26th of March 1652 |  | 16 | 0 |

|  | £ | s. | d. |
|---|---|---|---|
| Item laid out the 4th day of Aprill for two quarters pay for the Mained Soldiers due Our Lady last past |  | 17 | 4 |
| Item laid out the 9th of June to Thomas Turner for Sir Robert Cookes whit rent due from the towne att Our Lady last past[204] |  | 4 | 6½ |
| Item laid out to William Crosse for triming of the towne musquet |  |  | 8 |
| Item laid out the 23th day of June 1652 to my cozen John Fiske for his charge disbursed in the tyme of his being constable, as appeereth by his bill | 2 | 1 | 0 |
| Item laid out to Robert Milles the 26th day of July 1652, for his charges disbursed in the tyme of his being constable, as appereth by his bill | 3 | 0 | 7 |
| Item laid out to William Crosse for mending the church clocke |  | 13 | 4 |
| Item laid out to Robert Pacy for stoughing and making wood for the poore |  | 15 | 0 |
| Somme total | 8 | 8 | 5½ |

| Soe there remaine due to the towne just | 9 | 15 | 0½ |
|---|---|---|---|

This accoumpt, with the said nine poundes and fiftene shillinges, given and delivered up to John Rouse and other the townesmen the day and yere abovesaid
*Per me* William Fiske, junior                    [?]John Meene [*countersigned*]

[215]
The disbursmentes of John Rous, churchwarden for the towne of Cratfield for the yeare 1652, as followeth [*for 1652–3*]

|  | £ | s. | d. |
|---|---|---|---|
| Imprimis given to Edmund \Milles/ in the tyme of his sonnes siknes |  | 2 | 6 |
| Item for bread and wine for the Sacrament one Ester daye[205] |  | 2 | 4 |
| Item payd unto Willyam Carsie for weekly assesmentes and othere charges layd out as by his byll doe apere | 8 | 5 | 0 |
| Item payd unto Ruben Tallen for his quarters wages due at Our Lady |  | 10 | 0 |
| Item given unto Edmund Milles in his sonns sicknes, April 25 |  | 2 | 6 |
| Item layd out at the giveing in of the accoumpt for the pore, for our exspence and a warrant |  | 5 | 8 |
| Item for our exspence at Woodbridg,[206] and for the messenger that brought the towne word of a woman taken with the hue and crye uppon susspition to be the woman that left hir child in our towne, and John Stannardes hire that went to bringe hir[207] |  | 14 | 8 |
| Item given to Edmund Milles in the tyme of his sons siknes |  | 2 | 0 |
| Item given unto the Widow [Abre] Smyth in tyme of siknes |  | 2 | 0 |

204 Sir Robert Cook, as owner of Blything Hundred, received a quit rent (about 2s. 4d. a year) from the inhabitants of Cratfield for their property called Rose Lark's (account no. 208).
205 An unequivocal reference to an Easter communion (see Notes 164 & 184), which was illegal between 1644 and 1660.
206 Woodbridge, Suffolk.
207 See Introduction, p. 7.

|  | £ | s. | d. |
|---|---|---|---|
| Item payd unto Robert Milles for and towardes the repayre of Bourne and Martlesumm bridges[208] | 1 | 5 | 0 |
| Item payd unto Thomas Johnsons wife for keeping the child left in the towne | | 11 | 0 |
| Item payd unto the woman that did take the child left in towne | 1 | 0 | 0 |
| Item given unto John Edger bannished out of Germine for relegion[209] | | 1 | 0 |
| Item given unto the Widow [Ann] Newson in tyme of sicknes | | 2 | 0 |
| Item given unto Edmund Milles in the tyme of his sons sicknes | | 2 | 0 |
| Item layd out unto the Widow [Mary] Broadbancke for the pulverers dynners | 1 | 0 | 0 |
| Item exspended at Mr Willyam Fiskes, junior, accoumpt given to my selfe and other townes men, for drincke | | | 6 |
| Item given to Cornelious Morefield and Willyam Moone that lost £600 in goodes and £160 in landes *per annum* in Ireland as did apeare by there brefe[210] | | 1 | 6 |
| Item payd unto Ruben Tallion for his quarters wages due at Midsumer | | 10 | 0 |
| Item given unto the Widow [Ann] Newson in hir sicknes | | 2 | 6 |
| Item given unto Rose Browne for lokeinge unto the Widow [Ann] Newson in hir sicknes | | 1 | 6 |
| Item given unto Mary Rowles, widow, which lost in Ireland in landes £500 *per annum* and in goodes £1800 | | 1 | 6 |
| Summ | 15 | 4 | 8 |

Disbursments

| | | | |
|---|---|---|---|
| Item given unto Nicholas More in tyme of sicknes | | 2 | 0 |
| Item given unto Richard Basset, his wife and 5 children, which lost in Ireland £1000 as by ther certificat apered | | 1 | 0 |
| Item given unto Robert Adames to buy Milles his apprentice cloathes, bound by the towne | | 12 | 0 |
| Item layd out unto Robert Smyth de Coulshaw for 5 payre of indentures which he had of the Justice for the bynding of apprentices and for his charges | | 12 | 0 |
| Item layd out for my charges and other townes men, when we went unto Wrentam[211] about our valuation | | 2 | 6 |
| Item layd out unto the Widow [Margaret] Adames for 6 monthes assesmentes: Aprill, May, June, July, August, and September | 5 | 0 | 5 |

---

[208] Bourn Bridge, south of Ipswich, and Martlesham Bridge near Woodbridge.

[209] A unidentified refugee from Germany ejected, presumably, for his Protestantism.

[210] The first of a new string of payments to refugees from Ireland, which continue until 1655–6. This phenomenon is difficult to explain. Since the time of the Catholic rebellion in 1641–3 (Notes 38 & 82), the political situation had totally changed. Now, in the early 1650s, much of Ireland was being confiscated from Catholics and given to Protestants. Nevertheless, Irish immigrants continued to make their way to London in the 1650s, so perhaps their appearance in East Anglia is part of a larger pattern of movement. See K. M. Noonan, ' "The Cruell Pressure of an Enraged, Barbarous People" ' (1998), 151–77. I thank Jane Ohlmeyer for this reference.

[211] Wrentham, Suffolk.

|  | £ | s. | d. |
|---|---|---|---|

Item layd out unto Thomas Spatchet for his paynes in preaching
    amounghtes us[212] — 1 0 0

Item layd out unto Robert Rayner for 4 jurnies for the towne: 2 about
    the valuation and 2 about the woman that left hir child — 5 0

Item layd out unto Thomas Turner, the constable, for the repayreing of
    Claydon, Wilford and Stratford bridges[213] — 13 0

Item layd out for Marshalseas and Mayned Soulgers for halfe a yere
    from Our Lady unto St Micheall — 17 4

Item layd out unto Samuell Ludbroke for carryeinge of 18 loades of
    wood for the pore — 1 8 0

Item given unto thre pore people that came out of the hospitall at
    London and travelled by certificat — 6

Item payd unto <Robert> Joseph Smyth for the use of his £4 from Our
    Lady to St Micheall — 2 0

Item layd out unto Willyam Carsie for the weeklye assesment and
    Sepines charge for his paynes — 1 11 3

Item given unto 7 pore people that came from the hosptall in
    Southerucke[214] and went to Thorpe in Norffolk — 6

Item given unto Phinnis Smyth in tyme of his sicknes — 2 6

Item layd out unto Thomas Turner for the lordes rent of the towne
    landes and the common fyne, for St Micheall — 11 5½

Item layd out unto Ruben Tallion for a quarters wages due at
    St Micheall, and for weeding the stounes befor the porch — 11 0

Item given unto Elizabeth Butcher in hir siknes — 2 0

Item payd unto Willyam Crose for boultes and other worke for the great
    bell as by his bill doe apeare — 8 0

Item given unto M[r] Jefferye for his paynes in preaching — 1 0 0

Sum — 15 2 5½

Disbursmentes

Item for the dyet of six pore people that travelled by certficat, being
    mayned, for ther super and breakfast — 1 0

Item given unto thre pore people that that [sic] travelled by certficat — 4

Item given unto Elizabeth Butcher in hir sicknes — 1 0

Item payd unto John Willyames for his charges to Bongaye[215] for to
    loke for the woman that left hir child,[216] and for the accoumpt for
    the pore giving in unto the Justice, and divers other charges
    and thinges receyved of him for the use of the towne, as by his byll
    doe at large apeere — 2 2 10

Item payd unto Symon Warne for mendinge the stocke of the great bell — 4 0

---

212 Thomas Spatchet lived in nearby Cookley and preached regularly in Cratfield. His possession by a witch was later the subject of a contemporary pamphlet. (See Biography, p. 142.)

213 Bridges at Claydon, Wilford (near Woodbridge) and Stratford St Andrew, all in Suffolk.

214 Southwark, on the south bank of the River Thames, opposite the city of London. This could have been St Thomas's Hospital which provided for thousands of sick and maimed ex-servicemen.

215 Bungay, Suffolk.

216 See Introduction, p. 7.

| | | £ | s. | d. |
|---|---|---|---|---|
| Item payd unto Ruben Tallion for his quarters wages due at Christid | | | 10 | 0 |
| Item given unto Edmund Milles | | | 2 | 0 |
| Item payd unto Thomas Turner for charges in his office untill the 31th of January, as by his byll doe at large apeere | | | 10 | 4 |
| Item given unto the certificat for the burnng of Bongaye to make up that which was collected [to] £2 | | | 5 | 11 |
| Item given unto the certificat of Willyam Metcalfe of Sisewell[217] towardes the burning of a house and goodes | | | 2 | 6 |
| Item given unto a pore man that was robbed, as by his certificat did apeere | | | | 6 |
| Item given unto 2 pore people that travelled by certificat | | | | 6 |
| Item given unto the Widow [Margaret] Adams for doeing cost upon hir fearme and for ditching and spring layeing, being assigned by divers townesmen at our apoynting wood | | 1 | 0 | 0 |
| Summ | | 5 | 0 | 11 |

The collection for the pore

| | | weekly | yerely | | |
|---|---|---|---|---|---|
| Imprimis | Edmund Milles | 1s. 6d. | 4 | 1 | 0 |
| | Ruben Tallion | 1s. 0d. | 2 | 14 | 0 |
| | John Hartly | 1s. 0d. | 2 | 14 | 0 |
| | Widow [Elizabeth] Brissingham | 9d. | 2 | 0 | 6 |
| | Widow [Margaret] Adames | 1s. 0d. | 2 | 14 | 0 |
| | Rose Browne | 6d. | 1 | 7 | 0 |
| | Elizabeth Butcher | 6d. | 1 | 7 | 0 |
| | Widow [Abre] Smyth | 9d. | 2 | 0 | 6 |
| | Widow [Ann] Newson for 22 weekes | 1s. 0d. | 1 | 2 | 0 |
| | Summ | | 20 | 0 | 0 |

| | £ | s. | d. |
|---|---|---|---|
| Summe total | 55 | 8 | 0½ |

John Rous [signature]

Suffolk
Cratfield
The accoumpt of John Rous, chosen churchwarden for the towne of Cratfield for the yere Anno 1652, March the 25 [for 1652–3]

| Receyptes as followeth | £ | s. | d. |
|---|---|---|---|
| Imprimis receyved of John Newson, one of the ould churchwardens, uppon the last reckoning daye | | 4 | 10 |
| receyved of Joseph Smyth which he borrowed of the towne, the summ of | | 10 | 0 |
| receyved of Willyam Carsye for his halfe yeres rent for the fearme called Besnales due at Our Lady | 10 | 0 | 0 |
| receyved of the Widow [Mary] Broadbancke for hir yeres rent due at Our Lady last | 1 | 5 | 0 |

---

217 Sizewell, Suffolk.

|  | £ | s. | d. |
|---|---|---|---|
| receyved of Willyam Carsye for his halfe yere rent due at St Micheall | 10 | 0 | 0 |
| receyved of M$^r$ Willyam Fyske, junior, executor of M$^r$ Wyllyam Fyske his father, churchwarden for the yere 1652 deceased, the summ of | 9 | 15 | 0 |
| receyved of the Widow [Margaret] Adames the remaynder of hir halfe yers rent not receyved by M$^r$ [William] Fyske, due at Midsommer for Rose Larkes | 13 | 0 | 0 |
| receyved of Samuell Hayward for the halfe years rent of the scolehouse, for St Micheall | 1 | 0 | 0 |
| receyved of the Widow [Mary] Broadbancke for hir halfe years rent for the Towne Pyghtell due at St Micheall |  | 15 | 0 |
| receyved of John Willyames for the rent of the towne landes in his occupation for a yere, due at St Micheall last | 12 | 0 | 0 |
| Receyptes summ | 58 | 9 | 10 |
|  |  |  |  |
| Disbursments summ | 55 | 8 | 0½ |
| Remayneing due unto the towne upon this accoumpt | 3 | 1 | 9½ |
| John Rous [signature] |  |  |  |

[In a different hand] This accoumpt seene and allowed by the inhabbitantes of the towne the 25th daye of March 1653[218]


[217]
Cratfield
The accoumpt of John Rous churchwarden for the towne of Cratfield made and given up to the inhabitantes of the said towne the 31th day of March in the yeare of Our Lord 1654, for the yeare of Our Lord 1653 [for 1653–4][219]

| Receyptes | £ | s. | d. |
|---|---|---|---|
| Imprimis remayneing in my hands uppon my last accoumpt given up unto the towne the last reconing daye, Anno 1653 March the 25th | 3 | 1 | 10 |
| receyved of the Widow [Margaret] Adames for hir yeares rent and fearme of Roos Larks the summ of | 58 | 0 | 0 |
| receyved of Willyam Carsie for his years rent and fearme of Besnales the summ of | 20 | 0 | 0 |
| receyved of Samuell Hayward for his yeares rent and fearme of the scoolehouse | 2 | 0 | 0 |
| receyved of the Widow [Mary] Broadbancke for hir yeares rent and fearme of the Towne Pightell | 1 | 10 | 0 |
| receyved of John Willyames in part of his yeares rent and fearme for the land in his occupation, ending at St Micheall last | 8 | 4 | 3 |

---

218 This note clearly shows the process of submitting the annual 'reckoning' at around Lady Day, and its approval by the principal inhabitants of the parish.
219 During 1653, the Commonwealth was ended by Cromwell's dismissal of the Rump on 20 April, and of its successor, the Barebones Parliament, on 12 December. By means of the Instrument of Government, the Protectorate was established on 16 December.

|  | £ | s. | d. |
|---|---|---|---|
| receyved more of John Willyames | 3 | 15 | 9 |
| The totall summ of my receyptes is | 92 | 16 | 1 |
|  | and 3 | 15 | 9 |

Disbursmentes for the towne by me John Rous in the yeare of Our Lord 1653, as followeth

|  | £ | s. | d. |
|---|---|---|---|
| Imprimis layd out the last reconing daye for beere and Thomas Tallions attendance one the townesmen |  | 6 | 0 |
| Item layd out unto Samuell Hayward for fire the last reconing daye |  | 3 | 0 |
| Item layd out unto the Widow [Margaret] Adames for 6 monthes assesment: Occtober, November, December, January, February and March | 6 | 0 | 5 |
| Item given unto 4 pore people that traviled by certificat |  |  | 6 |
| Item payd unto Willyam Crose for lokeing unto the clocke and keeping it in repayre for a yeare, ending at Our Lady 1653 |  | 6 | 8 |
| Item given unto Edmund Milles towardes the buying of wood |  | 5 | 0 |
| Item given unto 8 pore travelling mayened people |  |  | 6 |
| Item payd unto Ruben Tallion for his quarters wages for Our Lady |  | 10 | 0 |
| Summ | 7 | 12 | 1 |

Disbursmentes

|  | £ | s. | d. |
|---|---|---|---|
| Item given unto the Widow [Abre] Smyth towards hir house fearme for Our Lady |  | 5 | 0 |
| Item given unto the Widow [Elizabeth] Sannard[sic] towards hir releafe |  | 2 | 6 |
| Item paid unto Goodman [Thomas] Gant for stowing the wood for the pore |  | 10 | 0 |
| Item payd unto the constable for Marshalseas and Mayemed Soulgers for halfe a yere from [St] Micheall to Our Lady |  | 17 | 4 |
| Item given unto 7 pore people that travelled by certificate |  |  | 6 |
| Item laid out unto Willyam Carsie for 3 monthes assesment: January February and March | 1 | 0 | 4 |
| Item layd out for mending the oven at Besnales |  | 1 | 8 |
| Item layd out for lordes rent for the towne lands |  | 4 | 6½ |
| Item layd out for the pulverers dinners | 1 | 2 | 0 |
| Item for my exspence for my selfe and my horse to Bliborough about our towne land |  | 1 | 6 |
| Item layd out unto Goodman Rackham for mending the windowes and threshould at Besnales |  | 2 | 3 |
| Item given unto the Widow [Abre] Smyth in tyme of sicknes |  | 2 | 6 |
| Item given unto many pore people <po> that travelled by certificat |  |  | 6 |
| Item payd unto Thomas Turner, constable, for his charges in his office | 2 | 8 | 8 |
| Item payd unto Wolfrine Bishop for 6 dayes worke and a halfe of himself and his man for thaching the scoolehouse and for 1000 broaches and 180 bindinges | 1 | 1 | 0 |
| Item payd unto Henerye Richardson for 2 loads of strawe |  | 17 | 0 |
| Item layd out unto Hammond Doughtie \for/ lords rent for 3 yeares at Our Lady last for Rose Larks, 1653 |  | 7 | 0 |

|  | £ | s. | d. |
|---|---|---|---|
| Item layd out unto John Stannard for a coat that he had taken to pane[*sic*] of a begger, that cam with the woman that was taken uppon suspicion for leaveing hir child in towne[220] |  | 1 | 0 |
| Item layd out unto Ruben Tallion for his quarters wages at Midsummer |  | 10 | 0 |
| Item paid unto Symon Warne for taking downe the clocke and mending the clocke chamber, and other worke in the steeple |  | 6 | 0 |
| Item paid unto Robert Raynar for his charges in tyme of his constableship as by his byll doe in particular apeare | 1 | 8 | 0 |
| Item layd out unto Robert Dowsinge the constable for the repayring of Beckles Bridg, which he had warrant for |  | 7 | 4 |
| Item layd out unto the Widow [Margaret] Adames for 6 monthes assesment ending at St Micheall last | 6 | 15 | 11 |
| Item given unto Thomas Johnsons wife in time of siknes |  | 3 | 0 |
| Item given unto the Widow [Elizabeth] Stannard |  | 2 | 6 |
| Item given unto the breefe of Sarath Egerton, widow, which lost £1000 |  | 1 | 6 |
| Item paid unto John Stannard for makeing a sawe pit and filling it up |  | 2 | 2 |
| Item payd unto Mr [Thomas] Bedingfield for the Marshalseas and Mayned Souldgers from Our Lady to St Micheall last |  | 17 | 4 |
| Summ | 19 | 19 | 1 |

Disbursmentes

|  | £ | s. | d. |
|---|---|---|---|
| Item paid unto Joseph Smyth for the use of his £10, from St Micheall unto the 18th of Aprill last |  | 6 | 0 |
| Item payd unto Ruben Tallion his quarters wagis for St Micheall ? |  | 10 | 0 |
| Item given unto 3 pore people that travelled by certificat |  | 1 | 0 |
| Item given unto the Widow [Abre] Smyth towardes the payment of hir rent, for St Micheall |  | 5 | 0 |
| Item layd out for bricke and the oven making at the scolehous |  | 5 | 6 |
| Item laid out for the lordes rent for the towne landes |  | 4 | 9½ |
| Item layd out for the comon fine for the towne |  | 6 | 8 |
| Item laid out unto Samuell Ludbroke for [?]cairieing the the [*sic*] wood for the pore and the seles[221] for the towne house |  | 19 | 0 |
| Item given unto Samuell Milles in time of his wifes siknes at severalles tymes and in leue of wood |  | 13 | 0 |
| Item layd out to John Willyames for wekly sessmentes and other charges | 3 | 15 | 9 |
| Item given unto John Stannard in leue of wood |  | 3 | 4 |
| Item given unto the ringers upon the powder treason daye[222] |  | 3 | 0 |
| Item given unto 6 Iresh people that had great lose |  |  | 6 |
| Item for my exspence at Halsworth when I went about apretizes |  | 1 | 6 |
| Item payd unto Mr Moulling for his charge and truble in indevoring [*to*] cure Samuell Milles wife of hir dropsie, November the 24th | 2 | 10 | 0 |
| Item layd out unto Willyam Carsie for the tax and assesment of 6 months | 2 | 0 | 8 |
| Item layd out unto Willyam Carsie for nayles to nayles[*sic*] the pales |  |  | 2 |
| Item given unto Nicholas More in leu of wood |  | 3 | 4 |

---

[220] See Introduction, p. 7.
[221] Sills, of windows.
[222] 5 November.

|  | £ | s. | d. |
|---|---|---|---|
| Item given unto 3 pore people that had great loses |  |  | 4 |
| Item given unto Thomas Johnson in leu of wood |  | 3 | 4 |
| Item given unto the Widow [Elizabeth] Stannard in leu of wood |  | 3 | 4 |
| Item given unto John Alldous in leu of wood |  | 3 | 4 |
| Item given unto Ruben Tallion for his quarters wagis at Christid |  | 10 | 0 |
| Item for beere and for fireing when the towne met about the survay[223] |  | 4 | 0 |
| Item payd unto Samuell Milles for ditching, hedging, and spring in the meadowes |  | 11 | 0 |
| Item payd unto Thomas Turner, the regester, for an act and his jurnye to Bliborough to take his oth[224] |  | 2 | 6 |
| Item layd out for lordes rent of the towne landes to Cratfeld Roos Mannor |  |  | 8 |
| Item for Willyam Aldous and my owne exspenc for 3 jurnyes to Bliborough about the survaye of the towne |  | 12 | 0 |
| Item layd out for a bell rope and a clock lyne |  | 5 | 0 |
| Item given unto Edmund Milles |  | 2 | 0 |
| Item layd out to Symon Warne for mending the churchyard pale |  | 6 | 6 |
| Item for spring for the ditching in the Sump Close being 1500[225] |  | 10 | 0 |
| Item payd unto Thomas Aldous the constable for the Marshalseas and Maymed Souldiers and for the repayre of Wolsie and East Bridges[226] | 1 | 13 | 4 |
| Sum | 17 | 16 | 9 |

The weklye collection to the poore in the yeare in the [*sic*] Our Lord 1653

|  | weeklye | monthly | yerlye | | |
|---|---|---|---|---|---|
| Edmund Milles | 1s. 6d. | 6s. | 3 | 18 | 0 |
| Ruben Tallion | 1s. | 4s. | 2 | 12 | 0 |
| John Hartly | 1s. | 4s. | 2 | 12 | 0 |
| Widow [Elizabeth] Brissingham | 1s. | 4s. | 2 | 12 | 0 |
| Elizabeth Butcher | 1s. | 4s. | 2 | 12 | 0 |
| Widow [Abre] Smyth | 9d. | 3s. | 1 | 19 | 0 |
| Robert Pacie | 6d. | 2s. | 1 | 6 | 0 |
| Widow [Margaret] Adames | 1s. | 4s. | | 16 | 0 |
| | | | and died Oct 31th | | |
| The summ | | | 18 | 7 | 0 |

| | £ | s. | d. |
|---|---|---|---|
| The whole summ of my disbursmentes is | 59 | 18 | 11 |
| | and 3 | 15 | 9 |
| Remayne due unto the towne uppon this accoumpt | 32 | 17 | 2 |

John Rous [*signature*]

---

[223] 'This 'survey' is certainly not the annual reckoning since, four items later, it is mentioned as requiring several journeys to Blythburgh.

[224] The parish register reads: 'Thomas Turner, taylor, chosen regester of the towne of Cratfeild according to the late Acte of Parliament dated the 24th of August 1653 was approved and allowed by us this 21 of October 1653'.

[225] A large number of cuttings, probably hawthorn, were bought for planting a new hedge.

[226] Wolsey Bridge, between Blythburgh and Southwold, and East Bridge in Theberton, both in Suffolk.

[218]
A note of what money I laye out for the towne in the tyme of my churchwarden
shippe in the yeere of Our Lord 1654 [*for 1654–5*][227]

|  | £ | s. | d. |
|---|---|---|---|
| Inprimis | | | |
| paid to the Widow [Mary] Brodbanke the 8th of Maye for flesh meate and bread and bread [*sic*] and beere for the townsmen \spent/ upon the pullverin daye, just | 1 | 7 | 5 |
| Item payd to William Carsy for 9 monthes asessmen[*sic*] ending att Mydsomer 1654, as appreth by his three billes, the sume of | 3 | 1 | 0 |
| Item paid to Thomas Alldus which he lay'd out in the tyme of his constableshippe the 29th of Maye 1654, the somme of | 2 | 7 | 7 |
| Item paid to John Ebbes and Nickolas Kempe the 26th of June 1654 to be bestowed for the repayring the high wayes, they being surveyors for this present yeere, the summe of | 6 | 10 | 0 |
| paid to Thomas Skeete the 27th of June for scouring the ditch against the Towne Pitell | | | 8 |
| Item payd to Thomas Turner for 2 quarters for the Marshells and Mayned Souldiers the 24th of September 1654 | | 17 | 4 |
| Item payd to John Clarke and William Ellis the 28th of September 1654 for daubing and making of floores att the gyld hall, the sume of | 1 | 6 | 6 |
| Item paid to Robert Addams for pining and mending the chimney stockes at the gyld hall the first of October 1654, just | | 8 | 0 |
| Item paid to Edmund Brodbanck then for brick | | 6 | 0 |
| Item lay'd out to 4 Yrish women and 20 children the 15th of October 1654 , the somme of | | 1 | 6 |
| Item paid to William Carsy which he layd out for 6 monthes asessment ending the 29° of December just £1 15s. 8d. and 4d. layd out to a carpenter as apereth by his bill in all | 1 | 16 | 0 |
| Item paid to Symond Warren for worke which he have done as appereth by his bill the somme of | 2 | 10 | 6 |
| Item payd to William Crosse the 7th of December 1654 for work att the towne howse and about the bells as appreth by his bill, the sume of | | 4 | 0 |
| Item payd to John Williams which he layd out for the weekely \asessment/ and other charges for the towne as by his bill appreth, the sume of | 5 | 14 | 4 |
| [*Sum of page*] | 26 | 10 | 10 |

A note of what moonyes I layd out for the towne as foloweth
| | | | |
|---|---|---|---|
| Item given to 14 poore distressed peopell which had lost all there estates in Yreland, January the 4th 1654 | | 2 | 0 |
| Item layd out for 2 bell ropes wayeing 18½ pounds | | 7 | 8 |

---

[227] This account is signed at the bottom by William Fisk.

|  | £ | s. | d. |
|---|---|---|---|
| Item layd out for M^r [Henry] Meene to redeeme Samuel Milses house, the 27^th March 1655, just[228] | 16 | 4 | 6 |
| [Sum] | 16 | 14 | 2 |

A note of what money I receive for the use of the towne in the tyme of my churchwardenshippe in the yeere of Our Lord God 1654 [for 1654–5]

|  | £ | s. | d. |
|---|---|---|---|
| Inprimis |  |  |  |
| received the last daye of March of John Rouse the last churchwarden the somme of | 16 | 0 | 0 |
| received the same daye of Sam[uel] Hayward for his Lady halfe yeere rent the somme of | 1 | 0 | 0 |
| received of the Widdow [Mary] Brodbank for her Lady halfe yeere rent the somme of \the 8^th of Maye/ |  | 15 | 0 |
| received of William Carsy the 16^th of Maye 1654, for his halfe yeeres rent due att Our Lady 1654, the sume of | 10 | 0 | 0 |
| received the last of October 1654 of Will[iam] Carsy for his halfe yeres rent due at Michallmas last, the somme of | 10 | 0 | 0 |
| received the 15^th of January 1654 of John Williams for his yeeres rent ending att Mychallmas 1654, the sume of | 12 | 0 | 0 |
| received the 26^th of March 1655 of Nick Kempe | 5 | 8 | 0 |
| Sume totall of my receiptes this yeere 1654 is just | 55 | 3 | 0 |
| Sume totall of my disbursments for the towne this yeere 1654 is just | 43 | 5 | 0 |
| Soe there remayne due unto the towne from William Fiske, senior, one of the churchwardins, the sume of | 11 | 18 | 0 |

For the yere of Our Lord 1654, ending att Our Lady day last
Viewed and allowed by the inhabbitants of the towne, the 6^th day of Apriell 1655
By me, William Fysk

[220]
Aprill the 6^th 1655
The accompt of William Aldus, one of the churchwardens of Cratfeild for the yeere of Our Lord 1654 as foloweth [for 1654–5]

|  | £ | s. | d. |
|---|---|---|---|
| Imprimus laid out for beere at the reckeninge day |  | 5 | 0 |
| laid out to Sameull Melles in time of his wifes sicknes |  | 5 | 0 |
| laid out to Samuell Haiward for fireing and tendance |  | 3 | 0 |
| laid out to Ruben Tallowing for his yeeres wages | ?2 | 0 | 0 |
| laid out to William Crose for mending the clocke, and for his yeeres wages | 1 | 0 | 0 |
| paid for the Widow [Abre] Smith her house fearme |  | 5 | 0 |
| given to [Robert] Paces wife in time of destres |  | 2 | 0 |

---

[228] Samuel Mills is an excellent example of how bad luck and illness could conspire to throw a household into poverty (see Biographies, pp. 137–8).

|  | £ | s. | d. |
|---|---|---|---|
| given to Samuell Meles in time of his wifes sicknes |  | 3 | 0 |
| laid out att Hallsworth when we had a warent for the ould church wardenes to give in there acompt, and the new ones to be alowed, and for a warent[229] |  | 3 | 6 |
| given to Joseph Smith to releve him in time of distrees |  | 5 | 0 |
| laid out for lordes rent for Our Lady to Thomas Turner |  | 4 | 6 |
| laid out to Samuell Meles in time of his wifes sicknes |  | 3 | 0 |
| laid out to Samuell Meles towardes the buringe of his wife |  | 10 | 0 |
| laid out to Thomas Brudbancke and Toby Ashby for mendinge the buttes |  | 5 | 0 |
| laid out for 9 pintes of sacke for the cort |  | 9 | 0 |
| given to a brefe for the burninge of Glascow in Scotland[230] |  | 5 | 0 |
| given to Samuell Meles to goo to the surgin with his daughters lege |  | 5 | 0 |
| given to an Irishman who came with a peticon |  | 1 | 0 |
| given to Thomas Culpeper who was taken by the Turke |  | 1 | 0 |
| given to Thomas Coke of Debnam[231] who came with a petcion for a burninge |  | 5 | 0 |
| laid out to the Widow [Margaret] Adams for Parlement charges and other charges as apeer by her bill | 8 | 0 | 2 |
| given to the Widow [Margaret] Adames | 1 | 0 | 0 |
| given to the Widow [Abre] Smith to releve her with all |  | 1 | 0 |
| given to 10 Irish people which came with a surteficat |  |  | 6 |
| paid to M<sup>r</sup> Clifar for learninge the pore children till Michellmas |  | 15 | 0 |
| laid out when we went to Hallsworth about [Thomas] Spatchet[232] |  | 4 | 0 |
| laid out when we went to Beckeles about the same |  | 5 | 0 |
| laid out to Richard Rushels of Bury St Edmontes for a lose by fire of £200 |  | 1 | 0 |
| given to the Widow [Elizabeth] Stanard to releve her with all |  | 5 | 0 |
| given to the Widow [Abre] Smith to releve her in her sicknes |  | 3 | 6 |
| given to 13 Irish peolple who came with a surteficat |  | 1 | 0 |
| given to a brefe for Thomas Trefusis, and Englishman [sic], who had great lose by sea |  | 2 | 0 |
| given to the Widow [Abre] Smith to releve her in her sicknes |  | 3 | 0 |
| given to Samuell Meles to goe to the surgin for his daughtars lege |  | 2 | 6 |
| given to the woman that had the child here[233] |  | 2 | 0 |
| given to the Widow [Mary] Tallowinge for loking to her |  | 4 | 0 |
| Item for a paier of shettes for her |  | 4 | 0 |
| given to a brefe to Edmond Blake and Mary Blake who were spoiled by the Turkes |  | 2 | 0 |
| given to Thomas Garet who came with a brefe from Ierland |  | 2 | 0 |
| laid out to Robart Dowsing for his cunstables bill |  | 3 | 6 |
| laid out to Joseph Smith to releve him with all |  | 5 | 0 |

---

[229] Purchasing a warrant to force the old churchwardens to relinquish their accounts was highly unusual, and suggests that there was a significant disagreement between members of the community.

[230] Glasgow, Scotland.

[231] Debenham, Suffolk.

[232] This may have been a delegation from Cratfield to the court in Halesworth to attest to Spatchet's upright character and the godliness of the many sermons he preached in the Cratfield church (see Biographies, p. 142).

[233] A vagrant gave birth while travelling through the parish. See following entry.

| | £ | s. | d. |
|---|---|---|---|
| given to M<sup>r</sup> Dason of Cheston[234] towardes his burninge | 2 | 0 | 0 |
| Sume is | 21 | 6 | 8 |

| | £ | s. | d. |
|---|---|---|---|
| geven to Thomas Johnson, senior, to by him wood | | 5 | 0 |
| given to John Stanardes wife to by her wood | | 3 | 4 |
| given to Edmond Meles to by him wood | | 3 | 0 |
| given to Samuell Meles to by him wood | | 3 | 6 |
| given to Thomas Johnson, junior, to by him wood | | 3 | 4 |
| given to the Goody [Mary] Tallowinge to by wood | | 2 | 6 |
| given to Joseph Smith to by wood | | 3 | 4 |
| to John Aldus his wife to by wood | | 3 | 4 |
| given to the Widow [Abre] Smith to releve her in her sicknes | | 3 | 6 |
| paid for the widow[235] for her house ferme September 29 | | 5 | 0 |
| given to Phenises [Smith] wife to releve her in her sicknes | | 2 | 0 |
| laid out att William Aldus is [sic] when we mett about the scholhouse and other busines for beer and for our dineres | | 16 | 0 |
| laid out to the Widow [Margaret] Adams for Parlement charges and other charges as apeereth by her bill[236] | 9 | 6 | 2 |
| laid out to Toby Ashby for stowinge and making the wood for the poore | | 9 | 0 |
| and for caringe of 9 lodes for the poore | | 15 | 0 |
| laid out to Thomas Turner for lordes rent for the towne | | 4 | 9½ |
| and for comon fine | | 6 | 8 |
| given to Thomas Johnson to releve him with all | | 10 | 0 |
| laid out to Robart Adams for reparing the pavementes in the church | | 2 | 0 |
| given to Joseph Smith to releve him with all | | 5 | 0 |
| given to two Irish women which came with a brefe | | 4 | 0 |
| given to the Widow [Elizabeth] Stanard to releve her with all | | 5 | 0 |
| paid to M<sup>r</sup> Clifar for his quarter for lerninge the poor children, due at Christmas | 1 | 0 | 0 |
| given to Samuell Meles to pay the surgon for his daughtars leg | | 3 | 0 |
| given to a brefe to two Irish men | | 2 | 0 |
| given to Joseph Smith to releve him with all | | 5 | 0 |
| given to a brefe to and Irish woman [sic] | | 2 | 0 |
| laid out to <the> Simon Warren for two cofines: on for the Widow [Abre] Smith and the other for Ruben Tallowing | | 13 | 4 |
| laid out upon the surendar of Samuell Meles his house | 6 | 0 | 0 |
| laid out to Simon Waren for treminge of the belles | | 2 | 0 |
| Sume is | 23 | 8 | 9½ |

laid out for colection for the fortnight begining the second of Aprill 1654 the sume of 9s.

| | £ | s. | d. |
|---|---|---|---|
| to the Widow [Elizabeth] Brisingham | | 2 | 0 |
| to John Hartly | | 2 | 0 |

---

[234] Probably Chediston, Suffolk.
[235] This is probably Abre Smith again.
[236] Widow Adams was a major tenant of parish land who in this year, 1654–5, paid £58 in rent.

|  | £ | s. | d. |
|---|---|---|---|
| to Elisabeth Buttcher |  | 2 | 0 |
| to the Widow [Mary] Tallowinge |  | 2 | 0 |
| to [Robert] Paces wife |  | 1 | 0 |
| for a month eightenne shilinges, for thertenne monthes | 11 | 14 | 0 |
| laid out to the Widow [Abre] Smith for 36 weekes 9 pence a weeke | 1 | ? | ? |
| laid out to Edmond Meles for 40 weekes colecion 1s. 6d. a weeke | 3 | ? | ? |
| Sume is | 16 | 1 | 0 |

| recived of John Rouse att the reckoninge day March the 31, 1654, the sume of | 16 | 17 | 0 |
|---|---|---|---|
| recived of the Widow [Margaret] Adams for her yeeres rent for 1654 | 58 | 0 | 0 |
| recived of Mr [Robert] Warner for breaking the ground in the church | 1 | 0 | 0 |

| Sume totall of the receiptes this yeere 1654, which William Alldus one of the churchwardens receive for the towne, the sume of | 75 | 17 | 0 |
|---|---|---|---|
| Sume totall of the disbursments this yeere 1654 of William Alldus one of the churchwardens, is just | 60 | 16 | 5½ |
| Soe there remayne due unto the towne from William Alldus one of the churchwardins for the yeere 1654 ending att Our Lady day last, the sume of | 15 | 0 | 6½ |

Veiued and allowed by the inhabbitantes of the towne the 6th of
Apriell 1655
*Per me*, William Aldus

[225]
Cratfeild
A note of what money William Fiske, senior, being one of the churchwardens
dissburseth in the behalfe of the towne in the yeere of Our Lord 1655
[*for 1655–6*]

| Inprimis | £ | s. | d. |
|---|---|---|---|
| paid to William Carsye for 3 monthes asessment: January, Febbruary and March the somme of |  | 10 | 2 |
| given to William Carsye by the order of the towne in regard of cheapness of cheese and butter[237] | 3 | 0 | 0 |
| paid to Samuell Hayward for a lock and a keye for the guild hall chamber dore, the some of |  | 1 | 0 |
| paid to William Alldus wife for meat and bread for the townsmens dinners the somme of | 1 | 4 | 0 |
| paid to Samuel Ludbroke for halfe a yeere for Maymed Soldiers the 24th of Aprill 1655 the somme of |  | 17 | 4 |
| paid to Samuel Ludbroke the same daye for strawe for the guyld hall the somme of |  | 2 | 6 |
| paid to Robert Smith for 13 pounds and a halfe of soder and for glaseing about the church, the somme of | 1 | 9 | 0 |

---

[237] Cheese and butter were the two principal products of local farmers, yet prices were damagingly low at this time. William Carsey was a tenant of parish land. The next year, Widow Adams was given similar help.

3. Extract from the account of William Fiske, senior, churchwarden of Cratfield, for the year 1655–6 (SROI, FC62/A6/225).

|  | £ | s. | d. |
|---|---|---|---|
| paid to Thomas Tallen for wood and for his worke the same tyme |  | 4 | 6 |
| paid to Samuel Ludbroke which he lay'd out in the tyme of his constableship as apereth by his bill, the somme of | 1 | 4 | 6 |
| paid to M<sup>r</sup> Pullham for makeing a newe feffement the 12<sup>th</sup> September, the somme of | 1 | 0 | 0 |
| paid to Thomas Turner for halfe a yeere for Maymed Soldiers the 23<sup>th</sup> September, the somme of |  | 17 | 4 |
| paid to John Warren for mending the bell wheeles and makeing a newe ladder, the somme of |  | 16 | 0 |
| layd out to Thomas Tallen for beere for John Warren |  |  | 6 |
| layd out more to him for weeding the stounes at the porch dore |  | 1 | 0 |
| layd out to William Crosse for makeing of sheires and mending of the bolts for the bell frames |  | 2 | 6 |
| layd out to Robert Smith for glaseing the church windowes the 22<sup>th</sup> of November, the somme of |  | 5 | 6 |
| layd out to William Carsye for the repayring of decayed bridges the 25<sup>th</sup> November |  | 9 | 0 |
| given to Joseph Smithes wife the 27<sup>th</sup> of December in tyme of his sickness, the somme of |  | 5 | 0 |
| paid to Robert Rayner for lords rent for the towne land |  |  | 4 |
| given to 10 poore people for theire releife |  | 1 | 0 |
| Somme is | 12 | 11 | 2 |

Dissbursements

|  | £ | s. | d. |
|---|---|---|---|
| layd out to James Brundish in tyme of his siknesse the 8<sup>th</sup> of Febbruary the somme of |  | 2 | 0 |
| layd out to William Fiske, senior, for his charges layd out in the tyme of his constableshipp the somme of |  | 14 | 0 |
| layd out to the Widow [Margaret] Addams for the townesmens dinners the somme of | 1 | 10 | 0 |
| given to her mayd with the consent of the towne |  | 1 | 0 |
| paid to John Williams for charges layd out as appereth by his bill, the somme of | 3 | 1 | 7 |
| paid to William Carsy which he layd out for the weekely asessment and other charges as appereth by his bill, the somme of | 1 | 16 | 10 |
| Somme is | 7 | 5 | 5 |

Cratfeild
A note of what money William Fisk, senior, being one of the churchwardens receiveth in the behalfe of the towne from the 6<sup>th</sup> of Aprill 1655 [for 1655–6]

|  | £ | s. | d. |
|---|---|---|---|
| Inprimis |  |  |  |
| received then which was in hand the last reckoning daye, the somme of | 11 | 18 | 0 |
| received of William Carsye the 6<sup>th</sup> of Aprill for his half yeeres rent due at Our Ladye 1655, the somme of | 10 | 0 | 0 |
| received of Samuell Hayward for his halfe yeeres rent for the schoole howse pitell the somme of |  | 5 | 0 |
| received of Luke Hunt for 5 scoore hoop staves |  | 1 | 3 |

|  | £ | s. | d. |
|---|---|---|---|

received of William Carsy for his halfe yeeres rent due at Mich'mas
    1655, the somme of              10   0   0

received of John Williams the 26th March for the yeeres rent for the
    land late in his fathers occupation, due at Mich'mas past the some of   11   0   0

Somme totall of the receipts this yeere is         43   4   3

Dissbursed by the abovesaid William Fiske churchwarden out of the
    abovesaid receipts          19   16   7

Soe there remayne due unto the towne from William Fiske upon this
    accoumpt the somme of          23   7   8

Memorandum that the howse of Samuell Milles that was morgaged by surender unto William Fiske thelder for £23 6s. 6d. was of the townsmens money, and I as feoffe or truste tooke the said surrender to the use of the inhabbitants of the towne aforesaid, which said morgage or surrender is fallen into my hands and I acknowledge it to be the townsmens use, in witnesse whereof I have heere unto set my hand
    William Fysk [*signature*]

Received by me John Williams of William Fiske in full discharg of his
    accoumpt the somme of          23   7   8
*Per* John Williams

[232]
Cratfeild
A note of what money John Williams, being one of the churchwardens, dissburseth in the behalfe of the towne from the 27th of March 1656 [*for 1656–7*]

| Inprimis | £ | s. | d. |
|---|---|---|---|

laid out to William Fiske and William Alldus which they had out of the
    money Samuell Milles had of the towne       1   8   ?

laid out to Bridget Spink the 15th Aprill towards her howse rent and
    fyerwood, the some of           13   ?

laid out to Giles Harcock for 2 new ropes waying 20 pounds ½ at 6d.
    per pound              10   ?

paid to Mr [Thomas] Beddingfeild the 25th Maye for Christmas and
    Our Lady quarters for Maimed Soldiers        17   4

laid out to Francis Alldus, taylor, the 6th of June in tyme of his sicknesse   10   0

paid to Samuel Claydon which he laid out in the tyme of his
    constableship            1   7   3

paid to Mr [Thomas] Beddingfeild the 23th of June for the repayring
    of Bungay Bridge           4   9

paid to Mr Clifford for the towne boyes schoole due at Midsomer   1   0   0

laid out to William Carsy which he laid out in the tyme of his
    constableship the somme of        1   13   2

laid out the 6th of July for 4 pintes ¾ of wine and 2 breads the somme
    of                4   11

|  | £ | s. | d. |
|---|---|---|---|
| more for fetching of it |  |  | 3 |
| laid out to the Widow [Elizabeth] Stannard the 16th September 1656 |  | 5 | 0 |
| paid to Mr [Thomas] Spatchet the 20th September for Midsommer and Mich'mas quarter for Maimed Soldiers |  | 17 | 4 |
| paid to Robert Rayner and William Elles for triming up the buttes and for rayles and crotches |  | 5 | 6 |
| laid out to William Alldus wife the 26th September for the townsmens dinners and for beere |  | 16 | 0 |
| paid to Hammond Doughty the 29th September for 1 yeeres rent for Rose Larkes due to John Cooke, esquire[238] |  | 2 | 4 |
| paid to Mr Clifford for the towne boyes schoole due at Mich'mas | 1 | 0 | 0 |
| paid to Robert Rayner for lords rent due at Mich'mas |  |  | 4 |
| laid out to Doll' Addams the 26th October towards her howse rent and fyerwood |  | 5 | 0 |
| laid out to the Widdow [Elizabeth] Brissingam in tyme of sickness |  | 5 | 0 |
| laid out to the ringers the 5th November 1656 |  | 5 | 0 |
| laid out to Nick Bicker for 23 pounds soder, 12d. per pound, and 4 dayes work of himselfe at 2s. per day | 1 | 11 | 0 |
| more to him for 1 pound bees wax and ½ pound rossen and 3 quarrells [of] glasse |  | 1 | 6 |
| laid out to \Thomas/ Tallen for 4 daye worke |  | 4 | 0 |
| more to him for fyerwood |  | 5 | 0 |
| laid out to [Robert] Pacyes boy for 4 day worke |  | 1 | 6 |
| laid out to Thomas Johnson, senior, towards his fyerwood |  | 5 | 0 |
| given to James Brundish and his wife in tyme of there sickness |  | 5 | 0 |
| laid out to Thomas Johnson, junior, towards his fyerwood |  | 3 | 4 |
| paid to Mr Clifford for the boyes schoole due at Christmas | 1 | 0 | 0 |
| laid out to John Stannard, senior, towards his fyerwood |  | 3 | 4 |
| laid out to Doll' Addams towards her fyerwood |  | 5 | 0 |
| laid out to John Alldus wife towards her fyerwood |  | 3 | 4 |
| laid out to John Cross for a screw for the Towne Pightell gate |  | 1 | 6 |
| laid out to the Widow [Elizabeth] Stannard toward her fyerwood |  | 5 | 0 |
| laid out to William Carsy which he laid out to the monthly asessment and other charges, and for fyerwood | 3 | 11 | 2 |
| paid to Mr Clifford for the 4 boyes schoole due at Our Lady the some of | 1 | 0 | 0 |
| laid out to the monthly asessment and other charges as appereth by my bill of parsells | 3 | 16 | 6 |
| paid to Mr [Thomas] Spatchet for Christmas and Our Lady quarters for Marshalls and Maimed Soldiers |  | 17 | 4 |
| laid out to the poore for 52 weekes collection | 13 | 13 | 0 |
| Somme toto[sic] of my disbursments | 39 | 17 | 3 |

[238] Hammond Doughty was bailiff to Sir John Cooke who was lord of Blything Hundred (see SROI, FC62/A6/236 which is a receipt to the parish from Doughty for paying for non-suit at the sheriff's tourn in 1657).

Cratfeild

A note of what money John Williams, being one of the churchwardens, receiveth in the behalfe of the towne from the 27th March 1656

|  | £ | s. | d. |
|---|---|---|---|
| Inprimis | | | |
| received of William Fiske the 29th of March which was in hand at the reckoning daye the some of | 23 | 7 | 8 |
| received the 29th September 1656 which was due uppon the morgage for Samuell Millses howse | 22 | 3 | 6 |
| received of William Carsy for his wholle yeeres rent due at Mich'mas the somme of | 17 | 0 | 0 |
| received more for the Towne Middow and Mollings Middow and the Towne Closs due at Mich'mas 1656 | 11 | 0 | 0 |
| Some toto of my receipts is | 73 | 11 | 2 |
| | | | |
| Somme toto of my disbursments is | 39 | 17 | 3 |
| Soe remayne in my hand due unto the towne | 33 | 13 | 11 |

John Williams [signature]

Seene and allowed by the inhabbitants of the towne abovesaid
[signatures of] John Smith, Robert Mynne, William Fiske, junior, John Rous, Robert Smyth, [?]junior, Thomas Turner, William Fysk

[235]

A true note of the charges which have bine laid out by me Robert Smith, one of the churchwardens for the towne of Cratfield, begining the 27th of March (1656) and given ine <the> to the townsmen the 23th of March following [for 1656–7]

|  | £ | s. | d. |
|---|---|---|---|
| Inprimis laid out to the Widdow [Margaret] Adames that shee paid as apeere by hir bill | | 5 | 13 | ?6 |
| given hir by conssent of the towne in regard of chepnes of cheese and butter | 8 | 0 | 0 |
| Item laid out to William Crose for mending the clock | | 10 | 0 |
| Item laid out to Thomas Tallant for one quarters wages | | 10 | 0 |
| more for beere and fiering and tendance at the reckning | | 10 | 0 |
| Item given to Joseph Smith in his nesesity | | 13 | 4 |
| Item paid to William Brodbanck for lokeing to the towne armore divers yeeres and other thinges | | 12 | 0 |
| Item laid out to William Alldis wiff for beer for the towns men 3 severall days | | 7 | 0 |
| Item given to [Thomas] Tallants dafter the 1th of Aprill for fiering and tendance at the survayors acount[239] | | 1 | 0 |
| Item laid out for the bynding of [William] Mynggyes boy the 10th of Aprill | 3 | 0 | 0 |
| Item laid out the 20th of Aprill for towne rent | | 4 | 6 |

---

[239] The principal inhabitants met to receive the accounts of their highway surveyors.

|  | £ | s. | d. |
|---|---|---|---|
| Item laid out the 9th of Maij to the towne soullgers | | 5 | 0 |
| Item at the same time to 2 townsmen for going to Blyborow | | 5 | 0 |
| Item about that time at the pulluren day | 2 | 0 | 0 |
| Item the 28th of Maij to the 2 towne soullgers | | 5 | 0 |
| Item about that time at Samuell Milleses | | 3 | 0 |
| Item the 6th of July to [Thomas] Tallant for wages and weeding | | 11 | 0 |
| Item the 20th of July sent to Joseph Smith | | 10 | 0 |
| Item the 26th of July given to Mr Clifford by consent | 2 | 0 | 0 |
| Item the 28 of July spent at the selling of [Samuel] Melleses house | | 3 | 4 |
| Item the 8th of August laid out to [Nick] Biker for glassing at the Widdowe [Margaret] Adameses house and at the church | 2 | 0 | 6 |
| Item laid out to William Crosse for a new cassment and othere iorns about the house | | 3 | 6 |
| Item laid out to Thomas Tallant for fiering and tendance for the glasar | | 2 | 6 |
| more to William Crose about that time for iorns for the bells | | 7 | 4 |
| Item to Simond Warne for timber and worke at the town house | 1 | 5 | 0 |
| Item for stowing and bratling of the pore folkes wood and carring of it | 1 | 5 | ? |
| Item laid out to William Crose the 4th of October for iorne work about the beelles | | 6 | ? |
| Item the 14th of October given to Joseph Smith | | ?11 | ? |
| more the same time to Thomas Tallant for wages | | ? | ? |
| | | | |
| Item the 20th of October laid out to Thomas Turner for rent and common fine for the feffes landes | | 11 | 7 |
| more to [Robert] Paces wiffe in sikenes | | 4 | 0 |
| Item the 2th of January given to Joseph Smith | | 10 | 0 |
| more the same time time [*sic*] to Thomas Tallin for wages | | 10 | 0 |
| Item to Simond Warne for timber and naylles, and worke about the towne groundes | | 4 | 3 |
| Item laid out for 6 months as apeere by the bill | 3 | 10 | 10 |
| Summe is | 38 | 4 | 10 |

March the 27th 1656

|  | £ | s. | d. |
|---|---|---|---|
| receyved then of the Widdow [Margaret] Adames for hir half yeeres rent then deue | 29 | 0 | 0 |
| receyved of William \Alldis/, one of the ould church wardens, the summe of | 23 | 13 | 9 |
| receyved mor of the Widdow [Margaret] Adames for Michellmis rent 1656 the summe of | 29 | 0 | 0 |
| Received the summe of | 81 | 13 | 9 |
| | | | |
| Disbursed the some of | 38 | 4 | 10 |
| Soe remayne in my hand due unto the towne just | 43 | 8 | 11 |

Robert Smyth [*signature*]

Seene and allowed by the inhabbitants of the towne abovesaid
[*signatures of*] John Smith, Robert Mynne, William Fiske, junior, [?]John Rous, Robert Smyth, junior, William Fysk, Thomas Turner

[239]

A note of what mone[*damaged*]ms, being one of the churchwardens, dissburseth in the be[*damaged*] towne from the 23th of March in the yeere of our Lo[*damaged*]56 unto the 18th of March 1657 [*expenses of John Williams, for 1657–8*]

|  | £ | s. | d. |
|---|---|---|---|
| Inprimis |  |  |  |
| laid out to Bridget Spink towards her howse rent and fyerwood the somme of |  | 13 | 4 |
| paid to Mr [Thomas] Spatchet for the repayring of Cataway Bridge[240] |  | 8 | 0 |
| given to the Widow [Elizabeth] Brissingam the 14th Aprill in tyme of sickness |  | 5 | 0 |
| laid out to a breife for a burning at Pargrave[241] \16th April/ |  | 5 | 0 |
| laid out to Doll' Addams towardes her howse rent and fyerwood the 15th of May |  | 10 | 0 |
| laid out to a breife for a burning at Brundish[242] the 24th May |  | 10 | 0 |
| given to Nick Mooer for his releife the 26th Maye |  | 5 | 0 |
| laid out to John Alldus wife in tyme of sicknesse |  | 5 | 0 |
| paid to Mr [Thomas] Spatchet for the repayring of Hoxne and Mendham bridges[243] the 26th Maye | 1 | 3 | 0 |
| laid out to Thomas Johnson, senior, in regard he had no wood |  | 5 | 0 |
| laid out to the Widow [Elizabeth] Stannard for beere when the townsmen met to take the surveyors accoumpts |  | 2 | 0 |
| laid out for bread and wine for the communion and for fetching of it the 30th Maye |  | 5 | 2 |
| paid to Mr Spatchet for Midsomer quarter for Maimed Soldiers |  | 8 | 8 |
| laid out to Thomas Johnson, junior, in regard he had no wood |  | 3 | 4 |
| paid to Mr Clifford for teaching the children due at Midsommer | 1 | 0 | 0 |
| given to Elezebeth Butcher in tyme of sickness |  | 5 | 0 |
| laid out to a breife the 12th July for a loss of £25C [244] |  | 4 | 0 |
| laid out to Doll' Addams towardes her releife |  | 5 | 0 |
| laid out to a brcife for a burning at Saffom Market[245] |  | 6 | 0 |
| laid out to Francis Alldus in tyme of sickness |  | 10 | 0 |
| laid out to the Widow [Elizabeth] Stannard towardes her releife |  | 5 | 0 |
| paid to Mr Clifford for teaching the children, due at Mich'mas | 1 | 0 | 0 |
| laid out to John Alldus wife the 24th July in tyme of sicknesse |  | 5 | 0 |
| paid to Hammond Doughty for 1 yeeres rent for Rose Larkes, due the 29th September 1657 |  | 2 | 4 |
| for the charges when we gave in the valuation of our towne at Blibrough when John Newson went |  | 7 | 6 |
| given more to Francis Alldus towards his releife |  | 5 | 0 |
| laid out to Samuel Mills towardes his releife |  | 4 | 0 |

---

240 Cattawade bridge, Suffolk.
241 Palgrave, Suffolk.
242 Brundish, Suffolk.
243 Hoxne and Mendham, both in Suffolk.
244 This appears to be £2500.
245 Saffron Walden, Essex.

|  | £ | s. | d. |
|---|---|---|---|
| laid out to a breife the 1th November to ransam a captive in Turky |  | 4 | 0 |
| laid out to a minister and his wife which came from Layson[246] the 4th of November |  | 3 | 0 |
| laid out to James Brundish towardes his releife the <6th December> |  | 5 | 0 |
| given to the Widow [Elizabeth] Stannard in tyme of sicknesse |  | 2 | 0 |
|  |  |  |  |
| laid out to William Carsy [*damaged*] to the monthly asessment and other charges [*damaged*] | 3 | 0 | 8 |
| laid out to the ringers the 5th [*damaged*]ember |  | 6 | 0 |
| laid out for the repayring of the butts |  | 5 | 6 |
| laid out to a breife for a burning at Holten[247] the 22th November |  | 6 | 8 |
| laid out to Francis Alldus for his releife the 24th November |  | 5 | 0 |
| laid out to a breife for a burning at Peterborough in Northampton[shire] the 6th December |  | 5 | 0 |
| laid out to the repaire of Bond bridge[248] the 18th December |  | 7 | 0 |
| laid out to James Brundishes wife for her releife |  | 5 | 0 |
| paid to Mr [Thomas] Spatchet for Christmas[249] quarter for Maimed Soldiers |  | 8 | 8 |
| paid to Robert Addams for mending the oven in the guildhall |  |  | 4 |
| laid out to Samuel Milles towards his releife |  | 5 | 0 |
| paid to Mr Clifford for the boyes schole due at Christmas | 1 | 0 | 0 |
| laid out to a breife for a burning at the Isle of [?]Luffe[250] the 3th of January 1657 |  | 4 | 0 |
| laid out to Samuel Millses sonne that day his father dyed |  | 4 | 0 |
| laid out more to Francis Alldus the 6th January |  | 5 | 0 |
| paid to Mr [Thomas] Spatchet for Our Lady quarter for Maimed Soldiers |  | 8 | 8 |
| given to James Brundish the 30th June |  | 2 | 6 |
| laid out to Thomas Johnson, junior, for his releife |  | 3 | 4 |
| laid out to John Stannards wife, senior, in regard she had no wood |  | 5 | 0 |
| laid out to the monthly asessment and other charges as appereth by my bill, the some of | 5 | 7 | 11 |
| paid to Mr Clifford for the boyes schole due at Our Ladye | 1 | 0 | 0 |
| paid to Simond Warren for tymber and for rayling of the caucy[251] and for plank for the ditch the some of | 8 | 5 | 0 |
| laid out to Joseph Smith for his releife the 14th March |  | 10 | 0 |
| paid to the poore for 52 weekes collection ending the 14th of March 1657 the some of | 13 | 13 | 0 |
| laid out for stoune for the repayre of the high wayes and for 44 dayes worke and to the surveyors the some of | 11 | 9 | 10 |
| laid out to the Widow [Elizabeth] Stannard for her releife |  | 5 | 0 |

---

246 Leiston, Suffolk.
247 Holton, Suffolk.
248 Unidentified.
249 Christmas is abbreviated to 'Xmas'.
250 An unidentified island.
251 Simon Warren, as one of the highway surveyors, was paid for mending a causeway. In this year the parish was paying major attention to the state of its roads.

|                                                              | £  | s. | d. |
|--------------------------------------------------------------|----|----|----|
| paid for the pullerrers dinners at the court[252]            |    | 13 | 4  |
| paid more for 2 loads of stoune                              |    | 6  | 8  |
| Some toto of this disbursments                               | 60 | 19 | 5  |

A note of [*damaged*] being one of the churchwardens [*damaged*] in the behalfe of the towne from the [*damaged*] of March 1656 [*receipts of John Williams, for year 1657–8*]

|                                                                                       | £  | s. | d. |
|---------------------------------------------------------------------------------------|----|----|----|
| Inprimis                                                                              | £  | s. | d. |
| received then which was in hand being the reckoning daye, the some of                 | 33 | 13 | 11 |
| received of William Carsy for his yeeres rent due at Mich'mas 1657                     | 18 | 0  | 0  |
| received for the yeeres rent for Mollings Middo and the Towne Closse due at Mich'mas 1657 | 10 | 0  | 0  |
| received of Sammuell Hayward for his yeeres rent for the Towne Pightell due at Mich'mas 1657 | 1 | 10 | 0 |
| received of John Rous which was mistaken in the rate which he gathered,[253] the somme of |  | 2  | 4  |
| received of Goodman [Robert] Smith [*of*] Collshall the some of                        | 5  | 0  | 0  |
| Some toto of the receipts                                                             | 68 | 6  | 3  |
|                                                                                       |    |    |    |
| Dissbursed out of the abovesaid receipts                                              | 60 | 19 | 5  |
| remayne in hand, due unto the towne                                                   | 7  | 6  | 10 |

|                                          | monthly |   |
|------------------------------------------|---------|---|
| to Elezebeth Butcher                     | 4       | 0 |
| to the Widow [Elizabeth] Brissingam      | 4       | 0 |
| to Robert Pacyes wife                    | 4       | 0 |
| to John Herctlyes wife                   | 4       | 0 |
| to the Widow [Mary] Tallen               | 2       | 0 |
| to Thomas Tallen                         | 3       | 0 |
| [*Sum*]                              | 1     1 | 0 |

Seene and allowed by the inhabbitants of the towne whose names are heere under written

[*signatures*] John Smith, Robert Mynne, John Rous, William Aldous, John Fyske, John Newson

[240]
A note of what moneys Robert Smith \of Coulshall/, being one of the church wardens, have dissbursed in the behalfe of the towne from the 23th of March (1656) to this 18th of March (1657) as followeth
[*for 1657–8*]

---

252 The annual reckoning of the principal inhabitants, or the 'pulvering day', was sometimes called a 'court' (see below, account no. 243 for 1658–9).
253 A rate collector had made a mistake, and made reimbursement through the churchwarden.

|                                                                                                                                                      | £  | s. | d. |
|------------------------------------------------------------------------------------------------------------------------------------------------------|----|----|----|
| Inprimis laid out to Edmund Balldry in regard of not ploughing the Great Closs and for fyerwood, greene and sare and for abatement for the fearme and for Neates Roakes and [*illeg.*] which were his, agreed by the consents of the townsmen | 10 | 0  | 0  |
| laid out more to him for the weekely assesment and other charges as appereth by his bill as                                                          | 3  | 16 | 8  |
| laid out to Thomas Tallen for his quarters wages                                                                                                     |    | 10 | 0  |
| laid out more to him for beere and fyerwood, and for his tendance on the reckening day                                                               |    | ?2 | 0  |
| laid out more at that time for beere                                                                                                                 |    | 3  | 6  |
| laid out to Joseph Smith towards his howse rent and fyerwood                                                                                         |    | 13 | 4  |
| Item laid out to William Crose at that time for lokeing to the clocke                                                                                |    | 10 | 0  |
| Item about that time to Thomas Turner for lordes rent                                                                                                |    | 4  | 6  |
| Item payd to Hamont Dowty the balife for Rosse Larkes for 8 yeeres                                                                                   |    | 16 | 0  |
| more at that time for a lode of straw and for carring of it to the towne howses                                                                      | 1  | 5  | 0  |
| Item to the thachars for there wages and naylles and ewfes bordes and othere things                                                                  |    | 10 | 0  |
| Item laid out to the 2 cunstables for there charges as apere by there billes                                                                         | 2  | 3  | 7  |
| Item laid out to John Williames for the hywayes[254]                                                                                                 | 5  | 0  | 0  |
| more to Francis Alldis wife                                                                                                                          |    | 2  | 0  |
| Item to Joseph Smith at Midsumer time                                                                                                                |    | 10 | 0  |
| more at that time to Thomas Tallen for his wages and for weeding                                                                                     |    | 11 | 0  |
| Item given at that time to Ould [Thomas] Johnson                                                                                                     |    | 10 | 0  |
| Item laid out to Tobee [Ashby] and Thomas Adames for stowing and bratling and carring of the poore folkes wood                                       | 1  | 6  | 0  |
| Item to the worke men about the belles                                                                                                               |    | 6  | 6  |
| more for our expences at Blyborow and our horses                                                                                                     |    | 4  | 6  |
| Item for Branson bridg[255] and Mained Soulgers                                                                                                      |    | 12 | 6  |
| Item laid out to William Ellis for worke at the poor \*illeg.*/                                                                                      |    | 1  | 0  |
| Item given to Joseph Smith for his Mich'mis rent                                                                                                     |    | 10 | 0  |
| more at that time to Thomas Tallen for his wages                                                                                                     |    | 10 | 0  |
|                                                                                                                                                      |    |    |    |
| Item given to 5 soulgers with horses                                                                                                                 |    | 2  | 0  |
| more for exspences and wages to Simon Warne                                                                                                          |    | 4  | 0  |
| Item at that time to Thomas Turner for rent and a common fine                                                                                        |    | 11 | 6  |
| Item laid out the 22th of October to John Willames for writting for the towne many yeeres by consent of some of the town                             | 2  | 0  | 0  |
| Item laid out about Joseph Smithes boy at Hallsar[256]                                                                                               |    | ?  | 0  |
| more to William Crose about that time for the clock                                                                                                  |    | 5  | 0  |
| Item at that time given to Samuell Milles in sicknes                                                                                                 |    | 5  | 0  |
| Item laid out at Hallsar about Joses boy                                                                                                             |    | 10 | 0  |
| more given to Samuell Milles in sickenes                                                                                                             |    | 5  | 0  |

---

[254] This is a money rate that had been collected for the repair of roads in the parish (see Note 251).
[255] Perhaps Brantham bridge, Suffolk.
[256] Halesworth, Suffolk.

|  | £ | s. | d. |
|---|---|---|---|
| Item at Mich'mis given to the pore folckes at the gild hall and to Ould [John] Stanard | | 12 | 0 |
| Item given to men cast at sea and [*illeg.*] | | 1 | 2 |
| more given to a pore minister passing throw the towne | | | 6 |
| Item laid out for 5 chimneys sweping for the pore | | 2 | 0 |
| Item given to Samuell Milles in time of neede | | 2 | 0 |
| more to Thomis Johnson, junior, in time of his need | | 2 | 0 |
| Item laid out to Anne Milles for the Widdow Barnbes \rent/ | | 5 | 0 |
| Item given to William Crose at Chrismis, a blind man | | 10 | 0 |
| more at that time to Thomas Tallen for his wages | | 10 | 0 |
| laid out for 6 months assesment as apeer by the bill | 2 | 19 | 3 |
| Item laid out to Gregory Rowse for M$^r$ Antalls bill | 2 | 10 | 0 |
| more for the lame boy for stockings and shooes, bonds and bocke, handcarchars and gloves and makeing of shurts, and to [William] Ellis for bying | | 6 | 6 |
| Item given to James Brundish in sicknes | | 5 | 0 |
| Item laid out to John Crose for sheers for the belles | | 1 | 6 |
| more given to Thomas Brodbanckes sarvants | | 1 | 6 |
| Item laid out to M$^r$ Rooffe for healling of Samuell Milles his daughter | 2 | 10 | 0 |
| Item laid out for ane actt for the cunstable[257] | | 1 | 6 |
| more for 2 new bell ropes | | 11 | 0 |
| Item paid to [William] Ellis for keping the towne boy tenne weekes | 1 | 0 | 0 |
| more given to William Crose being blind[258] | | 10 | 0 |
| more for keping of the clocke | | 5 | 0 |
| Some toto is | 48 | 19 | 6 |

[*in a different hand*] A note of what money Robert Smith, being one of the churchwardens, receiveth in the behalfe of the towne from the 23th of March 1656 unto the 18th of March 1657

|  | £ | s. | d. |
|---|---|---|---|
| received then which was in hand at the reckoning day | 43 | 8 | 11 |
| received for the yeeres rent for Rose Larkes due at Mich'mas last being the 29th September | 58 | 0 | 0 |
| whereof given with the consent of the townsmen in regard of the cheapness of comodityes and the hardness of the tymes fower pound | [4 | 0 | 0] |
| Some toto of the receipts | 101 | 8 | 11 |
| Dissbursed | 52 | 19 | 6 |
| Remayne in hand due unto the towne | 48 | 9 | 5 |

Seene and allowed by the inhabbitants of the towne whose names are heere under written [*signatures*] John Smith, Robert Mynne, John Rous, William Aldous, Robert Smyth, Ralph Baldry, John Newson, John Fyske

---

[257] An unspecified printed act of Parliament was bought for the parish constable.
[258] Though blind, William Crosse looked after the church clock for many years (see Biographies, p. 132).

[242]
Cratfield
The accounts of John Fiske, senior, being one of the churchwardens from March 18th 1657 to March 17th 1658 [for 1658–9][259]

|  | £ | s. | d. |
|---|---|---|---|
| given to James Brundish March 18th | 1 | 0 | 0 |
| William Carsy was then allowed for his monthly assesments and 2 load wood | 1 | 12 | 0 |
| to the minister 2s., to the sexton 3s. for graves of Samuel Milles and his wife |  | 5 | 0 |
| to Thomas Tallent for beer, firewood, and attendance on the reckoning day |  | 10 | 0 |
| April 3, for bread and wine at the communion[260] |  | 5 | 0 |
| [April] 8th, to Thomas Johnson, senior |  | 13 | 4 |
| [April] 15th, for Bridget Spinke from the towne |  | 14 | 4 |
| [April] 22, for Joseph Smiths releife |  | 3 | 0 |
| May 7, for Joseph Smiths releife |  | 3 | 0 |
| [May] 9, to the Widow [Elizabeth] Stannard for her releife |  | 5 | 0 |
| [May] 11, to Thomas Johnson, junior, for wood and for other releife |  | 10 | 0 |
| June 28, to John Williams as appeares in his bill | 2 | 2 | 10 |
| to Thomas Tallent for weeding the church \door/ porch |  | 1 | 0 |
| July 19 to William Crosse for his releife |  | 10 | 0 |
| to the Widow [Elizabeth] Brissingam towards her fireing |  | 5 | 0 |
| September 13 to Thomas Johnson, junior |  | 10 | 0 |
| [Sept] 20 to Thomas Johnson, senior | 1 | 0 | 0 |
| [Sept] 30 for John Milles his widow |  | 7 | 0 |
| October 6 to William Crosse for Midsummer to to [sic] this day, given for releife | 1 | 8 | 0 |
| [October] 11 to Joseph Smith for halfe a yeare ending at Mich'mas last | 1 | 0 | 0 |
| besides the former, towards a load of wood |  | 3 | 4 |
| to William Carsy for 6 moneths \assesments/ ending with the last September |  | 12 | 0 |
| another charge of reparation as in his bill | 1 | 10 | 0 |
| to the Widow [Elizabeth] Stannard for Mich'mas quarter |  | 5 | 0 |
| October 31 to Thomas Johnson, junior |  | 6 | 8 |
| towards fireing for the 4 towne schollers |  | 2 | 0 |
| November 5 to the ringers upon gun-powder treason |  | 7 | 0 |
| [November] 6 to John Williams as appeares by his bill | 2 | 16 | 9 |
| [November] 21 to Joseph Smith in his sicknes |  | 2 | 0 |
| December 6 to Goodman [John] Stannard for releife |  | 5 | 0 |
| [December] 31 to Goodman [Nicholas] Moore towards a load of wood |  | 3 | 4 |
| for a planke layd in the Towne Pightle |  | 2 | 6 |
| January 14 to John Garret whose petition was read publiq' |  | 2 | 0 |
| [January] 16 to Thomas Johnson, senior |  | 2 | 9 |
| [January] 19 to James Brundish |  | 2 | 9 |

---

[259] This account is unusually specific as to the dates of payments.
[260] Another illegal Easter communion (see Notes 164 & 205).

|  | £ | s. | d. |
|---|---|---|---|
| Febuary 6 to Richard Sagar of St Laurence, Ilkils-hall[261] whose petition was read at church |  | 4 | 6 |
| March 9 to James Brundish for releife |  | 3 | 0 |
| to Thomas Johnson, senior |  | 4 | 6 |
| for the 4 poor childrens schooling for the whole year (Smith, Gant, Thirton, Ellis)[262] | 4 | 0 | 0 |
| to Thomas Tallent his wages for the whole year ending at Christmas | 2 | 0 | 0 |
| to poor passengers who came with certificats upon the weeke dayes at severall times |  | 6 | 6 |
| to the bayleife of the hundred, Rose Larkes rent due upon Mich'mas last |  | 2 | 4 |
| The weekly collection for 24 weekes which ended August 29 at the rate [of] 5s. 3d. a week | 6 | 6 | 0 |
| for 4 weekes after the rate, 6s. 3d. the weeke | 1 | 5 | 0 |
| for the last 24 weekes ending the 13th instant, after the rate of 8s. 9d. the week | 10 | 10 | 0 |
| Sum total | 45 | 9 | 5 |

Received by the said John Fiske for the use of the towne from March 18th 1657 to March 17 1658

|  | £ | s. | d. |
|---|---|---|---|
| received of John Williams which was in his hand at the reckoning day | 7 | 6 | 10 |
| received of William Carsy for his yeers rent for Benshlins ending at Mich'ls last past | 20 | 0 | 0 |
| received of John Williams for his whole yeeres rent ending Mich' last | 10 | 0 | 0 |
| received of Sam' Heyward for his whole yeeres rent ending at Mich'l last | 1 | 10 | 0 |
| received of Mr [Robert] Meen | 2 | 16 | 10 |
| Sum' tot' | 41 | 13 | 8 |

[243]
Disbursments for the towne from March 18th 1657 untill March 17, 1658 [for 1658–9]

|  | £ | s. | d. |
|---|---|---|---|
| Inprimis given to Mr Clifford | 3 | 0 | 0 |
| given to Francis Barrow | 2 | 0 | 0 |
| given to the poore protestants of Bohemia | 1 | 0 | 0 |
| for an hat and bible for [Samuel] Mills's boy |  | 6 | 4 |
| to Thomas Turner for lords rent |  | 4 | 6 |
| to Edward Alding for constables charges | 1 | 15 | 0 |
| to William Mingy for the dinner of eleven men at the court for pulvering, after the rate for 18d. per man |  | 16 | 6 |
| to Samuel Ludbrook for carriing 6 loads of wood for the poore people |  | 10 | 0 |

261 Ilketshall St Lawrence, Suffolk.
262 In this year, exceptionally, the surnames of the four boys receiving education at parish expense are given (see Note 16).

|  | £ | s. | d. |
|---|---|---|---|
| paid to William Ellis for boarding [Samuel] Mills's boy 18 weekes from the 22 of March to July 26<sup>th</sup>, for mending his clothes and shoes[263] | 1 | 17 | 0 |
| to John Crosse for mending the wethercocke |  | 10 | 6 |
| to Symon Warren for mending the wethercocke |  | 9 | 6 |
| to Robert Addams for worke done at William Carsyes hous \and materialls/ | 4 | 1 | 0 |
| to Thomas Johnson for 2 loads of stone |  | 6 | 8 |
| to George Coale for 3 loads and an halfe of stone |  | 11 | 8 |
| given to Francis Aldus[264] towards paying his rent | 1 | 0 | 0 |
| given to Widdow [Francis] Mills in her sicknes |  | 5 | 0 |
| to Goodman [Samuel] Crane for 3 loads of stone |  | 10 | 0 |
| given to a breife for Desford in Leicester\shire/[265] |  | 10 | 0 |
| paid to Edward Alding for Marshallseas |  | 17 | 4 |
| paid to William Ellis for boarding [Samuel] Mills's boy from July 26 to September 26, and for shoes and mending shoes 3s. | 1 | 1 | 0 |
| paid to Samuell Ludbrooke for bricke and tile and worke done for the towne | 2 | 9 | 0 |
| payd to Robert Smyth of Colshall for wood to the poore folke | 2 | 15 | 0 |
| paid to John Rous for larth |  | 15 | 0 |
| paid to my partner John Fiske for nailes for Thomas Broodbanks hous, and for a bill which William Carsy brought in | 2 | 16 | 10 |
| given to James Brundish to pay for his wood and fetch it, and in his sicknes |  | 17 | 0 |
| given to John Broadbanke for mending the butts |  | 3 | 0 |
| given to Francis Aldus to releive him | 1 | 0 | 0 |
| paid to William Ellis for boarding [Samuel] Mills's boy 13 weekes from September 26<sup>th</sup> to December 27<sup>th</sup> 26s., and for 2 shirst and makeing them 3s. 9d. | 1 | 9 | 9 |
| given to Thomas Brood\banke/ for entertaineing <the> the townesmen at his hous | 2 | 0 | 0 |
| for 5 load of stone for my selfe |  | 16 | 4 |
| paid to Thomas Skeet for 3 loads of stone |  | 10 | 0 |
| given to Thomas Johnson the elder, \for wood/ |  | 8 | 0 |
| paid to Francis Aldus for makeing [Samuel] Mills's boy 2 payre of breeches, doublet, and coate |  | 5 | 0 |
| for 2 yards of twill for [Samuel] Mills's boys \breeches/ |  | 1 | 8 |
| paid to Symon [?Warne] for 2 bridges: one on Norwood Greene, the other on Littlehaugh \Greene/[266] |  | 6 | 0 |
| paid to Jeremy Gowin for constables charges |  | 12 | 0 |
| paid for [Samuel] Mills's boyes cloth for his suite and coate | 1 | 6 | 10 |
| given to Nicholas Moore |  | 13 | 0 |

---

263 Samuel Mill died earlier that year, and his son, Henry, was boarded with William Ellis.

264 In this account the surname Aldus is spelt with the medieval abbreviation for a final -us, looking like an Arabic number 9.

265 Desford, near Market Bosworth, Leicestershire

266 These are local greens and bridges within Cratfield parish (see Map 1 on p. xi).

|  | £ | s. | d. |
|---|---|---|---|
| given to Thomas Johnson, junior |  | 5 | 0 |
| laid to Thomas Broodbanke as appeareth by his bills for the whole |  |  |  |
| yeere | ? | 2 | 5 |
| Summ | 56 | 3 | 10 |
|  |  |  |  |
| Received of Robert Smyth | 48 | 9 | 5 |
| received of Thomas Broodbanke | 50 | 0 | 0 |
|  |  |  |  |
| Remainder in my custody | 42 | 5 | 7 |

[244]
A note of what money John Fiske, being one of the churchwardens, dissburseth in the behalfe of the towne from the 18th March 1658 [for 1659–60]

|  | £ | s. | d. |
|---|---|---|---|
| Inprimis |  |  |  |
| laid out to Doll Addams for her releife |  | 10 | 0 |
| remayne due to me upon the reckoning daye | 3 | 15 | 9 |
| more allowed me for keping the poore woman | 2 | 0 | 0 |
| allowed to William Carsy for 6 months asessment ending the |  |  |  |
| 25th March, the somme of |  | 12 | 0 |
| more allowed him for 2 loads of wood |  | 15 | 0 |
| April 5th, laid out for bread and wine for the communion |  | 5 | 0 |
| May 3th, for my journy to Halsworth concerning the minister |  | 1 | 6 |
| allowed to John Williams for 6 months asessment ending the |  |  |  |
| 25th March 6s., and 2s. 9d. for tobacko and pipes |  | 5 | 9 |
| June 6th, given to William Cross in tyme of sickness |  | 6 | 0 |
| July 17th, given to the Widow [Elizabeth] Brissingam in tyme of |  |  |  |
| sicknesse |  | 5 | 0 |
| for my horse to Blibrow[267] 2 severall tymes to carry the towne soldier |  | 2 | 0 |
| laid out for the towneship called Rose Larkes [sic] |  | 2 | 4 |
| laid out to William Carcy for 9 monthes asessment ending the 24th June |  |  |  |
| next |  | 18 | 0 |
| laid out more to him for 6 months begining the 24th June |  | 12 | 0 |
| November 3th, given to John Campion and 2 seamen with a certeficate |  |  |  |
| to London |  | 1 | 0 |
| November 9th, given to Wollman Wilson and there company being 15 |  |  |  |
| maimed people |  | 1 | 0 |
| to John Cross for 1 pound nayles to use about the Widdow [Mary] |  |  |  |
| Tallens house |  |  | 7 |
| December 4th, laid out to the ringers for ringing the 5th November |  | 6 | 0 |
| given to William Crosse |  | 6 | 0 |
| January 4th, laid out to James Brundish for his releife |  | 3 | 0 |
| laid out to John Williams which he paid for 15 months asessment |  |  |  |
| ending the 24th June next |  | 7 | 6 |

267 Blythburgh, Suffolk.

|  | £ | s. | d. |
|---|---|---|---|
| January 25, laid out to M<sup>r</sup> Clifford for Christmas quarter for 4 towne boyes schoole | 1 | 0 | 0 |
| 25<sup>th</sup> January, laid out to William Cross in tyme of his sicknesse |  | 7 | 0 |
| laid out to William Carcy for moneys he laid out |  | 2 | 6 |
| laid out to William Cross for his releife |  | 7 | 0 |
| laid out to the Widow [Elizabeth] Brissingam for her releife |  | 10 | 0 |
| laid out to the poore for 14 weekes collection at 7s. 3d. per weeke | 5 | 1 | 6 |
| laid out more for 38 weekes collection to the poore at 7s. 9d. per weeke, the somme of | 14 | 14 | 6 |
| ending the 11<sup>th</sup> of March 1659 [*1650*] |  |  |  |
| Some totall of my dissbursments | 33 | 17 | 11 |

Cratfeild

A note of what money John Fiske, being one of the churchwardens, receiveth in the behalfe of the towne from the 18<sup>th</sup> of March 1658

|  | £ | s. | d. |
|---|---|---|---|
| Inprimis |  |  |  |
| received then of William Carcy for his Lady halfe yeere rent for Benslins, the somme of | 10 | 0 | 0 |
| received of the Widow [Margaret] Hayward for her yeeres rent for the Towne Pightell | 1 | 10 | 0 |
| received of John Williams for his yeeres rent for the Towne Middowes and the Towne Closse ending the 29<sup>th</sup> September, the some of | 11 | 0 | 0 |
| received of William Carcy for his halfe yeeres rent for Benslins ended the 29<sup>th</sup> of September, the somme of | 10 | 0 | 0 |
| received of M<sup>r</sup> [Henry] Meene the 9<sup>th</sup> September 1659 the somme of | 1 | 10 | 0 |
| Somme totall of my receipts this yeere is | 34 | 0 | 0 |
|  |  |  |  |
| Some totall of my dissbursments this yeere is | 33 | 7 | 11 |
| Soe remayne due unto the towne to be delivered to the new churchwardens from John Fiske, the somme of |  | 2 | 1 |

[246]

A note of the disbursments of mee Robert Mynne for the towne of Cratfeild [*1659, in different hand*]

|  | £ | s. | d. |
|---|---|---|---|
| given to William Aldus, the butcher, the last reckoning day for provision, fireing and makeing ready the dinner | 1 | 4 | 0 |
| given to James Brundish |  | 11 | 0 |
| paid to William Crosse for keepeing the clocke for the yeere befor the last |  | 10 | 0 |
| paid to Thomas Turner, the elder, for lords rent |  | 4 | 4 |
| paid to Robert Spatchet for Marshallseas for 2 quarters |  | 17 | 4 |
| given to Francis Aldus to buy him wood | 1 | 0 | 0 |
| paid to William Ellis for boarding [Samuel] Mills's boy 15 weekes from December 27 to April 11<sup>th</sup>, and for mending his shoes | 1 | 10 | 6 |
| paid to M<sup>r</sup> Clifford for mending the schoole hous windowes |  | 5 | 0 |

|  | £ | s. | d. |
|---|---|---|---|
| given to Thomas Johnson, the elder, to pay his hous rent | | 12 | 0 |
| paid to Thomas Tallowin for his quarters wages | | 10 | 0 |
| given him more for beere and fireing and attendance at the reckoning day | | 10 | 0 |
| paid to John Gosse and Thomas Skeet surveyors[268] | | 2 | 8 |
| paid likewise to John Gosse for Francis Aldus his rent due the 25th of March | | 15 | 0 |
| paid to Joseph Smyth for his halfe yeeres rent due the 25th of March | 1 | 0 | 0 |
| paid to Francis Barrow for 12 loads of stone | 2 | 0 | 0 |
| paid to the surveyors for workemen that wrought in the high wayes | 2 | 8 | 6 |
| paid to George Cole for 2 loads of stone | | 6 | 8 |
| paid to William \Carsy/ for a load and halfe of stone | | 5 | 0 |
| paid to Robert Rayner for 10 loads of stone | 1 | 13 | 4 |
| for 7 loads of stone which I laid | 1 | 3 | 4 |
| given to the towne of Southwold[269] being burnt | 10 | 0 | 0 |
| paid to Edward Alding his constables charges | 2 | 5 | 6 |
| given to Thomas Johnson <...> a trained soldier goeing to Blyburgh | | 2 | 6 |
| given to Joseph Stannard, the elder, and his wife | 1 | 0 | 0 |
| given to Rose Pacy, her husband being a trained soldier | | 2 | 6 |
| given to Joseph Smyths wife to relieve him [sic] | | 2 | 0 |
| given to a breife | | 5 | 0 |
| paid to Mr Clifford for schooleing 4 poore boyes | 1 | 0 | 0 |
| paid to William Ellis for boarding [Samuel] Mills boy 14 weekes from Aprill 11th to July 18th, and for a paire of shoes, a payre of gloves, and a payre of stockings | 1 | 13 | 2 |
| paid to Thomas Tallowin for his quarters wages and weeding the stones before the porch | | 11 | 0 |
| given to Joseph Smyth his wife to releeve him | | 3 | 0 |
| paid to William Mingy for dineing 15 pulvering men after the rate of 18d. per man | 1 | 2 | 6 |
| given away at Thomas Broodbankes when the townes men dined there | | 5 | 0 |
| given to a breife for a burning at London | | 7 | 6 |
| given to Rose Browne and Widdow [Mary] Tallowin for a key | | | 4 |
| given to Joseph Smyth | | 5 | 0 |
| paid to the Widdow [Rose] Pacy for boards | | 2 | 6 |
| given to [John] Thirton being sicke | | 5 | 0 |
| paid to my partner John Fiske when he wanted money | 1 | 10 | 0 |
| given to the Widdow [Mary] Tallowin when her daughter lay in | | 4 | 0 |
| given to the Widdow [Elizabeth] Stannard | | 5 | 0 |
| | | | |
| paid to William Aldus for being a trained soldier and goeing to Blyburgh | | 2 | 6 |
| paid to Edmond Mills, the nacker, for being a soldier for the towne | | 1 | 6 |
| paid to James Gosse for Francis Aldus's rent due the 29 of September | | 15 | 0 |
| paid to William Mingy for wood which was given to [John] Thyrton when he was sicke | 1 | 2 | 0 |

---

[268] Gosse and Skeet were the highway surveyors of the parish. Subsequent entries show that workmen were paid, and quantities of stone bought, to maintain or improve local roads.
[269] Southwold, Suffolk.

|  | £ | s. | d. |
|---|---|---|---|
| given to Thomas Johnson, the elder | | 15 | 0 |
| paid to Joseph Smyth's wife for her halfe yeeres rent and for wood | 1 | 3 | 0 |
| given to [John] Thyrton | | 5 | 0 |
| paid to William Ellis for boarding [Samuel] Mills's boy 12 weekes | 1 | 4 | 0 |
| paid to Robert Spatchet for the Marshallseas for 2 quarters | | 17 | 4 |
| given to Thomas Johnson, junior, to buy him wood | | 3 | 4 |
| paid to [Nick] Bicker, the glasier, for worke done at the church | 1 | 13 | 0 |
| paid to Thomas Tallowin his quarters wages | | 10 | 0 |
| paid to Thomas Tallowin for fireing and worke when [Nick] Bicker wrought on the leads[270] | | 7 | 0 |
| given to Joseph Smyth | | 2 | 6 |
| given to [John] Thyrton | | 5 | 0 |
| given to a woman with a passe | | 2 | 0 |
| given to [John] Thyrton | | 5 | 0 |
| paid to Mr [John] Williams for cloth for a suite for Phenice Smyths boy and severall other things | 1 | 9 | 0 |
| paid to Widdow [Temperance] Ludbroke for fetching home [John] Thirtons wood | | 6 | 0 |
| paid to Bryan Clarke for makeing Phenice Smyths boyes suite | | 3 | 0 |
| paid to Mr Clifford for schooleing 4 towne boyes | 1 | 0 | 0 |
| given to [John] Thyrton | | 6 | 0 |
| laid out for [John] Thyrtons coffin | | 6 | 0 |
| paid to William Ellis for boarding [Samuel] Mills's boy 13 weekes from October 3rd to January 2nd, and for a paire of shoes and mending his shoes twice | 1 | 9 | 2 |
| given to Nick Moore to buy him wood | | 3 | 4 |
| given to William Aldus, the butcher, towards his repayres | 1 | 0 | 0 |
| paid to Thomas Turner, the elder, for lords rent and for a common fine | | 11 | 5½ |
| paid to Edmond Mills for going a soldier to Blyburgh | | 1 | 6 |
| paid to William Aldus for goeing a souldier | | 2 | 6 |
| given to Thomas Johnson, the elder, to releeve him | | 5 | 0 |
| given to Thomas Johnsons wife, the younger, when shee was sicke | | 5 | 0 |
| paid to Thomas Tallowin for his quarters wages | | 10 | 0 |
| given to Robert Addams for [Samuel] Mills's boyes indentures makeing | | 2 | 0 |
| paid [John] Thirtons debts to severall persons | 3 | 13 | 0 |
| paid to Symond Warren for worke done | 6 | 0 | 0 |
| given away at Thomas Broodbanks when the townes men dined there | | 5 | 0 |
| paid to Thomas Broodbanke for stowing, bratling, and carrying the poore peoples wood, and for straw and thatching | 1 | 7 | 4 |
| paid to Mr Clifford for schooleing 4 towneboyes | 1 | 0 | 0 |
| given to Dorothe Addams when shee was sicke | | 5 | 0 |
| given to Dorothe Addams | | 10 | 0 |
| given to Elizabeth Butcher when shee was sicke | | 5 | 0 |
| allowed Thomas Broodbanke for his bills out of the first halfe yeeres rent | 6 | 13 | 0 |
| allowed Thomas Broodbanke out of his last halfe yeeres rent | 5 | 10 | 4 |

---

[270] The glazier was here working on the lead roofs of the church.

|  | £ | s. | d. |
|---|---|---|---|
| given to John Rous's wife a sugar loafe for her husbands release[271] |  | 5 | 0 |
|  |  |  |  |
| paid to William Aldus, the butcher, for the townesmen dinner this day | 1 | 5 | 0 |
| paid to [William] Crosse for keepeing the clocke for this yeere |  | 10 | 0 |
| paid to Thomas Tallowin for makeing 2 graves |  | 3 | 0 |
| Summe | 84 | 4 | 11 |

|  | £ | s. | d. |
|---|---|---|---|
| Received of the towne for rent | 50 | 0 | 0 |
| Remaining of towne money in my hands \at the last reckoning/ | 42 | 5 | 7 |
| Expended out of the abovesaid receipts | 84 | 4 | 11 |
| Remaine due to the towne | 8 | 0 | 8 |

[250]
Cratfeild

A note of what money John Newson, being one of the churchwardens, receiveth in the behalfe of the towne from the 19th of March 1659 [for 1660–1]

| Inprimis | £ | s. | d. |
|---|---|---|---|
| received then of John Fiske the last churchwarden which |  |  |  |
| was in his hand then, the somme of |  | 2 | 1 |
| received of John Stannard for his yeeres rent due the 29th of September |  |  |  |
| 1660 for Benslins, the somme of | 20 | 0 | 0 |
| received of John Williams for his yeeres rent for the Towne Middowes |  |  |  |
| and Mollings Mid° and the Towne Close | 12 | 0 | 0 |
| received of Thomas Turner for his yeeres rent for the Towne Pightell |  |  |  |
| due the 29th September 1660, the somme of | 1 | 10 | 0 |
| Somme totall of my receipts | 33 | 12 | 1 |

Cratfeild

A note of what money John Newson, being one of the churchwardens, disburseth in the behalfe of the towne from the 19th of March 1659

| Inprimis | £ | s. | d. |
|---|---|---|---|
| to the poore for 28 weekes collection at 7s. 9d. per weeke | 10 | 17 | 0 |
| to the poore for 6 weekes collection at 6s. 3d. per weeke | 1 | 17 | 6 |
| to the poore for 18 weekes collection at 8s. 3d. per weeke | 7 | 8 | 6 |
| Somme totall of the collection | 20 | 3 | 0 |

|  | £ | s. | d. |
|---|---|---|---|
| given to 3 menn which were imprissoned by the Spanyard and sent |  |  |  |
| home per passe |  | 1 | 0 |
| given more to 3 poore passengers |  |  | 6 |
| given to 3 pore soldiers coming from London and goeing to Holle[272] to |  |  |  |
| lye in garison there |  | 1 | 0 |

---

271 This John Rous cannot be identified with certainty. The parish may have been contributing to a celebration when a soldier or prisoner was released.
272 Kingston-upon-Hull, in eastern Yorkshire.

|  | £ | s. | d. |
|---|---|---|---|

paid to John Williams as apereth by his bill the somme of — 4 4 5
paid to John Stannard which he laid out to the monthly asessment as
   appereth by his bill, the some of — 2 8 0
allowed him more for 2 loads of wood — 17 6
   Somme totall of my dissburshments — 27 15 5

Soe remayne due unto the towne from John Newton uppon this
   accoumpt, the some of — 5 16 8

[252]
Cratfield
The accoumpt of John Rous, one of the churchwardens, made and given up to the inhabitants of the towne the 21th daye of March, for the yeare of Our Lord 1660 [*for 1660–1*]

Receypts — £ s. d.
Imprimis, receyved of Robert Meene gent', one of the ould
   churchwardens, the last recconing day — 8 0 8
receyved of Thomas Broadbancke for his yeares rent ending at
   St Micheall last — 50 0 0
receyved of James Brundish for the use of Margaret Milles, widow, in
   part of her debt to the towne — 10 0
   Summ is — 58 10 8

Disbursed
Imprimis, payd unto Willyam Youngs the last recconing daye the bill
   of charges that was oweing to John Newson, senior, deceased, ever
   since he was constable — 16 10
Item payd unto Willyam Aldous for beere the last recconing daye — 5 0
Item given to Carter of Houlton[273] that had his house and goods burnt — 2 6
Item given unto George Turrell that had great lose by Turkes as by his
   certificat did apeare — 3 0
Item payd unto Thomas Tallion for beere and fire the last recconing daye — 10 0
Item payd unto the sayde Thomas Tallion for his yeares wages \and
   weeding before the porch/ — 2 1 0
Item for a stop for a bell — 6
Item given unto Nicholas More towards his rent — 5 0
Item given unto Ould [Thomas] Johnson towards his rent — 10 0
Item payd unto Symond Warren for mending the pales about the
   churchyard and the gate — 7 10
Item payd unto Willyam Ellice for Henery Miles dyet, a payre of
   stockings and gloves, for a quarter of a yeare at Our Lady last — 1 16 11
Item payd unto Goodman [Edward] Aldinge for carryeing of the
   Widow Smythes stufe, being 2 loads — 6 6
Item given unto the sayd Widow Smyth towards her rent — 1 0 0

273 Holton, Suffolk.

|  | £ | s. | d. |
|---|---|---|---|
| Item payd unto Thomas Broadbancke for 3 monthes assesment, and for wood he bought in lew of allowance | 5 | 5 | 8 |
| Item payd him more for the townesmens dinners [when] thay went to apoynt wood the last yeare[274] | 2 | 0 | 0 |
| Item layd out for the lords rent at Our Lady |  | 4 | 6 |
| Item layd out for bread and wine for 2 sacraments |  | 8 | 4 |
| Item layd out for the Marshalseas and Maymed Soulgers for halfe a yeare at Our Lady last |  | 17 | 4 |
| Item layd out to the 2 towne soulgers for traying[sic] |  | 5 | 0 |
| Item for my owne exspence when I gave in my accoumpt for the pore |  | 2 | 6 |
| Item given unto Thomas Gant for loking to his mother |  | 15 | 0 |
| Item layd out to the 2 towne soulgers for 2 dayes traying |  | 10 | 0 |
| Item given to the ringers for ringing that the king was com into England[275] |  | 5 | 0 |
| Summ | 18 | 8 | 5 |
|  |  |  |  |
| Item given to Ould [Thomas] Johnson the 17th of June |  | 5 | 0 |
| Item given to Ould [John] Stannard being not well |  | 5 | 0 |
| Item given to Edmund Baldrye for carrieing the wood for the pore |  | 8 | 0 |
| Item payd to Goodman [William] Elice for Henery Milles bord for 9 weeks and shooes mending |  | 18 | 6 |
| Item payd unto Jeremy Gowinge, constable, for his charges in the tyme of his office | 1 | 11 | 0 |
| Item given to eleven soulgers that had bin wounded, and traveled with a certificat from Generall Munk[276] |  | 2 | 0 |
| Item payd unto Mr Clifford for 4 pore chilldren teaching from Our Lady to <Midso> St Micheall | 2 | 0 | 0 |
| Item payd to Jeferye Crane, constable, his charges | 2 | 4 | 0 |
| Item layd out for the Widow [Mary] Milles to take her out of the jayle,[277] the charges of sute to Clements, Mr Nelson and Mr Wright as under ther hands apere | 3 | 0 | 0 |
| Item payd unto Micheall Barfot of Halsworth that he was to have with Henery Milles his apprenty'[278] | 15 | 0 | 0 |
| Item payd him more for to apparell him and indenturs mak | 1 | 15 | 0 |
| Item for 2 jurnyes to Halsworth to bynd him |  | 2 | 6 |
| Item for my jurnye to Halsworth to have the Justice hands to [Henry] Miles indentures |  | 2 | 0 |
| Item payd unto Robert Adames for Marshalseas |  | 17 | 4 |
| Item given unto the breefe of Robert Nuham and Edward Peake of South Bukingham in Norffolk,[279] lose by fire £200 |  | 3 | 6 |

274 This was the meeting of the principal townsmen to determine which poor households would receive free or subsidised firewood, and how much.

275 May, 1660 saw the return and restoration of Charles II.

276 For General George Monck, see Biographies, p. 138, and Introduction, p. 19.

277 Mary Milles was released from gaol as an act of mercy.

278 A premium of £15 was paid for a parish orphan to be apprenticed in the nearby town of Halesworth. Further costs are given in subsequent entries.

279 New Buckenham, in south Norfolk.

| | £ | s. | d. |
|---|---|---|---|
| Item given to James Carye of Stowbridg in Norffolk,[280] haveing had lose by fire £300 | | 1 | 0 |
| Item given unto Thomas Johnson to buy wood | | 4 | 0 |
| Item payd unto Goodman [Thomas] Turner the lords rent <for> at St Micheall \for the towne land/ | | 11 | 5½ |
| Item given unto Willyam Crose to paye his yers rent ending at St Micheall last | 1 | 0 | 0 |
| Item layd out to Thomas Broadbancke for assesments and for wood for the pore and other charges, as by his bill apere | 5 | 18 | 10 |
| Item given unto the Wapping[281] breefe of £1929 | | 4 | 0 |
| Item given unto the ringers the 5 of November | | 6 | 0 |
| Item given unto James Brundish to hynd his sonn aprentiz to Goodman [Robert] Hayward £2, and £2 more lent him and to be payd agayne in four yeares | 4 | 0 | 0 |
| Item given unto M^r Wright, the collector for the Poll Mony, to ingrose the duplycots[282] | | 1 | 6 |
| Item given to the 2 towne soulgers for a dayes traying[sic] | | 5 | 0 |
| Item given the 18^th of November to the breefe for a burning in London, the lose were £5000 | | 5 | 0 |
| Item layd out for a sword and belt for the towne | | 10 | 0 |
| Item layd out to [William] Crose for 3 scrue nayles for a bell | | 2 | 3 |
| Item given unto Thomas Johnson in his wifes siknes | 1 | 0 | 0 |
| Item given unto Elizabeth Butcher | | 5 | 0 |
| Item given unto John Stanards wife being sick | | 2 | 0 |
| Item given to the tow soulgers for traying | | 5 | 0 |
| Item given unto 3 saylores that had ther ship cast away | | 1 | 0 |
| Item layd out for 2 head peeces for the towne | | 11 | 0 |
| Item given to Thomas Broadbancke for the townesmens dinners when thay apoynted wood | 1 | 5 | 0 |
| Item given to Dorrithie Adames | | 10 | 0 |
| Item given to John Crose for triming a head peece for the towne | | | 6 |
| Summ | 46 | 2 | 4 |
| | | | |
| Summ totoll | 64 | 10 | 9 |
| | | | |
| Remayne due from the towne uppon this accoumpt to John Rous churchwarden the summ of | 6 | 0 | 1½ |

John Rous [signature]

[253]
Cr[. . . . .] [heading damaged]
A note of what money John Newson, being one of the churchwar[. . . . . ], receiveth in the behalfe of the towne from the 21^th March 1660 [for 1661–2]

---

280 Stowbridge, in west Norfolk.
281 Wapping, in east London.
282 To write out a duplicate copy of the Poll Tax returns.

| | £ | s. | d. |
|---|---|---|---|
| Inprimis | | | |
| received which was in my hand then being the last reckoning daye, the | | | |
| somme of five pound, sixtene shillings, eight pence, I say | 5 | 16 | 8 |
| received of John Stannard for one yeeres rent for Benslins due the | | | |
| 29th September 1661, the somme of | 20 | 0 | 0 |
| received of John Williams for one yeeres rent due the 29th September, | | | |
| the somme of | 12 | 0 | 0 |
| received of Thomas Turner for one yeeres rent for the Towne Pightle, | | | |
| due the 29th September 1661 | 1 | 10 | 0 |
| [Sum] | 39 | 6 | 8 |

A note of what money John Newson, being one of the churchwardens, dissburseth in the behalfe of the towne the 21th March 1660

| | £ | s. | d. |
|---|---|---|---|
| Inprimis | | | |
| laid laid out to the poore for 34 weeke collection at 8s. 9d. per weeke | 14 | 17 | 6 |
| laid out to the poore for 9 weekes collection at 8s. 9d. per weeke | 6[sic] | 19 | 6 |
| allowed to John Stannard for 9 months asessment | 1 | 16 | 4 |
| and more for 2 loads wood | 1 | 0 | 0 |
| paid to Goodman [John] Goss for 1 yeres rent for Francis Alldus | 2 | 0 | 0 |
| given to Thomas Johnsons wife in tyme of sickness | | 5 | 0 |
| laid out for my diner when I gave in the accoumpts for the poore | | 2 | 6 |
| allowed to John Stannard for glaseing and for nayles | | 5 | 6 |
| more for fetching of plank out of John Fishes grownd | | 2 | 0 |
| and more for one months asessment | | 4 | 0 |
| for my journy to Blithbrow to be sworne | | 1 | 0 |
| laid out for one pike for the towne | | 6 | 0 |
| given to 3 seamen | | 1 | 0 |
| given to 5 woemen comeing from London to Norwich | | 2 | 0 |
| allowed to John Williams which he laid out to the asessment and for | | | |
| other charges | 2 | 11 | 3 |
| Some totall of my dissbursments, £30 13s. 7d. | 30 | 13 | 7 |

| | £ | s. | d. |
|---|---|---|---|
| Soe remayne in my hand due unto the towne to be paid unto the new | | | |
| churchwardens, the some of | 8 | 13 | 1 |
| paid unto the new churchwardens in full of this accoumpt | 8 | 13 | 1 |

Received by me, Robert Milles [signature]

# Appendix 1

# Biographies

The following biographical notes assemble information for individuals mentioned in this volume. They are based on a full reconstitution for the parish, using the church-wardens' accounts, parish registers, other manuscript sources, and printed sources where available. No claim is made to completeness. Where individuals have the same name, there is always a danger that their biographies have been conflated. The dominant spelling of each surname has been used, and major variations indicated where necessary.

ADAMS, Doll or Dorothy: (no baptism or marriage information; buried 2 September 1662). A poor, old woman supported by the parish. She collected a regular pension of 3d. a week from 1644 to 1650. In 1651 she began to collect 1s. a week, and did so through the first sixteen weeks of 1653, at which point her pension ceased but she continued to live in the parish. She also collected miscellaneous relief periodically from the churchwardens.

ADAMS, Finet: (no vital information). She received 2s. a month in 1641 from the overseers 'for her child of Base' and the same amount during the following year. Her only child, Sarah, was baptised on 9 April 1640 and buried 1642. The father's name was not recorded.

ADAMS, Margaret: (baptised c.1611; married Thomas c.1637; buried 28 November 1656). From 1652 Margaret was a substantial rate-payer at 1s.10d. a month, but in 1656 she ceased contributing to poor relief. She also rented the Rose Larks property from the parish, at an annual rent of £53. In 1652, she began to experience financial difficulties, and was assisted by the town with her assessment. She had one child, Thomas.

ADAMS, Robert, bricklayer: (baptised c.1620; married Ann c.1647; buried 12 October 1703). He was assessed at four hearths in the Hearth Tax of 1674. In 1651 he took one of Samuel Mills's boys as an apprentice. He also did some work on the guild-hall in 1654 and 1656. Robert was first assessed for the poor rate in 1654 at 5d. a month. His assessment increased over time, and his last recorded entry was in 1694 at 3s.3d. a month. He had four children: Gregory, James, Mary and Robert.

ADAMS, Stephen: (no vital information). Churchwarden in 1659. He was reimbursed for expenses in 1649. He was assessed for the rate in 1646 at 4d. a month, and again in 1650 at 8d.

ADAMS, Thomas: (baptised c.1610; married Margaret c.1637; no burial information). Thomas did odd jobs around the parish, such as cutting and delivering wood for the poor. He had one child, Thomas.

ADAMS, Widow: (no vital information). A poor woman of the parish who received both a regular pension and miscellaneous relief.

ALDING, Edward: (baptised c.1626; married Ann Page, 6 November 1654; no burial information). A widower by 1655. Constable in 1657 and 1659. Originally from

Stradbroke, Suffolk. He was assessed for the poor rate in 1685 at 1s. a month. He had one still-born child.

ALDUS, Francis, senior, yeoman: (baptised 4 November 1576; married Catherine Smith, 16 June 1613; buried 1657). Constable in 1639. Overseer in 1635. Churchwarden in 1636 and 1637. He was assessed at £1 3s.8d. for the Ship Money of 1640. In 1625 he was assessed at 1s.8d. a month for the poor rate. He leased Benselin farm from the town in 1641 at £17 a year, and was still renting land from the parish in 1642. In 1646, he was assessed at 1s. a month. According to the parish register, 'Francis Aldus was buried the 23th day of November. He had drunk anneseed water the 21 day and went to goe home and fell into a ditch, and could not gett out and for want of helpe thear he died Anno Dom 1657'. He had four children: Ann, Margaret, Sarah and William.

ALDUS, Francis, tailor: (baptised c.1615; married Margaret c.1642; buried 30 September 1668). Churchwarden in 1651. Francis was assessed at 7s.10d. for the Ship Money in 1640. He was first assessed for the poor rate in 1646 at 4d. a month, and paid until his forty–ninth year when the assessment dropped to 2d. a month. He continued to pay the rate until his death in 1668. Illness, in 1656, forced Francis to accept relief from the churchwardens and in 1657 they paid his rent. On 20 September 1662, 'a still borne childe of Francis Aldous secretly in the night [was] put into a grave without Christain buriall'. This probably was a failed attempt to hide an act of infanticide to which the authorities turned a forgiving eye and which they did not pursue fully. He had one child, Sarah.

ALDUS, Joan: (baptised c.1585, maiden name Sudbrooke; married John, 1 November 1611; buried 10 August 1657). In 1629 Joan was one of the women paid to care for Olive Eade during her final illness and to assist with her laying-out and burial. She had four children: Margaret, Sarah, Susanne and William.

ALDUS, John: (baptised 2 May 1591; married Joan Sudbrooke, 1 November 1611; buried 24 January 1675). Because of sickness, John and Joan were frequent recipients of miscellaneous relief, which was usually paid to her rather than him. They received a great deal of firewood from the parish. In 1664 John was in some sort of trouble and Mr Meene made 'severall journeys to Halsworth when John Aldus went to the Justices'. In 1667 a warrant was issued for John and his daughter. For the last two years of his life John collected regular relief at 4s. a month. Eventually, he received a pauper's burial. He had four children: Margaret, Sarah, Susanne and William.

ALDUS, Thomas, tailor: (baptised 26 February 1610; married Margery Smith, 16 June 1637; buried 4 May 1685). Constable in 1653. Listed with four hearths in 1674. He began paying the poor rate in 1651 at 8d. a month and stopped only in 1684 at 1s. a month. In 1670, Thomas pledged 1s. to 'A true certificate of the contribution of the general inhabitants of Cratfield afforesaid towards the redemtion of Christian slaves in Turkey as apereth by his majesties leters pattens and for their freedom is required 3,000 pound so gathered by the chirchwardings with fower other of the inhabitants of the parish to assiste them'. He had one child, Hanna.

ALDUS, William: (baptised 2 February 1607; son of William, thatcher, and Sarah; no burial information). Probably this is the William Aldus who served as one of the town's soldiers in 1640 and 1642 when they were sent to Yoxford. William again served as a soldier in 1643 and 1659. He did odd jobs for the parish. In 1642, for example, he went to Laxfield to collect wine for the local court. He had no children.

ALDUS, William, junior, yeoman and butcher: (baptised 1 June 1614; married Sarah Dowsing, 26 September 1637; buried 3 November 1675). Overseer in 1651, 1653,

1656 and 1662. Churchwarden in 1642–3, 1654–5 and 1664. One of chief inhabitants in 1656–1666, and 1668–1673. Assessed at four hearths in 1674. It is probable that this is the 'Master Aldus' who taught the four poor boys in 1641 and 1643–1644. He contributed 1s.6d. in 1670 for the redemption of Christian slaves (see p. 128). His poor rate assessment began in 1650 at 1s. a month, and continued until his death in 1675 when it was 1s.8d. a month. In 1659, he was host to the chief inhabitants when they drew up their annual accounts. His will suggests discord between his wife and children: 'And lastly I leave this legacye to my said wyfe and children desering them all to live as mother and children out to doe accordinge to the rule of gods holly [wholly] holy word lovinge and comfortinge one another upon all occasions.' He had four children: William, Francis, Sarah and Ann.

ANTALLS, Master: (no vital information). He submitted a bill to the parish in 1656–7.

ASHBY, Toby: (no vital information). He did odd jobs in the parish, such as mending the butts in 1654.

BALDRY or BALLDRY, Edmund: (baptised 17 June 1599; married Elizabeth Broadbank, 30 June 1625; buried 20 May 1670). Assessed at 4d. for the Ship Money in 1640, and first assessed for the poor rate in 1652 at 3d. a month. He continued paying rates until his death in 1670, when his assessment stood at 1s. 4d. a month. Edmund was paid for not ploughing the Great Close in 1656–7. He had no children.

BALDRY, Jeremy (baptised c.1601; married Ann Gowing, 3 October 1642; buried 29 February 1648). Constable in 1642. He was assessed for the poor rate between 1625 and 1644 at 1s.8d. a month. His wealth dropped in 1664–6, when his rate fell to 8d. a month. He had four children: Mary, Ann, Jeremy and an unnamed infant.

BALDRY, Ralph: (no baptism or marriage information; buried 27 April 1695). Overseer in 1665 and 1666. A chief inhabitant in 1657. His first assessment for rates came in 1658 when he paid 1s.6d. He paid increasing amounts until 1695, when his last payment was 2s.4d.

BANCKES or BANKS, Master ———, minister of religion: preached at Cratfield in 1641–3.

BARNABLY or BARWBY, Thomas, thatcher: (no baptismal information; married Elizabeth, n.d.; no burial information, but he was still alive in 1687 when his wife died). He was assessed for the poor rate between 1687 and 1692 at roughly 8d. a month.

BARNBY or BARNBE, widow: (no vital information). She received miscellaneous relief from the churchwardens in 1656–7.

BARROW, Francis: (baptised c.1601; married Mary c.1628; buried 18 June 1670). Constable in 1639. He was assessed at 6s. for the Ship Money in 1640. In 1645 he was paid by the parish 'to make upp the rate for our good bretherin of Scotland'. Francis was first assessed for the rate at 8d. a month, but payments rose as his social standing improved. At his death, his assessment stood at 1s.2d. a month. In 1670, he pledged 6d. for the release of Christian slaves (see p. 128). He had four children: Ann, Amy Francis and Sarah.

BEDDINGFIELD, Thomas, Mr: (no vital information). He collected money from the parish for things such as Marshalseas and Maimed Soldiers and the repair of bridges.

BISHOP, Wolfrine, thatcher: (baptised c.1638; married Elizabeth Wincop, 21 September 1665; buried 12 February 1679). Between 1668 and 1670 he was assessed for the poor rate at 6d. a month. He seven children, five of whom died in early childhood: Ann, Ann, John, Sarah, Wolfran, Wolfran and a stillborn child.

BOTTRES, ———: (no vital information). He was paid by the town to find the woman who in 1650 left a child in the church porch.

BRISSINGHAM, Elizabeth: (baptised c.1576, maiden name Baldry; married Thomas, 13 September 1602; buried 11 June 1660). Widowed in 1628. Elizabeth received miscellaneous poor relief after her husband's death, and suffered from the 'pockes' in 1629. Throughout the 1630s she helped with the townsmen's dinners, and continued to receive assistance from them for her rent. In 1642, Elizabeth became a regular pensioner at 2s. a month. By 1646 she shared accommodation with another widowed pensioner, Ann Newson. As she aged, the amount of Widow Brissingham's pension increased; in the last eight weeks of her life it was 3s. a week. In 1651 an unidentified Brissingham was 'routed' from the town. This may have been Elizabeth, who was later buried in Cratfield, or it could have been her son. She had seven children: Ann, Elizabeth, Jeremy, Rachel, Rose, Simon and Susanna

BROADBANK, Edmund: (baptised 10 October 1590; married to Mary Stannard, 20 February 1611; buried 20 January 1661). Churchwarden in 1626. In the decade immediately after his marriage, Edmund earned additional income by carrying wood for the poor of the parish, a practice that he continued sporadically throughout his life. The first surviving record of his poor rate assessment was in 1625, at 1s.4d. a month. In the 1630s, Edmund and his wife hosted the chief inhabitants when they drew up their accounts, as well as entertaining visitors to the town. In 1640 he and his cousin's widow, Mary Broadbank, paid the rent of the town pightle for three years. He was assessed at 10s. for Ship Money in 1640. It may be this Edmund or his son who killed Thomas Cox, 'stabd with a knife', in 1640. He had seven children: Robert, Ann, Edmund, Mary, Samuel, Thomas and William.

BROADBANK, Mary: (baptised 2 February 1565; married to Robert, 2 October 1595; buried 11 October 1656. The parish register recorded her burial: 'She dyed at Linstead Magna and was buried at Cratfield, a woman a great deale above fower score yeares of age'). She was widowed in 1633. In the 1640s, she was primarily responsible for feeding and entertaining the chief inhabitants on the day of the reckoning, as well as visitors to the town. Mary was economically successful. In 1642 she was assessed at 13s. 'for a pike & a sword for the towne'. In the following year, she was reimbursed 'at 5 severall times for provision for the soldiers and ther kepers, £6'. In 1643, Mary was assessed for the poor rate at 4d. a month. In the same year, she was fined 20s. for 'drawinge of beere without lycenc': the money was distributed amongst the poor. She also rented the town pightle from 1641 until 1654. Her last assessment for the rate, at 7d. a month, was in 1654. Given her advanced age, it is probable that she spent the final two years of her life 'retired'. She had six children: Elizabeth, Margaret, Ann, Edmund, Mary and Priscilla.

BROADBANK, Robert: (baptised 20 February 1620; no marriage or burial information). He served as a town soldier in 1648. He was assessed for the poor rate between 1662 and 1674 at 4d. a month. In 1675 his wife fell ill and Robert collected miscellaneous relief to provide for his family. In the next year, Robert was again assessed for the rate, but once again he ended up receiving assistance from the parish. Eventually he collected a weekly pension of 1s. until he disappeared from the records in 1698.

BROADBANK, Thomas: (baptised 20 December 1632; married Mary c.1661; buried 15 March 1717). He hosted the townmen's dinner in the late 1650s when they drew up the accounts for the year, and was probably in the brewing and victualling trade. In 1658 he was assessed for the rate at 1s.4d. a month, but in the following year the parish actually paid his for him. His assessment remained roughly level throughout the rest of his life. He had one child, Thomas.

BROADBANK, William: (baptised 20 January 1616; never married; buried 10 March 1662). He was paid by the parish for farm labour in 1649–50. In 1651 he worked around the parish and kept the town's arms in repair. He was never assessed for the poor rate.

BROWNE, Rose: (baptised 18 January 1595; never married; no burial information). A poor, single woman who collected both miscellaneous relief and a weekly pension, Rose earned additional money from the overseers by taking care of the sick poor, such as the widow Ann Newson in 1646 and again in 1651.

BROWNING, Captain: (no vital information). In 1645, the parish paid him for the colours of the town soldiers.

BRUNDISH, James: (no vital information). In 1655–7 he collected relief from the churchwardens when ill. He had no children baptised in the parish, but he had at least one son, who was apprenticed to Robert Hayward in 1660.

BUCKER or BICKER, Nick, ?plumber: (no baptismal information; married Margaret, n.d.; no burial information). He was paid by the churchwardens for twenty-three pounds of solder and four days work in 1656, and for more work in 1659. He was never assessed for the poor rate.

BUTCHER, Elizabeth: (no baptismal information, maiden name Sterrer; married Hugh, 17 September 1596; no burial information). She collected a weekly pension and miscellaneous relief from the churchwardens. No children were baptised in the parish.

CADY, Samuel: (baptised 23 January 1596; married Elizabeth c.1618; buried 6 December 1678). A man who suffered fluctuating fortunes. He first appears in parish records in 1629 when the churchwardens provided £2 to pay his debts. In 1632 the parish provided a new suit of clothes for his son. Samuel collected miscellaneous relief nearly every year thereafter. However, he and others were paid 'for ther charges concerning the Perlements cause', and in 1644 he served in the town's arms. By 1652 his income had risen for he was assessed at 1s.2d. a month for the poor rate. Samuel continued paying the rate until 1669, when sickness again drove him onto the relief rolls where he remained until his death. He had six children: Ann, Margaret, Thomas, William, Bridget and John.

CADY, Sarah or Sarye: (baptised 22 August 1594; no marriage or burial information). Unmarried daughter of John Cady and Margaret Baile, she collected miscellaneous and regular relief from 1639 to 1650, at which point she dropped from the record.

CAMPE, Goodman: (no vital information). Constable in 1651. He was not assessed for the poor rate.

CARSY, Edward, yeoman: (baptised 21 December 1608; married Maud c.1631; buried 11 October 1675). Edward was first assessed for the rate in 1643 at 4d. a month. He continued to be assessed until 1675 at 5d. a month. In 1670 he contributed 6d. for the redemption of Christian slaves (see p. 128). He had four children: Alice, James, John and Sarah.

CARSY, William: (no vital information). Constable in 1656. He rented Benslins Farm in 1652–8. He also received £3 in 1655 'by the order of the towne in regard of cheapness of cheese and butter'. He was assessed for the poor rate between 1656 and 1660 at 6d. a month. In 1657 and 1658, he was given money to pay his assessment.

CARTER, Robert: (no vital information). The Carters are an old Cratfield family.

CLARKE, Brian, tailor: (baptised 8 April 1632; married Mary Bootan, 25 September 1654; buried 28 December 1702). He was assessed for the poor rate in 1658 at 4d. a month, and again in 1660 at 6d. a month. His son's death was of a questionable nature, and a coroner's inquest was held in 1699. He had one child, Brian.

CLARKE or CLERKE, John: (baptised 18 January 1628; married Mary Peirce, 4 October 1664; buried 22 June 1676). John was one of the poor children educated at the expense of the parish in 1637–8. He served as a soldier in 1643. John also did odd jobs about the parish, such as cutting wood for the poor in 1650. He received miscellaneous relief from the overseers from 1670 to 1676. He had four children: Brian, Henry, John and Mary.

CLARK, Master, physician: (no vital information).

CLAYDON, Samuel: (no vital information). Constable in 1656. He was assessed for the poor rate at 3d. a month in 1655–6.

CLIFFORD or CLIFAR, Master: (no vital information). School teacher 1654–9. Among his pupils were four poor boys whose fees were provided by the parish. In 1656–7 he received miscellaneous relief from the churchwardens. It may be his son Edward who served as vicar at the end of the seventeenth century.

COALE, George: (no vital information). He was paid by the parish in 1657 for stone, and again in 1659. He was assessed for the poor rate at 1s.6d. a month in 1658 and at 2s. in 1659. He had one child baptised in the parish, George.

COOK, John, esquire: (no vital information). Presumably he was the son of Sir Robert. John collected the rent for Rose Lark's in 1656.

COOK, Sir Robert: (no vital information). High constable of the hundred of Blything.

COOPER, William: (baptised c.1619; married Margaret Alde, 19 January 1636; no burial information). Constable in 1643. His mare was used by the town soldiers in 1644. He was assessed for the poor rate once in 1644 at 8d. a month. He had four children: George, Margaret, William and John.

COX, ———, shoemaker: (no baptismal or marriage information; buried 12 May 1653). This is probably Robert, son of the Robert Cox who was also a shoemaker. In 1640, Cox was paid for making two pairs of shoes for the town's soldiers.

CRANE, Geoffrey: (no vital information). Constable in 1660.

CRANE, Samuel: (no baptismal information; married Elizabeth c.1660; married Mary Parker, 21 January 1666; no burial information). The churchwardens purchased three loads of stone from Samuel in 1657. He was assessed for the poor rate at roughly 1s. a month between 1662 and 1664, and once again in 1674 at 7d. a month. He had two children by Elizabeth, Ann and James; he had one child by Mary, Beata.

CROSBY, Master [Thomas]: (died 1658). A preacher who gave the town lecture in 1642, 1644 and 1646–7. Educated at Christ's College, Cambridge 1613–18, licensed to preach at Huntingfield 1618,; vicar of Laxfield 1645.

CROSS, John: (baptised 16 December 1632; no marriage or burial information). John followed his father (William) as clock-keeper, general mechanic and iron-worker. He was never assessed for the poor rate.

CROSS, Mary: (baptised c.1596; married William c.1622; buried 23 December 1666). She had three children: Francis, John and Mary.

CROSS, William: (baptised c.1595; married Mary c.1622; buried 17 May 1668). Clock-keeper, general mechanic and iron-worker. Blind by 1656, William still continued to keep the clock. He received miscellaneous poor relief after losing his sight. By 1660 the parish paid his rent annually. He had three children: Francis, John and Mary.

DALLEN, ———: (no vital information). He worked on the church bells in 1651.

DEALLINGE, Henry: (no vital information). He mended the bell-stop in 1641.

DOUGHTY, Hammond: (no vital information). Bailiff for Rose Larkes, 1649–57.

DOWSING, Robert: (no vital information). Constable in 1653–4. He was probably related to the Dowsing family of Laxfield and thus to William Dowsing the iconoclast.

EBBES, John: (baptised *c.*1628; married Mary Harrison, 29 September 1655; buried 4 April 1657). Surveyor in 1654. He first paid the poor rate in 1646 at 8d. a month, and did so at roughly the same level until his death in 1657. He had four children: Elizabeth, John, Mary and Sarah.

EDGER, John: a religious refugee from Germany, given relief by Cratfield in 1652–3.

ELAND, Gabriel, minister: (baptised 24 December 1568; married Elizabeth *c.*1602; buried 16 August 1652). Matriculated Pembroke College, Cambridge 1585. Vicar of Cratfield 1602–52. His father, Francis, had been vicar before him in 1566–1602. Gabriel's religious leanings were radical, resisting Laudian reforms, but legally conforming. He was a dynamic force within the parish, actively promoting the use of wills. He was also responsible for most of the marginal notes (written in English, Latin and Greek) in the parish register. He had three children: Damaris, Elihema and Eunke.

ELLIS, William, yeoman: (baptised *c.*1615; married Penelope Mille, 11 October 1642; married Dorothy n.d.; buried 23 August 1667). His first wife was buried 23 October 1648. He served as a town soldier in 1654–5. Between 1657 and 1660, he was paid by the parish to board Henry Mills, the son of Samuel. Henry Mills was the lame 'town boy' that William also boarded in 1656 and 1657. William also performed a number of jobs throughout the parish. In 1662, he is first assessed at 3s. a month for the poor rate, which he paid in ever-decreasing sums until his death. Ann may have been one of the four children educated at the expense of the parish. He had two children by Penelope: Ann and a still-born child.

FILBY or FYBY, John: (no vital information). A chief inhabitant in 1657. He was not assessed for the poor rate.

FISKE, John, junior: (baptised *c.*1611; married Francis *c.*1638; buried 29 December 1667). Constable in 1644 and 1652. He was assessed at £1 9s. 3d. for Ship Money in 1640. He was first assessed for the poor rate in 1644 at 8d. a month. His assessment varied widely over the course of his life, with a final payment in 1666 of 6d. a month. He was the cousin of William Fiske. He had one child, Francis.

FISKE, John, senior: (baptised 22 February 1606; married Elizabeth Day, 30 March 1631; buried 21 January 1675). A chief inhabitant in 1656, 1659–60 and 1664. Churchwarden in 1632–3, 1648–9, 1657–8 and 1671. He was assessed at three hearths in 1674. John rented a meadow from the town in 1642. By 1643, he was assessed at 4d. a month for the poor rate. His local worth grew over time, with a peak assessment of 2s.2d. in 1665–6. In 1670 he pledged 6d. for the redemption of Christian slaves (see p. 128). His final poor rate assessment was in 1672, three years before his death, at 1s.6d. a month. In the same year he served as Master of the Town Arms. He had three children: John, William and Elizabeth.

FISKE, William, senior: (baptised 17 August 1609; married Mary *c.*1633; buried *c.*1652). Overseer in 1648–50. Churchwarden in 1639, 1646 and 1652, at which point he was identified as a gentlemen. Paid to make the rate in 1644 and 1646, he also made the rate 'for the 5 garrisons'. He was assessed for the poor rate between 1643 and his death in 1652. He was the cousin of John Fiske. He had six children: Elizabeth, Francis, Margaret, Tobias, William and Ann.

FISKE, William, junior: (baptised 22 December 1635; never married; will dated 24 April 1673). Churchwarden in 1654–5. A chief inhabitant in 1656. He probably had no children, as he left his estate to his nephew, John Borrett, on the condition that his servant, Elizabeth Stobard, receive £10 a year.

FRIER, James: (baptised 18 August 1588; never married; buried 19 April 1659). He was the son of William and Alice Frier. Churchwarden in 1648. Paid to make up the rate in 1644. There is no record of his having been assessed for the poor rate.

GANT, Thomas: (baptised c.1615; married Susan, c.1642; buried 31 March 1686). He first appeared in the parish records in 1653, cutting wood for the poor. In 1657, he was paid to teach the four poor children of the parish. He collected miscellaneous assistance, including money to look after his mother, until the last year of his life when he collected a pension of 1s. a week. His son, Henry, was one of the four poor boys educated at the parish's expense. He had two children, Henry and Susan.

GLEMHAM, Colonel Sir Thomas: (no vital information). He was the leader of Charles I's 4th Regiment. Governor of York, surrendered 16 July 1644; governor of Carlisle, surrendered 28 June 1645; governor of Oxford, surrendered 20 June 1646. He was sentenced to the Fleet Prison by Parliament, and he died in Holland prior to the Restoration.

GOODING, Master: (no vital information). Constable in 1649. He was assessed for the rate in 1650 at 2s. a month.

GODBALL or GORBALD, John: (no vital information). Churchwarden in 1650. He was rated in 1650–1 at 8d. a month.

GOLDSMITH, John, gent: (baptised c.1603; married Elizabeth c.1630; buried 15 September 1683). Overseer in 1639–40. Churchwarden in 1667–8. A chief inhabitant 1670–7. He was assessed at six hearths in 1674. In 1667 his poor rate assessment was 2s.2d. a month, rising in 1678 to 3s.4d., where it remained until his death. In 1670 he contributed 5s. towards the redemption of Christian slaves (see p. 128). He had two children, Elizabeth and John.

GOOCH, John: (baptised c.1590; married Ann Gadd, 1 October 1618; no burial information). In 1650 John was paid by the town for a warrant.

GOSSE, John: (no vital information). In 1659, the churchwardens paid Frances Aldus' rent to John. He was assessed for the poor rate between 1657 and 1677 at between 2d. and 6d. a month.

GOWN or GOWINGE, Jeremy: (no baptism information; married c.1655; no burial information). Constable in 1657 and 1660. He was rated in 1657 at 4d. a month. He had two children, Jeremiah and Ann.

GRENE, Robert: (baptised 22 November 1590; married, but not in the parish; no burial information). In 1643 the parish gave 6d. to Robert, his wife and children.

GRIMSTON, Mother: (no vital information; widow in 1640). She took care of a number of local people, for example 'healing Stannard's son' in 1640–1 and helping Joseph Smith when he was in need in 1649–50.

HARCOCK, Giles: (no vital information). He sold two new ropes to the parish in 1656.

HARTLEY, John: (baptised 24 February 1596; married Margaret Stips, 8 December 1628; buried 18 September 1665). John was chronically ill in the early 1640s, which forced him to collect miscellaneous relief from the parish. In 1643 occasional assistance was supplemented by a regular dole of 4d. a week, rising to 1s. a week in 1652.

In the early 1660s, as John entered old age, payments to ease his burdens were resumed. By the final year of his life, John was collecting 8s. a month from the overseers, in addition to 6s. to cover the costs of his illness. He had one child, Elizabeth.

HAYWARD, Amy or Ann: (no baptismal information, maiden name Rowwer; married John, 4 June 1607; buried 9 January 1653). Widowed in 1625, and was rated at 8s. a month in 1626. Also immediately upon widowhood, she began to receive regular relief from the parish at 8s. a month, probably because she had five young children. Her pension gradually decreased as her children grew up, and finally ceased altogether in 1645. She had five children: Rose, Samuel, Thomas, Robert and Michael.

HAYWARD, Margaret: (no vital information). Widowed in 1659. She assumed her husband's rental of the town pightle in 1658–9. She was assessed for the poor rate only once, in 1660 at 8d. a month. She had four children: Alice, Margaret, Samuel (who died at one month) and Samuel.

HAYWARD, Robert: (baptised 27 July 1617; married Mary c.1654; buried 27 July 1695). He took James Brundish's son as his apprentice in 1660. However, Robert struggled with poverty for the rest of his life, accepting both a regular parish pension and miscellaneous relief. He had one child, Thomas.

HAYWARD, Samuel, cordwainer: (baptised 8 January 1620; married Margaret c.1643; buried 8 June 1659). Rented land, including the schoolhouse and the town pightle, from the town in the 1640s and 1650s. In 1648 Samuel built the new floor in the school house. In the 1650s, he was reimbursed regularly for money spent on behalf of the town. His will directed his executrix, his wife Margaret, 'to have a speciall care for the bringing up of my children'. He had four children: Alice, Margaret, Samuel (who died at one month) and Samuel.

HEARCLES, John: (no vital information). He and his wife received a combination of miscellaneous and regular relief between 1643 and 1667.

HOVELL or HOWELL, John: (no vital information). The Howell family were from nearby Metfield. In 1639–41 he was heavily involved with major repairs to the bell-frame and tower of Cratfield church.

HUDSON, Samuel: (no vital information). Rented the town land of Rose Larks in 1639–40.

HUNT, Luke: (no vital information). Paid by the churchwardens for five hoop staves in 1655.

JEFFERY, Master [Devereux], minister of religion: preached in Cratfield in 1652–3. Devereux Jeffray was educated at Christ's College, Cambridge; curate of Sotherton; vicar of Blyford and Wenhaston, 1650.

JOHNSON, Ann: (baptised c.1628; married Thomas c.1654; buried 27 July 1694). Widowed in 1688. She earned extra money from the parish, in 1650 for example when she nursed a poor child. After her husband's death she collected a weekly pension of 2s. a week, which continued until her death. She had no children.

JOHNSON, Thomas, senior: (baptised c.1580; married Elizabeth c.1607; buried 2 July 1662). He received miscellaneous relief throughout his adult life, beginning in 1613, probably as a result of having a large family. He had eight children: Elizabeth, Thomas, Ann, Gregory, James, Margaret, Mary and William.

JOHNSON, Thomas, junior: (baptised c.1627; married Ann c.1654; buried 22 January 1688). Engaged as a soldier during the Civil War, he was sent to Yoxford in 1642, 1643 and 1644, to Yarmouth in 1651, and to Blyburgh in 1659. Due to poverty his single hearth was exempted from tax in 1674. He collected miscellaneous relief for his entire adult life, but never a weekly pension. Thomas was an excellent example of the marginally poor. He had no children.

KEMPE, Nicolas: (no vital information). Surveyor in 1654. His servant, Mary Bacon, died in 1656. He was assessed for the poor rate between 1650 and 1663 at between 6d. and 1s. a month. The Kempes are an old Cratfield family.

KEMPE, Thomas: (no vital information). In 1639–40 he paid a fee to have his case dismissed from an ecclesiastical court.

KEABEL or KOABLE, Robert, junior: (baptised 3 August 1587; married Ann c.1607; no burial information). Overseer in 1626, 1632 and 1638. Churchwarden in 1631. He was assessed for the poor rate at 4d. a month nearly every year between 1626 and 1646, at which point he disappeared from the record. Trained as one of the town's soldiers in 1644, he served as an auxiliary in 1645–6. He had two children, Robert and William.

KEAMAR, Thomas: (no vital information). He rented land from the town in 1649–50.

LANEY, Benjamin: son of John Laney who was recorder of Ipswich and patron of Cratfield (qv); was educated at Ipswich School under James Leman, a noted conservative who had a long battle with the radical preacher, Samuel Ward. A high churchman, Benjamin became Master of Pembroke Hall, Cambridge (1640–4), chaplain to Charles II in exile, and after the Restoration successively bishop of Peterborough (1660–3), of Lincoln (1663–8) and of Ely (1668–75). While at Cambridge, he was involved in vigorous controversy with the iconoclast William Dowsing, a native of Laxfield and holder of land in Cratfield. As a bishop, Laney always treated nonconformists leniently, a fact which may be connected with his own family's mixed allegiances. (See *DNB*)

LANEY, John: (no vital information). The Laneys were originally gentlemen from London who entered Cratfield through marriage. Grandson of the first Laney at Cratfield, John was the recorder of Ipswich, counsellor at law, and a JP for forty-eight years. He died in 1663 at the age of eighty-one. His wife, grand-daughter of Lord Thomas Wentworth, died in the same year at eighty-six. His monument is in St Margaret's church, Ipswich. His eldest son, John, succeeded him as both a counsellor and recorder of Ipswich, while his youngest son, Benjamin, was a distinguished academic and divine (qv).

LAWNE, ———, knacker: (no vital information).

LEGGITT, Thomas: (baptised 1604; married Priscilla c.1636; no burial information). Constable in 1642; he had the charge of the three town soldiers when they were at Ipswich. He was assessed for the poor rate in 1643–4 at 8d. a month.

LOWE, John: (baptised c.1617; married Ann Dew, 23 October 1645; no burial information). He was assessed for the poor rate between 1650 and 1657 at roughly 4d. a month. He had three children: Ann, Mary and another daughter.

LUDBROKE, Samuel: (baptised c.1626; married Temperance c.1653; buried 20 June 1659). Constable: in 1655. He worked at odd jobs around the parish. Samuel was assessed for the poor rate between 1652 and 1659 at between 6d. and 9d. a month. He had three children: Temperance, Richard, and Robert who died as a child.

LUDBROKE, Temperance: (no baptismal information; married Samuel c.1653; no burial information). Widowed in 1659. In 1659 Temperance collected wood from John Thirton, and in 1660 she collected 1s. a month in poor relief. She had three children: Temperance, Richard, and Robert who died as a child.

MEENE, Henry: (baptised *c*.1602; married Mary Warner, 7 December 1630; no burial information). He was identified as a gentleman in the marriage register. His wife's former husband was also identified as a gentleman in the same document. He was one of the most substantial rate payers in the 1650s. He had one child, Robert.

MEENE, Robert: (baptised 21 February 1631; no marriage or burial information). Churchwarden in 1659. Robert was first assessed for the poor rate in 1658 at 3s.6d. a month, and continued as a substantial rate-payer throughout his life. The last recorded assessment was for 1699 when he contributed 9s.6d. a month.

MILLES, Anne: (baptised *c*.1576, maiden name, Gowinge; married Robert, 16 November 1602; buried 30 March 1670). She was in gaol in 1660. She had eight children: John, Robert, Susanna, William, Grace, Mary, Ann and Sarah.

MILLES or MILES, Edmund: (baptised *c*.1571; married to Rose *c*.1598; buried 24 December 1654). The parish register records: 'Edmond Milles was buried the four and twenty day of December Anno Domini 1654. He was a very old man, well on to five score yeares of age'. He was poor, and received his first formal relief from the parish in 1605. By 1640, the parish was paying his rent on a steady basis. In 1649 he collected a parish pension at 2s. a month, rising to 4s. in 1651, and to 6s. in 1654 when he died. On numerous occasions he received miscellaneous relief in the form of cash and rent rebates, particularly when illness struck him or his family. He had three children: Samuel, Ann and Penelope.

MILLES, Edmund, knacker: (baptised 5 January 1633; no marriage or burial information). Apprenticed in 1647. He served as a town soldier in 1659. He was the son of James and Joane Milles.

MILLES, Frances: (no baptism information; married John, 1 November 1608; no burial information). She collected miscellaneous relief from the churchwardens starting in the mid-1650s. She had four children: Gregory, Frances, Henry and Richard.

MILLES, Henry: (no vital information). Raised at the expense of the town by William Ellis, Henry was apprenticed to Michael Barfot of Halesworth in 1660.

MILLES, James: (baptised 17 October 1587; married Mary Peirce, 5 June 1617; buried 13 March 1643). In 1631 he received assistance from the parish for his son, Samuel, in the form of '2 yeards of cloath & skines' worth 8s.4d. At the age of 47 he collected his first known relief because of illness, a process which was repeated in 1638, 1639 and 1643, the year of his death. He had four children: Susan, Mary, John and James.

MILLES, John: (baptised 4 October 1604; married Elizabeth, 28 January 1634; no burial information). Widowed in November 1658. Constable in 1639, 1641 and 1652. He was paid to make up the rate in 1644. He had three children: Elizabeth, Susan and John.

MILLES, Margaret, widow: (no vital information). She was in debt to the town in 1660.

MILLES, Mary: (baptised *c*.1589; married James, 5 June 1617; no burial information). Her husband collected 18s. in 1643, but died in March 'in the time of sicknes and distresse'. She had four children: Susan, Mary, John and James.

ROBERT MILLES, Robert, carter: (baptised 4 March 1570; married Ann Gowinge, 16 November 1602; buried 2 August 1659). Overseer in 1625. Assessed at 6s.9d. for the Ship Money in 1640, and for the poor rate at roughly 1d. a week from 1626–59. He had eight children: John, Robert, Susanna, William, Grace, Mary, Ann and Sarah.

MILLS or MELES, Samuel: (baptised 25 June 1603; married Joanne Mingie, 3 October 1626; buried 31 December 1656). Samuel was 'over burdened by his children' and was relieved by the parish. In 1651 one of his sons was apprenticed to Robert Adams. In 1654, Samuel's wife became ill and died, and his daughter had to undergo surgery on a leg. In the same year he defaulted on his mortgage with William Fiske, senior, and the parish paid to support him in his house. One of his sons was given 4s. the day Samuel died. He had five, possibly six, children: Mary, Robert, William, Edmund, Henry and Samuel.

MINGAY or MYNGGYE, William, tailor: (baptised c.1600; married Susan c.1627; married Rose c.1649; buried 16 August 1670). He trained as a soldier for the town in 1645. The parish paid for the apprenticeship of one of his sons in 1656. In 1657–9 he provided the dinner of the eleven men who drew up the parish accounts. He had three children by Susan: Matthew, Susan and Elizabeth; and one child by Rose, William.

MONCK, General George: (died 3 January 1670). Commander of the king's army in Ireland, he was taken prisoner in 1644, and spent two years in the Tower of London. Released after negotiation with Parliament, took both the negative oath and the covenant, and from 1646 served Parliament and Cromwell as commander of land and naval forces. After Cromwell's death, Monck navigated the murky political waters of the interregnum with prudence and finesse. His military prowess and ability to broker agreements between many quarreling factions in Ireland and Scotland, guaranteed him a position of power which he used to secure the Restoration. Thereafter, Charles II made him Earl of Albermarle and he served as commander in the Dutch War.

MORE, Nicholas: (baptised c.1610; married Ann Smith, 23 May 1637; buried 10 July 1686). Sickness struck Nicholas' family in 1652 and permanently relegated them to the ranks of the marginally poor. He received miscellaneous relief in the form of cash and wood annually until his death. Only during his last year did he collect a regular pension of 4s. a month. Nicholas was listed as having one hearth in 1674. He was considered one of the 'worthy' poor, as shown by repeated references to 'Goodman More' in the parish records. He had four children: James, Nicholas, William and Elizabeth.

MOULLING, Master, physician: (no vital information).

MYNNE, Robert: (no vital information). Churchwarden in 1658. Overseer in 1660–1. A chief inhabitant in 1656–7. His son, Robert, lived in the parish and was identified as a gentleman. Between father and son, they were assessed for the poor rate virtually every year between 1658 and 1699 at amounts that ranged between 5s.8d. to 9s. a month.

NELSON, Master: (no vital information). He was involved with Ann Milles' release from gaol in 1660.

NEWSON, Ann: (baptised c.1567; married Henry c.1593; buried 16 August 1652). Widowed in 1637. The next year she became a regular parish pensioner at 4s. a month. Illness struck her particularly hard in 1651, and the churchwardens provided nursing and additional cash until her death in 1652. She had four children: Elizabeth, Henry, John and Robert.

NEWSON, John, senior: (baptised c.1580; married Grace c.1607; buried 14 October 1655). Constable in 1644–5. Churchwarden in 1622–3, 1639, 1646 and 1650–1. Overseer in 1630–1 and 1638. He was a rate payer from 1625 until his death in 1655 at amounts ranging between 1s. and 1s. 4d. a month. John loaned money to the parish, the interest of which was recorded by the churchwardens in 1641. Another loan was made sometime before 1659–60, when £5 was returned to him by a churchwarden.

NEWSON, John, junior: (baptised 30 November 1626; married Elizabeth c.1641; no burial information). Churchwarden in 1647 and 1660–1. Overseer in 1654–5, 1662–3 and 1686. A chief inhabitant in 1656–7. He was a rate payer from 1643 until 1686 at approximately 1s.4d. a month. He had six children: Elizabeth, Margaret, Robert, Sarah, William and John.

NEWSON, Samuel: (baptised 30 September 1610; married Ann Smith, 22 July 1638; no burial information). In 1639–40 the parish bought straw from him when repairing the town hall and other properties. He had two children baptised in Cratfield, Ann and Elizabeth.

NEWSON, William: (no baptismal information; married Audry Barret, 30 August, 1632; no burial information). The parish paid his rent in 1642. He was a soldier for the town in 1644. William was assessed for the poor rate between 1642 and 1646 at approximately 8d. a month. He had one child, Mary.

NEWSON, William senior: (baptised 18 April 1613; married Mary c.1641; no burial information). He provided arms for the town in 1644. He had two children, Elizabeth and William.

PACY, Robert: (baptised c.1607; married Catherine Worlich, 25 April 1637; married Rose, n.d.; no burial information). He was a soldier for the town, and a poor man. His wife collected a weekly pension while he was a soldier. The couple received a great deal of miscellaneous relief and they did odd jobs in the parish. Robert collected a pension in 1652, but thereafter it was directed to his wife at 2s. a month. They had four children: Ann, Francis, Margaret and Mary.

PACY, Rose: (no baptismal information; married Robert, n.d.; buried 28 November 1677). She collected assistance from the parish, including a regular pension of 4s. a month, while her husband Robert was serving as a soldier in 1659. She continued to collect this amount until her death in 1677.

PARKES, Robert: (no vital information). Bailiff of Blything hundred.

PEARSE, Widow: either Christian, the wife of Matthew Peirce, or Ann, the wife of Edward. Two children were born to each couple, but no one from either nuclear family was buried in the parish. The children of Matthew and Christian were Mary and Matthew; the children of Ann and Edward were Edward and John.

POE, Captain William: was one of the most notoriously corrupt captains in the Eastern Association, requisitioning supplies (especially horses) at whim. He led Parliamentary troops during the siege of King's Lynn.

POWERS or POWIS, Richard: (no vital information; married to Lettis). In 1639–40, when the parish bought a new surplice, Richard was paid to bring it. He had two children baptised in the parish, Richard and Lettis.

PULHAM, Master: (no vital information). He was paid by the churchwardens to draw up a new feoffment in 1655.

RACKHAM, Raynold, carpenter: (no baptismal or marriage information; buried 7 April 1659). He was employed periodically by the parish, as in 1653 when he mended 'the windowes and threshould at Besnales'. He was assessed for the poor rate in 1652–3 at roughly 1s. a month, and at 2s. in 1657–8.

RAYDON, Richard: (baptised 22 June 1626; married Elizabeth Richardson, 1 February 1648; no burial information). In 1645 he made up the rate to assist another community, and in the same year he assessed the town on behalf of the 'British armye'. He rented the town meadow in 1646. In 1651 he provided the parish with 'wood and rayels and a calves cribe'. He was assessed for the poor rate between 1626 and 1630 at 1s.8d. a month, and between 1543 and 1650 at 8d. a month. He had six children: Elizabeth, Mary, Richard, Robert, Robert and William.

RAYNAR or RAYNER, Robert: (baptised c.1621; married, Elizabeth c.1648; no burial information). Constable in 1653. Widowed in 1662. Robert also provided services on behalf of the village. He was assessed for the poor rate between 1651 and 1662 at a rate between 1s.1d. and 3s. a month. He had six children: Elizabeth, John, Benjamin, Grace, Mary and Edmund.

RICHARDSON, Henry: (baptised 30 July 1592; married Joan c.1621; died in Linstead Magna and buried in Cratfield on 7 July 1655). Overseer in 1625. He first appeared in the record with a poor tax assessment of 2s. a week. He continued to pay the rate until his death, with a final assessment of 1s.6d. a month. He had four children: Alice, Ann, Elizabeth and Henry.

ROOFFE, Master, physician: (no vital information).

ROUSE, Frances: (baptised c.1597; married Gregory c.1623; buried 15 May 1675). Widowed in 1639. Her husband was constable in 1625; churchwarden in 1628–9. She was assessed at £1 3s.6d. in 1640 for the Ship Money. Frances rented Rose Larks and Sallow Pightle from the town at £45 a year. In 1641 the churchwardens 'doe appoynt that Frances Rouse, widow, shall leave Sallowe Pichtels to the nex fearmer'. She became a rate payer in 1643, at 8d. per month, and continued to be assessed until 1664, at which point she paid 10d. a month. Widow Rouse appeared in the record only once between 1664 and her death. In 1670 she contributed 6d. for the redemption of Christian slaves (see p. 128). She had four children: John, Prudence, Robert and Ann.

ROUSE, Gregory, senior: (baptised c.1615; married Ann Alde, 23 August 1642; buried 30 August 1690). Churchwarden in 1689–90. A chief inhabitant in 1680–88. Gregory was assessed for the poor rate at 8d. a month between 1644 and 1646. He was paid to assess the rate in 1645. He had two children, William and an unnamed daughter.

ROUSE, John, gent: (baptised 1 January 1598; married Margaret c.1628; buried 22 May 1671). Churchwarden in 1640–1, 1652–3 and 1660–1. A chief inhabitant in 1656–7. As a young man he served as clerk, and was paid for 'takynge the acownte for the poore' in 1617. He began paying the poor rate in 1626 at 2d. a week. John was the cousin of William Aldus, churchwarden in 1642, and John Williams, churchwarden in 1644. He again made up the poor rate in 1645. In 1670, he pledged 7s. for the redemption of Christian slaves (see p. 128). During the year of his death, he was rated at 2s. a month. He had three children: William, Margaret and Ann.

ROUSE, William: (baptised 29 January 1636; no marriage or burial information). He was paid to make up the rate for the relief of Ireland in 1646. There is no evidence that he was assessed for the poor rate.

ROYDEN, Richard: (no baptismal information; married Elizabeth, n.d.; no burial information). He had six children: Elizabeth, Mary, Richard, Robert, Robert and William.

SAWARD, Widow: (no vital information). A poor widow with children. She collected assistance from the parish in 1649.

SKEEKE or SKEET, Thomas: (baptised c.1613; married Margary Else, 8 March 1640; no burial information). Surveyor in 1659. Thomas was employed by the churchwardens in 1654; in 1657 they purchased stone from him. Thomas was assessed for the poor rate between 1652 and 1693 at an ever increasing amount, beginning in 6d. and ending at 1s.4d. a month. He had no known children.

SMITH, Abre: (no baptismal information; married James c.1607; buried 21 November 1654). Widowed in 1647, the parish paid part of her rent that year. She also began collecting a weekly pension at this time. Starting at 3d. a week, her pension grew steadily until her death. She had five children: Ann, Elizabeth, Mary, Henry and John.

SMITH, Elizabeth: (baptised *c*.1625; married Finis *c*.1651; buried 9 December 1681). She contributed to her household economy by doing odd jobs in the parish. She had two children, Finis and William.

SMITH, Gregory, yeoman: (baptised 1 December 1588; married Jane Helwis, 20 May 1614; buried 6 March 1643). Churchwarden in 1618–19 and 1635. Overseer in 1631. Assessed for the poor rate in 1625–6, and 1629, at 5d. a week. His children are not recorded, but grandchildren are mentioned in his will.

SMITH, James, thatcher: (baptised *c*.1580; married to Abre *c*.1607; buried 19 February 1647). In 1621 illness forced him to accept assistance from the parish annually until 1625. In 1635 illness once more pushed him into relief, and again in the early 1640s. In 1644, James became a regular parish pensioner, at 1s. a month, until his death. He had five children: Ann, Elizabeth, Mary, Henry and John.

SMYTH, John, esquire, described as 'of Norward' or 'of Northwood': (baptised *c*.1615; married Penelope, 22 August 1652; buried 19 September 1664). Identified as a gentleman at his death. Churchwarden in 1645–?6. A chief inhabitant in 1656–7 and 1660–3. He had three children: Mary, Lidea and Penelope.

SMITH, John: (no baptismal information; married Alice *c*.1643; no burial information). A soldier for the town in 1642. He had three children: Margaret, Alice and Mary.

SMITH, Joseph: (baptised 14 July 1588; married *c*.1616; buried 15 November 1659). Joseph began collecting miscellaneous relief in 1625 when ill. He and his wife continued to be sickly until the early 1650s. At this point, he must have come into money because he was able to repay a loan from the parish. Furthermore he lent money to the churchwardens in 1652, which they repaid in 1653. But by the following year, Joseph was again in receipt of parish relief, which continued until his death in 1659. He had three children: Phineas, Sarah and Prudence.

SMITH, Phinelias or Finis, tailor: (3 March 1617; married Elizabeth, 3 December 1651; buried 19 April 1680). Beginning in 1652 and continuing until his death, he collected miscellaneous relief and did odd jobs for the parish. One of his sons may have been among the four poor children educated at the expense of the parish. He had two children, Finis and William.

SMITH, Robert, junior, described as 'in the Close' or 'de Colltshawe' or 'de Coushall': (no baptismal information; married to Finet in August 1629; buried 20 January 1662). Constable in 1642. Collector's deputy in 1641. Churchwarden in 1641, 1649–51 and 1656–7. A chief inhabitant in 1656–7. He had one child, Margaret.

SMITH, Robert, senior, glazier: (baptised *c*.1586; married Alice *c*.1614; buried 1 March 1651). Churchwarden in 1620s and 1643–4. Overseer in 1620s and 1642–3. He was assessed at £1 10s.6d. in 1640 for Ship Money. He paid the poor rate between 1625 and 1650 at approximately 1s. a month. In 1645 a child was baptised in his house and not in church. Robert also kept the church windows in repair. He had four children: Ann, Margery, Robert and John.

SMITH, Sir Thurston: (no baptismal information; married Willybe, n.d.; will written 20 July 1647, burial not recorded in the parish). He was the brother of John Smyth, gent. and Thomas Smith, gent. At some date his goods were seized. His will recorded: 'that all those goods that Capteyn Robert Nollson by his pretented warrant took away from me' are to be returned as a result of John Smith's legal action. His will requested that what he had 'writt and composed wither in prose or meter be colected, digasted into forme and impretted and published to the world in my name', but nothing was published. He had no known children.

SPATCHET, Robert: (no vital information). Probably the son of Thomas. Robert became collector for Maimed Soldiers and Marshalseas in 1659.

SPATCHET, Thomas: (no vital information). A preacher from the neighbouring parish of Cookley. He was possessed by a witch, and suffered a large number of fits which were witnessed by Samuel Petto. Petto became 'minister of the Gospel' at Sudbury, Suffolk, where he published Spatchet's story in *A Faithful Narrative of the Wonderful and Extraordinary Fits which Mr Tho. Spatchet (Late of Dunwich and Cookly) was under by Witchcraft. . .* (London, 1693). The trips to Beccles and Halesworth undertaken by Cratfield's townsmen were presumably to attest to the truth of Spatchet's claims. Thomas was also a regular collector for Maimed Soldiers and Marshalseas.

SPINK, Ann: (baptised *c.*1561, maiden name Swain; married 27 May 1588; buried 10 April 1641). Widowed in 1608, Ann is a regular parish pensioner by 1625 at 2s. a month. At the time of her pauper's burial in 1641, she was collecting 3s.4d. a month from the overseers. She had three children: Bridget, Elizabeth and Ann.

SPINK, Bridget: (baptised 8 April 1589; never married; buried 30 August 1658). Despite an impoverished childhood, she lived successfully by makeshift. She called upon the parish for relief only twice in her sixty-nine years: in 1656 and 1658.

STANNARD, Elizabeth: (baptised *c.*1616; married Richard *c.*1642; buried 27 February 1675). Elizabeth was widowed in 1645, having one child nearly two years old and the other an infant. As a widow with small children she was constantly plagued by poverty, and had to be relieved by the parish. For example, in 1645 Elizabeth was given £1 4s. 8d. 'for her releife in the tyme of her great want and extreame nesessety'. Thereafter, she received assistance 'for ye releife of her poore chilldren'. The town occasionally paid her rent and bought firewood for her. In turn, she worked for the parish by providing beer 'when the townsmen met to take the surveyors accoumpts', as in 1656, or by washing the vicar's surplice. Elizabeth Stannard managed to survive on the edge of poverty until 1672, when at age of 56 she began to collect regular relief from the overseers. She received 2s. a month, in addition to miscellaneous relief, until she died. She had two children, Elizabeth and Richard.

STANNARD, John, senior, sometimes described as 'of Laxfield': (baptised 28 December 1589; married Elizabeth *c.*1616; buried 12 February 1669). John and Elizabeth were amongst the poor relieved by the parish in 1634 when a virulent illness was raging. He and his wife were frequently employed by the parish to perform odd jobs. For example in 1642 John collected bread and wine for the Christmas communion, and Elizabeth nursed Mary Tallant during her illness. In 1653 John was sent to collect the 'woman taken with the hue and crye upon susspition to be the woman that left hir child in our towne'. By 1656 'Ould Stannard' lived with 'the pore folckes at the gild hall'. He continued to receive cash sporadically from the parish until 1666 when he became a regular pensioner at 2s. a month. He died after a long illness during which he collected 6s. a month from the overseers. He had four children: John, Richard, William and Margaret.

STANNARD, Joseph, senior: (no vital information). He received money from the churchwardens in 1659.

STEBBING, John: (no vital information). He signed the overseers' accounts in 1675–7.

TABRE, ———: (no vital information). He was paid by the churchwardens in 1656–7 for cutting and delivering wood for the poor.

TALLANT or TALLOWINGE, Mary: (baptised *c.*1597, maiden name Cob; married Ruben, 5 June 1624; buried 5 September 1669). Mary collected a weekly pension which was continued after the death of her husband. She had five children: Robert, Mary, Anna, Elizabeth and Thomas.

TALLANT, Ruben, sexton: (baptised c.1597; married Mary Cob, 5 June 1624; buried 21 February 1654). He was constantly employed by the churchwardens in a variety of odd jobs around the parish, and at the same time collected a weekly pension. Apparently, his domestic situation was not always harmonious: in 1632 the churchwardens gave him 1s., 'being throwne out and lyeing abroad'. He died after a long illness. He had five children: Robert, Mary, Anna, Elizabeth and Thomas.

TALLANT, Thomas, sexton: (baptised 5 September 1629; never married; buried 29 June 1700). He assumed his father's position as sexton, and did many odd jobs around the church and parish. Yet in 1655 began collecting a regular parish pension of 2s. a month. In 1674 he was listed with one hearth, and on grounds of poverty exempted from the Hearth Tax.

THIRTON, John: (baptised c.1610; married Damaris Eland, 7 February 1638; married Sarah c.1644; buried 13 December 1659). His first wife died in 1642. One of his children was educated at the expense of the parish. In 1659, he collected relief when ill. He had one child by Damaris, John; and five by Sarah: Sarah, Benjamin, Mary, Robert and an unnamed child.

TOWNESEN, William, minister of religion: was given relief by Cratfield in 1639–40 while travelling from Germany to Flegg in east Norfolk.

TREDSKIN, Robert: (no vital information). Constable in 1643.

TURNER, Thomas, tailor: (baptised 4 June 1621; married Mary, n.d.; buried 1 July 1696). Constable in 1644–5, and 1652–3. Churchwarden in 1668–71. A chief inhabitant in 1656. In 1653 he was appointed the official 'regester of the towne of Cratfeild'. He was first assessed for the rate at 1d. a month in 1652. In 1659, he rented the Town Pightle. His final rate payment was in 1694 at 3d. a month. In 1670, Thomas pledged 6d. for the release of Christian slaves (see p. 128). He had no children, and divided his estate between his nephew and nieces: Samuel Hayward, Alice Benns and Margaret Manning.

WARNE, Simon: (baptised 13 January 1613; no marriage or burial information). Simon did odd jobs about the parish, such as working on the bells.

WARNE or WARREN, William: (baptised c.1590; married Mary c.1617; buried 28 April 1651). He was assessed at 2s.3d. for Ship Money. He became active in parish life in 1621, and began to pay the rate in 1625 at 3d. a week. He paid until his death in 1651, with a final assessment of 1d. a week. In 1639–41 the parish paid him for supplying brick and lime, some of it for the repair of the church tower. He had three children: Thomas, James and William.

WARNER, Robert, gent: (baptised c.1578; married Elizabeth c.1605; buried 3 August 1641). He was assessed for the poor rate at 2s.8d. a month for his lands in Linstead and Cratfield. His last assessment was in 1629 for the same amount. He was assessed at £1 11s.6d. for Ship Money in 1640. Robert rented Rose Larks from the parish, paying fourteen years of back rent in 1651. He had four children: Elizabeth, Francis, Mary and Robert.

WARREN, John, carpenter: (no vital information). Paid by the churchwardens to do carpentry in the church in 1655.

WARREN, Symond, yeoman and carpenter: (baptised c.1634; married Mary Aldous, 26 September 1661; buried 31 August 1684). Constable in 1668. He was first assessed for the poor rate in 1660, at 8d. a month. His final assessment in the year before his death was at 2s.8d. a month. He had no children.

WATTLINGE or WATLIN, Edmund, bailiff: (no vital information). In 1645, he was fined 'for not doing service att the sherifes turne'.

WIETH or WYITH, William: (no vital information). Paid by the parish to attend the assize court at Bury St Edmunds in 1646. He was assessed for the rate beginning in 1644 at 8d. a month, and continued to pay 4d. a month until 1650.

WILLIAMS, John: (no baptismal information; married Ann Hayward, 23 October 1600; married Rachel Cooke, 23 January 1621; no burial information). Constable in 1643. Overseer in 1644, 1646–7 and 1658. Churchwarden in 1644, 1650 and 1656. John rented land from the town and provided services to the community. For example, in 1642 he was reimbursed for raisons, almonds, figs, and sugar, probably consumed at a town dinner. In 1639 and 1642 he supplied the town's soldiers with powder, bullets, and match to take to their 'traininge', and did the same in the following year. He, or his son John, rented the Town Meadow and Mollings Meadow in 1659. He and his son were major rate-payers from 1643 until the end of the century; their rates ranged between 2s. and 5s. a month. He had least one child, John.

WILLIAM(SON), John, described as 'of Norwood Green': (baptised 8 December 1605; married Ann Dowsing, 18 December 1632; buried 23 February 1655). Church-warden in 1645. He was reimbursed for expenses on behalf of the town in 1649–50. He had seven children: Ann, Elizabeth, Henry, John, Mary, Sarah and Susan.

WORLICH, Henry: (baptised c.1608; married Elizabeth Kirke, 7 May 1635; buried 14 March 1663). Although his earlier civic career looked promising, he spent most of his life on the edge of poverty. He figured briefly in the churchwardens' accounts in 1639, and by 1643 was serving as constable. While constable he was paid 'to make upp the weekly rate the 17th of Apriell for two monthes', and was given £3 0s. 8d. to share between 'constabell Henery Worlich and other poore men for ther charges concerning Perlements cause'. It appears that he eventually fell foul of more prominent villagers, particularly the vicar Gabriel Eland, for in 1645 the parish register records: 'Henry Worlich had a child baptzd without aquainting the minister at the place rightly called, and it is an usrpuption and an unlawfull invasion of any man so to performe, besidest the malice of mind of them that invite such invader to thrust sickle into another's corn'. Whether Henry's decision to have his child baptised by another minister was driven by purely religious concerns or by more mixed motives, the result was the abrupt curtailment of his involvement in local affairs. The churchwardens' accounts mention him only briefly the following year, but are then silent until his death when John Cross was paid 'for a lock for Henry Worliche's doore'. He had two children, Henry and Richard.

WRIGHT, Master: (no vital information). He was involved with Ann Milles' release from gaol in 1660. He collected the Poll Money in 1660.

YOUNGS, William: (no vital information). William was a soldier for the town in 1644. He was paid to make up the weekly rate in 1646, and to write out the indentures of Edmund Milles in 1647. William was assessed for the rate in 1645 at 4d. a month. He resumed paying the rate in 1655, first at 1d. a month, but in 1567 his assessment shot up to 1s.6d. where it remained until 1686.

# Appendix 2

## Chief Inhabitants of Cratfield, 1656–1700

The chief inhabitants of East Anglian villages were individuals of the 'better sort', those who were either economically or socially successful, or both. The most substantial landholders were generally amongst their number, as were the local clergymen, despite what was often their relative poverty. These men met at least annually to make significant decisions on behalf of their community: to approve the accounts of the previous year, and to elect officers for the next. In most cases this group also constituted the more cohesive unit of the vestry, which was responsible for the on-going administration of the village, deciding for instance which individuals would receive poor relief and the nature of that assistance. In the case of Cratfield, these men also determined who would be allowed to rent which piece of the community's extensive 'town lands'. No 'vestry book' as such survives for Cratfield, but it is highly probable that the chief inhabitants functioned as, and were considered to be, 'vestry men'. It is not an overstatement to conclude that the public order, reputation and economic well-being of the parish of Cratfield was determined in large measure by the decisions of the chief inhabitants listed below.

Their names are given in the order of their signatures and marks in two sources: principally from the town books of Cratfield,[1] for the period from 1658 onwards, but also from the churchwardens' loose accounts for the years 1656–7.[2] As a result much is revealed about the hierarchical nature of early modern society for, undoubtedly, these men belonged to Cratfield's highest social order. That did not mean, however, that they were necessarily social equals. The most important man present signed his name first, and every other man signed in turn, according to a rough assessment of his place within the ruling elite. Robert Mynne, Cratfield's largest landowner, signed first in nearly all instances when he attended a meeting. Similarly, Edward Clifford, the much poorer vicar at the end of the century, was always amongst the leading signatories, if not the first, because of his high social and moral standing as a clergyman. In many cases, individuals such as Proctor Verdon entered the group at the lowest level, and gradually rose in the ruling hierarchy as they prospered. Others were less certain of their position amongst the local elite. For example, William Drane signed only occasionally and then was always amongst the last.

The following list, therefore, represents the highest level of Cratfield's society in the later seventeenth century. These are the people whose decisions and approval were necessary for the smooth and prosperous functioning of the village, but who were often above the day-to-day running of the parish. And, interestingly, their names sometimes do not even appear amongst the churchwardens' entries.

---

[1] SROI, FC62/E1/1–2.
[2] See above, pp. 107, 108, 111 & 113.

**[from churchwardens' accounts]**

1656   John Smith, Robert Mynne, William Fiske, junior, John Rous, Robert Smyth, ?junior, Thomas Turner and William Fysk[3]

1657   John Smith, Robert Mynne, John Rous, William Aldous, John Fyske and John Newson

1657   (2nd account) John Smith, Robert Mynne, John Rous, William Aldous, Robert Smyth, Ralph Baldry, John Newson and John Fyske

**[from town book]**

1658   John Rouse, William Fisk, Ralph Baldry and Robert Smith

1659   Robert Mynne, Robert Smith, John Smith, John Rouse, William Youngs, Ralph Baldry and William Aldous

1660   John Smith, William Youngs, John Smith, William Aldous and Robert Smith

1661   John Rouse, John Smith, William Youngs, William Aldous, John Williams, John Newson and Ralph Baldry

1662   John Rouse, John Smith, William Aldous and John Newson

1663   John Smith, Robert Mynne, John Rouse, William Aldous and John Newson

1664   Robert Mynne, John Rouse, Leonard Peirson, William Aldous, John Newson, Robert Milles, John Fiske and William Fiske, senior

1665   Robert Mynne, John Rouse, William Aldous, John Williams and John Newson

1666   Robert Mynne, John Rouse, Robert Drane, John Goldsmith, Jeremy Baldry, Ralph Baldry, William Aldous and Robert Milles

1667   [no information]

1668   Robert Mynne, Thomas Hayes, John Rouse, William Barnes, Leonard Peirson, Ralph Baldry and William Aldous

1669   Robert Mynne, John Rouse, William Barnes, Leonard Peirson, Ralph Baldry, William Aldous and Jeremy Baldry

1670   Robert Mynne, John Rouse, John Goldsmith, William Aldous, Jeremy Baldry, Robert Milles and John William

1671   Robert Mynne, Thomas Hayes, William Barnes, John Goldsmith, William Aldous and William Newson

1672   William Barnes, Ralph Baldry, William Newson, Jeremy Baldry and William Aldous

1673   Robert Mynne, John Goldsmith, William Barnes, William Newson, William Aldous, Ralph Baldry and John Williams

1674   Robert Mynne, Thomas Hayes, William Barnes, William Newson, Ralph Baldry and Robert Milles

1675   Robert Mynne, Thomas Hayes, John Goldsmith, William Barnes, William Newson, Ralph Baldry and John Williams

1676   Robert Mynne, Thomas Hayes, William Barnes, John Goldsmith, Leonard Peirson and Robert Milles

1677   Robert Mynne, Thomas Hayes, William Barnes, John Goldsmith, Robert Milles, John Fiske and Francis Aldous

1678   Robert Mynne, Thomas Hayes, Ralph Baldry, John Williams, John Fiske, Robert Milles and John Stannard

---

[3]  In the second account of 1656 (No. 235), the names of Thomas Turner and William Fysk were reversed.

1679  Robert Mynne, Thomas Hayes, Alexander Barnes, Ralph Baldry, John Fiske, John William, Robert Milles and William Drane
1680  Edward Clifford, vicar, William Barnes, Alexander Barnes, William Newson, Ralph Baldry, Gregory Rouse, John Fiske, Robert Milles, Francis Aldous, William Drane and John Williams, junior
1681  Robert Mynne, William Barnes, Gregory Rouse, Ralph Baldry, William Newson, Robert Milles, John Fiske, John William and Francis Aldous
1682  Robert Mynne, Edward Clifford, vicar, William Newson, Gregory Rouse and John Williams
1683  Robert Mynne, Edward Clifford, vicar, Alexander Barnes, William Newson, Gregory Rouse and John Williams
1684  Robert Mynne, Edward Clifford, vicar, Alexander Barnes, William Barnes, Gregory Rouse, William Newson and Proctor Verdon
1685  Robert Mynne, Alexander Barnes, William Newson, William Barnes, Gregory Rouse, Ralph Baldry, Robert Milles and William Drane
1686  Robert Mynne, Edward Clifford, vicar, William Barnes, William Newson, Gregory Rouse, Robert Milles, John Fiske and John Williams
1687  Edward Clifford, vicar, Alexander Barnes, William Barnes, Gregory Rouse, Ralph Baldry, John Fiske and William Aldous
1688  Edward Clifford, vicar, Alexander Barnes, Proctor Verdon, John Williams, Robert Milles, Ralph Baldry and William Aldous
1689  Robert Mynne, Edward Clifford, vicar, William Barnes, Proctor Verdon, John Williams, William Aldous and Edmund Tallifer
1690  Alexander Barnes, Proctor Verdon, John Williams, William Aldous, William Newson and Gregory Rouse
1691  Alexander Barnes, Proctor Verdon, John Williams, William Aldous, Gregory Rouse and William Newson
1692  Edward Clifford, vicar, William Newson, Proctor Verdon, William Borrett, William Aldous, John Barber, William Drane and John Williams
1693  Edward Clifford, vicar, William Newson, Proctor Verdon, William Borrett, William Aldous, John Barber, William Drane and John Williams
1694  Edward Clifford, vicar, Proctor Verdon, William Newson, William Borrett, William Aldous, John Williams and William Drane
1695  Edward Clifford, vicar, Thomas Hayes, Proctor Verdon, William Newson, William Aldous and John Williams
1696  Edward Clifford, vicar, Thomas Hayes, Proctor Verdon, William Newson, John Barber and John Williams
1697  Robert Mynne, William Newson, John Barber, William Aldous and John Newson
1698  Edward Clifford, vicar, Proctor Verdon and William Newson
1699  Edward Clifford, vicar, Robert Mynne, William Aldous and John Newson
1700  Edward Clifford, vicar, Thomas Hayes, Proctor Verdon, John Barber and William Newson

# Appendix 3

## Churchwardens of Cratfield, 1639–1661

The third column gives the number of each man's relevant account in SROI, FC62/A6/176–253. These numbers are also given in the text of this volume, at the start of each account. It should be noted that such loose manuscript accounts are not particularly tidy or orderly: hence some of them are without numbers, and more than one account may survive for a particular warden's year.

| Year | Name of churchwarden | Account |
|------|----------------------|---------|
| 1639–40 | William Fisk, junior | 176 |
| | John Newson | 176 |
| 1640–1 | Robert Smith, junior | 177 |
| | John Rous | 178 |
| 1641–2 | Robert Smith, junior | 179 |
| | John Rous | 180 |
| 1642–3 | Robert Smyth, senior | 181 |
| | William Aldus | 182 |
| 1643–4 | Robert Smyth, senior | 183 |
| | William Aldus | 184 |
| 1644–5 | John Williams | no number |
| | John Smith of Norwood Green | 185 |
| 1645–6 | John Smith of Norwood Green | 186, 189 |
| | John Williams | 187–8 |
| 1646–7 | William Fisk, senior | 190 |
| | John Newsone, junior | 191 |
| 1647–8 | John Newsone, junior | 192 |
| | William Fisk, senior | no number |
| 1648–9 | John Fisk | 193 |
| 1649–50 | John Fisk | 197 |
| 1650–1 | Robert Smith de Coulshall | 200–1, 204 |
| | John Newson, senior | 203 |
| 1651–2 | John Newson, senior | no number |
| | Francis Alldus | 210 |
| | Robert Smith de Coulshall | 211 |
| 1652–3 | William Fisk, gent. | 214 |
| | John Rous | 215 |
| 1653–4 | John Rous | 217 |
| 1654–5 | William Fiske | 218 |
| | William Aldus | 220 |

# Bibliography

*Manuscript Sources*

Bodleian Library, Oxford
  Tanner MS 324: List of manors in Suffolk with their chief inhabitants, 1655

British Library, London
  Harleian MS 595: Archbishop Whitgift's Return, 1603

Cambridge University Library
  Ff.V.13: abstract of the *Valor Ecclesiasticus* of 1535
  Vanneck MSS: Records of Cratfield Manor

Lambeth Palace Library, London
  Comm. XIIa/15/520–22: Parliamentary Survey, 15 October 1650

Suffolk Record Office, Ipswich
  Cratfield:
    FC62/A3/1: Solemn Vow and Covenant, 1642
    FC62/A6/178–253: Churchwardens' Accounts
    FC62/D1/1–3: Parish Registers
    FC62/E1/1–2: Town Books
    Probate Inventories
    Wills


*Printed primary sources*

Achesone, J., *The Military Garden; or Instructions for All Young Souldiers* (Edinburgh, 1629)
*Archbishop Parker's Diocesan Articles* (London, 1563)
*Archbishop Parker's Articles for Norwich Diocese* (London, 1567)
*Articles to be Enquired of by the Church-Wardens and Questmen in the Ordinary Visitation of the Right Worshipfull Mr Robert Pearson, Doctor of Divinitie, and Archdeacon of Suffolk, or his Officall* (London, 1618)
*Articles . . . of John Lord Bishop of Norwich* (Cambridge, 1619)
*Articles . . . of Master Doctor Pearson, Archdeacon of Suffolke* (London, 1625)
*Articles . . . of Richard, Lord Bishop of Norwich* (Cambridge, 1633)
*Articles . . . of Master Doctor Pearson, Arch-Deacon of Suffolke* (London, 1633)
*Articles to be Enquired of in the Metropoliticall Visitation of the Most Rev. Father William . . . Lord Arch-Bishop of Canterbury . . . and for the Diocese of Norwich* (London, 1635)
*Articles . . . of Master Doctor Pearson, Archdeacon of Suffolk* (London, 1636)
*Articles of . . . Matthew Bishop of Norwich* (London, 1636)

*Articles . . . of Richard Mountaigu Bishop of Norwich. This Book of Articles, being extremely negligently printed at London, (which impression I disavow) I was forced to review it and have it printed at Cambridge* (Cambridge, 1638)

*Articles of . . . Mr. Doctor Pearson, Archdeacon of Suffolke* (London, 1638)

*Articles of . . . Doctor Bostock, Arch-Deacon of Suffolk* (London, 1640)

*Articles of . . . Edward Lord Bishop of Norwich* (London, 1662)

*Articles Agreed upon by the Archbishop and Bishops* (London, 1669)

*Articles Agreed upon by the Archbishop and Bishops* (London, 1686)

*Articles Agreed upon by the Archbishop and Bishop* (London, 1693)

Barriffe, W., *Military Discipline; or the Young Artilllery Man* (London, 1635)

*The Chorography of Suffolk*, edited by D. MacCulloch (Suffolk Records Society, 19, 1976)

*The Concise Dictionary of National Biography*, part I (Oxford, 1983)

Defoe, D., *A Tour thro' the Whole Island of Great Britain* (London, 1968)

Evelyn White, C. H. (ed.), *The Journal of William Dowsing* (Ipswich, 1885)

*Hodskinson's Map of Suffolk, 1783*, edited by D. P. Dymond (Suffolk Records Society, 15, 1972)

*Injunctions Exhibited by John by Gods Sufferance Bishop of Norwich in his First Visitation beginning the seconde date of May in the third year of our Sovereign Lady Elizabeth* (London, 1561)

*The Military Discipline* (London, 1623)

*Orders Taken the X Day of October for Roods Loftes* (London, ?1561)

*Parkhurst's Injunctions for Norwich Diocese* (London, 1569)

*Diocese of Norwich, Bishop Redman's Visitation 1597: Presentments in the Archdeaconries of Norwich, Norfolk and Suffolk*, edited by J. F. Williams (Norfolk Record Society, 18, 1946)

*The Royal Articles of Queen Elizabeth* (London, 1559)

Ryece, R., *Suffolk in the XVIIth Century: The Breviary of Suffolk by Robert Reyce*, edited by Lord Francis Hervey (London, 1902)

Strype, J., *The Life and Acts of Matthew Parker*, vol. I (Oxford, 1821)

*Suffolk in 1524, Being the Return of a Subsidy Granted in 1523*, Suffolk Green Books, no. 10 (Woodbridge, 1910)

*Suffolk in 1674, Being the Hearth Tax Returns*, Suffolk Green Books, no. 11, vol. 13 (Woodbridge, 1905)

*Suffolk and the Great Rebellion, 1640–1660*, edited by A. Everitt (Suffolk Records Society, 3, 1960)

*Valor Ecclesiasticus*, iii (London, 1817)


*Secondary Sources*

Ashton, R., *The English Civil War: Conservatism and Revolution, 1603–49* (London, 1989)

Baker, J. H., 'Criminal Courts and Procedure at Common Law, 1550–1800' in J. S. Cockburn (ed.), *Crime in England, 1550–1800* (Princeton, 1977), 15–48

Barnard, T. C., *Cromwellian Ireland, 1649–60* (Oxford, 1975)

Beier, A. L., 'Vagrants and the Social Order in Elizabethan England', *Past and Present*, 64 (1974), 3–29.

Blackwood, B. G., 'The Cavalier and Roundhead Gentry of Suffolk', *The Suffolk Review*, 5 (1985), 2–10

Blackwood, B. G., 'The Gentry of Suffolk during the Civil War' in D. Dymond & E. Martin (eds), *An Historical Atlas of Suffolk* (Bury St Edmunds, 1988), 84–5

Botelho, L. A., 'Accommodation for the Aged Poor of Cratfield in the Late Tudor and Early Stuart Period', *The Suffolk Review*, n.s. 24 (1995), 19–31

Botelho, L. A., 'Provisions for the Elderly in Two Early Modern Suffolk Communities', Cambridge University Ph.D., 1995

Cheney, C. R., *Handbook of Dates for Students of English History* (Royal Historical Society, 1978)

Collinson, P., *The Elizabethan Puritan Movement* (Oxford, 1967)

Copinger, W. A., *Manors of Suffolk*, ii (1908)

Cornwall, J., *Wealth and Society in Early Sixteenth Century England* (London, 1988)

Coward, B., *The Stuart Age: England, 1603–1714*, 2nd edn (London, 1994)

Craig, J. S., 'Co-operation and Initiatives: Elizabethan Churchwardens and the Parish Accounts of Mildenhall', *Social History* 18 (1993), 357–80

Cressy, D., *Bonfires and Bells: National Memory and the Protestant Calendar in Elizabethan and Stuart England* (London, 1989)

Dobson, M. J., *A Chronology of Epidemic Disease and Mortality in Southeast England, 1601–1800*, Historical Geography Research Series, 19 (London, 1987)

Dow, F. D., *Cromwellian Scotland, 1651–60* (Edinburgh, 1979)

Duffy, E., *The Stripping of the Altars: Traditional Religion in England, 1400–1580* (New Haven, 1992)

*The English Dialect Dictionary*, ed. J. Wright, 6 vols (Oxford, 1981)

Everitt, A. E., *Suffolk and the Great Rebellion* (Suffolk Records Soc., iii, 1961)

Farnhill, K., 'Religious Policy and "Parish Conformity": Cratfield's Lands in the Sixteenth Century' in K. L. French, G. C. Gibbs & B. A. Kümin (eds), *The Parish in English Life, 1400–1600* (Manchester UP, 1997), pp. 217–29

Fissel, M., *The Bishops' Wars: Charles I's Campaigns against Scotland, 1638–1640* (Cambridge, 1994)

Fletcher, A., *The Outbreak of the English Civil War* (New York & London, 1981)

French, H., 'Chief Inhabitants and their Areas of Influence: Local Ruling Groups in Essex and Suffolk Parishes, 1630–1720', Cambridge University Ph.D., 1993

Gardiner, S. R., *History of the Great Civil War, 1642–1649*, 4 vols (1893, reprint New York, 1965)

Haigh, C., *English Reformations* (Oxford, 1993)

Herlan, R. W., 'Poor Relief in London during the English Revolution', *Journal of British Studies*, 18 (1979), 30–51

Herlan, R. W., 'Relief of the Poor in Bristol from Late Elizabethan Times until the Restoration Era', *Proceedings of the American Philosophical Society*, 1262 (1982), 212–28

Hexter, J. H., *The Reign of King Pym* (Cambridge, Mass., 1941)

Holmes, C., *The Eastern Association in the English Civil War* (Cambridge, 1975)

Holmes, C., *Seventeenth-Century Lincolnshire* (History of Lincolnshire, 7, 1980)

Holland, W., *Cratfield: A Transcript of the Accounts of the Parish, from A.D. 1490 to A.D. 1642, with Notes*, edited by J. J. Raven (London, 1895)

Hudson, G. L., 'Ex-Servicemen, War Widows and the English County Pension Scheme 1593–1679', Oxford University D.Phil., 1995

Hudson, G. L., 'Negotiating for Blood Money: War Widows and the Courts in Seventeenth-Century England' in J. Kermode & G. Walker (eds), *Women, Crime and the Courts in Early Modern England* (London, 1994) 146–69

Hughes, A., *Politics, Society and Civil War in Warwickshire, 1620–1660* (Cambridge, 1987)

Hutton, R., *The Restoration: A Political and Religious History of England and Wales, 1658–67* (Oxford, 1985)

Kerridge, E., *The Agricultural Revolution* (London, 1967)

Kirby, J., *The Suffolk Traveller: or a Journey through Suffolk* (Ipswich, 1735)

Lake, P., 'The Laudian Style: Order, Uniformity and the Pursuit of the Beauty of Holiness in the 1630s' in K. Fincham (ed.), *The Early Stuart Church, 1603–16* (Basingstoke, 1993), 161–85

MacCulloch, D., *The Later Reformation in England, 1547–1603* (Basingstoke, 1990)

MacCulloch, D., *Suffolk and the Tudors: Politics and Religion in an English County, 1500–1600* (Oxford, 1986)

Macfarlane, A. (ed.), *The Diary of Ralph Josselin, 1616–1683*, Records of Social and Economic History, New Series III (London, 1976)

*Middle English Dictionary*, ed. R. E. Lewis (Ann Arbor, MI, 1956–97)

Milward, R., *A Glossary of Household, Farming and Trade Terms from Probate Inventories* (Derbyshire Record Society, Occasional Paper no. 1, 3rd edn 1989)

Mill, A. D., *A Dictionary of English Place-Names* (Oxford, 1991)

Morrill, J., *Cheshire 1630–1660: County Government and Society during the English Revolution* (London, 1974)

Morrill, J., 'The Ecology of Allegiance in the English Revolution', *Journal of British Studies*, 26 (1987), 451–67.

Morrill, J., *The Revolt in the Provinces: Conservatives and Radicals in the English Civil War, 1630–50* (London, 1989)

Nichols, A. E., 'Broken Up or Restored Away: Iconoclasm in a Suffolk Parish' in C. Davidson & A. E. Nichols (eds), *Iconoclasm vs. Art and Drama*, Early Drama, Art, and Music Monograph, no. 11 (London, 1989), 164–96

Noonan, K. M., ' "The Cruell Pressure of an Enraged, Barbarous People": Irish and English Identity in Seventeenth-Century Policy and Propaganda', *The Historical Journal*, 41, 1 (1998), 151–77

Palliser, D. M., 'Popular Reactions to the Reformation during the Years of Uncertainty, 1530–70' in C. Haigh (ed.), *The English Reformation Revised* (Cambridge, 1988), 94–113

Patten, J., 'Village and Town: An Occupational Study', *The Agricultural History Review*, 20 (1972), 1–16

Pearl, V., 'Social Policy in Early Modern London' in H. Lloyd-Jones, V. Pearl & B. Worden (eds), *History and Imagination: Essays in Honour of H. R. Trevor-Roper* (London, 1981), 115–31

Pennington, D. H., 'The Accounts of the Kingdom, 1642–1649' in F. J. Fisher (ed.), *Essays in the Economic and Social History of Tudor and Stuart England in Honour of R. H. Tawney* (Cambridge, 1961), 182–203

Pound, J., *Poverty and Vagrancy in Tudor England* (London, 1971)

Seaver, P. S., *The Puritan Lecturerships: The Politics of Religious Dissent, 1560–1662* (Stanford, CA, 1970)

Scarfe, N., 'Medieval and Later Markets' in D. Dymond & E. Martin (eds), *An Historical Atlas of Suffolk* (Bury St Edmunds, 1988), 64–6

Scarfe, N., *The Suffolk Landscape* (London, 1972)

Spurr, J., *The Restoration Church of England, 1646–1689* (New Haven, 1991)

Thirsk, J., *The Agrarian History of England and Wales, IV: 1500–1640* (Cambridge, 1967)

Todd, H. & Dymond, D., 'Population Densities, 1377 and 1524' in D. Dymond & E. Martin (eds), *An Historical Atlas of Suffolk* (Bury St Edmunds, 1988), 64–7

Underdown, D., 'A Reply to John Morrill', *Journal of British Studies*, 26 (1987), 467–79

Underdown, D., *Revel, Riot and Rebellion: Popular Politics and Culture in England, 1603–60* (Oxford, 1985)

Underdown, D., *Somerset during the Civil War and Interregnum* (Newton Abbot, 1973)

Venn, J. & Venn, J. A., *Alumni Cantabrigienses*, part I (Cambridge, 1922)

Whiting, R., *The Blind Devotion of the People* (Cambridge, 1990)

Williamson, T., 'Ancient Landscapes' in D. Dymond & E. Martin (eds), *An Historical Atlas of Suffolk* (Bury St Edmunds, 1988), 40–1.

Williamson, T., 'Parish Boundaries and Early Fields: Continuity and Discontinuity', *Journal of Historical Geography*, 12 (1986), 241–8

Williamson, T., 'Sites in the Landscape: Approaches to the Post-Roman Settlement of South Eastern England', *Archaeological Review from Cambridge*, 4 (1985), 51–64

Wrightson, K., 'The Politics of the Parish in Early Modern England' in P. Griffiths, A. Fox & S. Hindle (eds), *The Experience of Authority in Early Modern England* (Basingstoke, 1996), 10–46

Young, A., *General View of the Agriculture of the County of Suffolk* (London, 1794)

# Glossary

The original spelling of the churchwardens' accounts is retained. In the case of words which were spelt in more than one way, some (though not necessarily all) of the variants are indicated below. It should be remembered that where alternative spellings occur, the overall alphabetical order is to some extent distorted. The document number is given where the word is used rarely or in a particular way; similarly a secondary source is quoted for the less obvious definitions. The sources normally used are the *Oxford English Dictionary* (2nd edn, 1989) and the *Middle English Dictionary* (1956–). Other definitions have been found in R. Forby, *The Vocabulary of East Anglia* (1830), J. O. Halliwell, *Dictionary of Archaic and Provincial Words* (1847), Samuel Johnson, *Dictionary of the English Language* (1755) and E. Moor, *Suffolk Words and Phrases* (1823).

**admission fee:** a fee to be admitted to a court, probably ecclesiastical (*cf.* 'dismission fees')

**alaromes, allarams:** alarms, the call to arms

**amons:** almonds [182]

**arerages, arrerages:** arrears

**assis', assises:** assizes, court of

**awxilleres, awxilleris, awxilleryes:** auxiliary troops

**baily, bally, ballye, baly:** bailiff of a manor or hundred

**bandelears:** bandoliers, a broad belt worn over the shoulder to support a musket and carry shot-cases

**bar postes:** [of uncertain meaning]; either posts acting as bars, or posts supporting bars [182]

**beel stoopes:** bell-stops; devices to prevent church-bells from turning over [180]

**beell wheele, bell whelle:** bell-wheel; a wheel to which a church-bell is attached, and by which it is swung

**beelles:** bells, in church tower

**beil, beles:** bill(s), account(s)

**belleropes:** bell-ropes; ropes hanging from bells to ringing chamber

**bessenes:** business

**billes indented:** indented bills or indentures. An indenture was a legal document on which two identical texts were written and then separated by being cut along an irregular wavy line. In the event of a dispute, the two halves could be brought together to make sure that the cut edges matched.

**bindings, byndeings:** bindings, used by a thatcher

**blockes:** blocks; logs of wood for fuel

**bocke, bokes:** book(s)

**bolts, boultes:** denotes stout pins for fastening a church-bell

**braches:** [see 'broaches']

**bratling, bratlyng, bratlling, brattlling:** brattling; lopping the branches of trees after felling (Forby)

**breeches:** describes a garment covering the lower body and thighs, akin to trousers

**breefe, bref, brefe, breffe, briefe:** brief, a written document issued by official or legal authority; usually a licence for collecting money for a specified charitable object

**broaches, broatches:** broaches; sticks pointed at both ends, used by thatchers to pin their straw or reed; usually a split rod of hazel

**buttes:** butts; mounds bearing targets for the practice of archery, required in every parish

**byllett:** billets; pieces of wood cut and split for fuel; firewood

**bynding forth/of:** binding of an apprentice, formally engaging him to a master

**cairieing, caring(e), carring:** carrying (of wood, etc.)

**certifficate:** denotes a written document giving authorisation to the bearer; a licence or pass

**chimney stockes:** denotes fire-backs; metal plates at back of fires [218]

**Christed, Christid:** Christ-tide or Christmas, 25 December; a quarter-day for the payment of rents, wages, etc.

**church:** used specifically for the nave of Cratfield church, which parishioners had the responsibility of maintaining [185]

**clock lyne:** denotes a wire for suspending the weights of the church clock; the wire was regularly purchased at Cratfield.

**coatt, cot:** cote, a small building; a hog's cote or pigsty [185]

**cofines:** coffins

**colection, collection:** denotes the gathering of a parochial rate to relieve the poor

**collectors:** officers of parish or hundred appointed to gather rates and taxes; specifically the collector of a parliamentary subsidy [180], and of a Poll Tax [252]

**collor:** collar (?for clothing, or a horse collar) [191]

**commens fine, common fine:** a fine due to the lord of a manorial leet

**companies :** used to describe bands of poor people who travelled together

**composecion, composistione, composition, compossition, compostistion:** composition, sometimes mentioned as 'composition oats'; used to describe the royal prerogative of purveyance, whereby parishes were expected to contribute towards the provisioning of the royal household

**conductinge mony:** money paid to meet the cost of transporting troops [178]

**corslet, coslet:** corslet, a piece of body armour

**course:** coarse (wheat)

**cribe:** crib, a rack holding hay for horses or cattle to eat

**cronyer:** coroner, a royal officer who maintained the private rights and property of the crown within a particular county or region [197]

**crotches:** crutches, meaning posts with a fork at the top to take an horizontal rail

**cryplle:** cripple

**cullering:** colouring; seems to refer to the colours of a corslet [178]

**cullurs, culours:** colours; coloured devices to distinguish particular troops or regiments of soldiers [189]

**dabinge:** daubing; coating walls with clay, etc.

**dafter:** daughter [235]

**dich:** ditch

**dismission fees:** fees paid to an ecclesiastical court, when a party was discharged

**doubell refine sewger:** sugar purified or cleansed by a double process [187]

**doublet:** denotes a close-fitting garment for the upper body, with or without sleeves

**dragoneers, dragoners:** dragoons; mounted soldiers who carried short muskets called 'dragons'

**drosse:** dross or chaff; the waste of wheat [211]

**ducketes:** ducats; the ducat was a gold coin of varying value used in most of Europe [178]

**Dunkardes:** Dunkirkers; people from Dunkirk on the coast of French Flanders; hence, privateering vessels of that town

**destres, distrees:** distress (of poor people)

**dropsie:** dropsy, a disease which causes watery fluids to accumulate in the body

**duplicots:** duplicates

**dyett:** diet; food and drink; victuals in daily use

**euse:** use; applied to money lent at interest [200]

**exercise, exercising:** military training, drilling of troops

**evfes bordes:** eaves boards; boards protecting the overhanging edges of roofs

**eyes:** in sense of round fastenings used on doors, gates, etc.; usually mentioned with hooks

**faggott:** faggot, a bundle of firewood or kindling

**faning:** fanning, winnowing; separating grain from chaff by creating an artificial breeze

**fearme:** farm or rent paid for a manorial holding

**feffement:** feoffment, enfeoffment; the act of conferring possession of a property, and the relevant legal document

**feffes, feofees, feoffe:** feoffees or trustees, entrusted with a freehold estate

**fiering, fioring, fire, fireinge, fyring:** firing; wood used as fuel

**flesh meate:** meat of butchered animals, as opposed to other kinds of 'meat'

**fram:** (bell-)frame; a framework of heavy timbers in a church tower, from which bells are hung and swung

**gathered:** refers to money collected for special purposes, public or charitable

**generall:** general court of an archdeacon, held twice a year

**gimers:** gimews, hinges

**glaasers, glasar, glaser, glasur, gleasur:** glazier(s), who worked with glass, lead and solder

**glassen, glassene:** glazing (windows)

**Goodman:** used as a vague title of respect or dignity for a man of 'middling' social rank (e.g. a yeoman farmer)

**Goodwife:** used for the mistress of a house and wife of a substantial citizen; again a civil form of address

**Goody:** an abbreviated form of 'goodwife'

**gudgin:** gudgeon; a pivot, usually of metal, on which a wheel turns or bell swings

**handcerchars:** handkerchieves

**har, hir:** her

**headlans:** headlands; strips of land in ploughed fields where the plough turned at the end of furrows; 'wheat headlands' [211]

**headpeeces:** headpieces, helmets; pieces of armour to protect the head

**heare:** hair for mortar [191]

**heweing:** hewing; cutting or felling timber

**horsmeat(e):** horse-meat; food or provender for horses

**house fearme, housfearme, howsse fearme:** farm or rent paid to tenant a house

**hue and crye:** hue and cry; a public outcry calling for the arrest of a malefactor

**impresed:** describes a man forcibly compelled to serve as a soldier; *cf.* 'prest'

**indentures:** (see 'billes indented'); specifically describes a formal document binding an apprentice to a master

**ingrose:** engross; write a fair copy of a document

**inprimis, imprimis:** *in primis* (Latin) meaning 'in the first things' or 'firstly'

**iorn, iorne:** iron (adjective)

**iornes, iorns:** irons (noun)

**Justes, Justice:** Justice of the Peace or magistrate, appointed to serve in a particular district, county or town [182]

**Ladday:** Lady Day, 25 March; a quarter-day for the payment of rents, wages, etc.

**laiinges ought:** layings out, expenses

**larth:** laths; thin strips of wood

**layeing:** laying (a hedge or 'spring'); cutting the boughs half through, bending and entwining them to thicken a hedge and make it animal-proof

**learning:** teaching [220]

**leaveing moneys:** money ?paid to soldiers about to leave home [181]

**leags:** leagues; a measure of distance, usually about 3 miles

**leckter, lecktor, lector, lectuer, lectur, lecture:** lecture, a special sermon delivered regularly on a particular weekday, supported by an endowment

**lining:** linen

**lokeing to:** looking after, maintaining (armour)

**lose:** loss; financial ruin

**mained, mayened, mayned:** maimed; Maimed Soldiers was the name given to a county rate levied to support injured soldiers

**makeing , making (of a rate):** assessing and collecting a new levy on the ratepayers of a parish [183]

**making (of wood):** trimming felled timber before it is transported [220]

**malignants:** a pejorative term which in 1640–60 supporters of Parliament and the Commonwealth applied to their adversaries, such as royalists and papists

**maner:** manor

**mansmeate:** man's meat; food and drink for a man (*cf.* 'horsemeat')

**Marchallseas, Marciallseas, Marshalls, Marshalseas, Marshells:** Marshalsea, a prison in Southwark belonging to the marshal of the king's household; used to denote a county rate for the support of prisons

**marsement:** amercement; an arbitrary fine imposed in a manorial court, left to the 'mercy' of those inflicting it

**meades, meddes, middows, mido, myddowes:** meadows

**Michalmis, Mich'mas, Mychallmas, Mychalltid, Mychelltid, Mykilltide:** Michaelmas or Michaeltide, the feast of St Michael the Archangel, 29 September; a quarter-day for the payment of rents, wages, etc.

**Midsumer, Mydsomer:** Midsummer, the feast of the Nativity of St John the Baptist, 24 June; a quarter-day for the payment of rents, wages, etc.

**musquet, mussket:** musket, a hand-gun ('matchlock') used by infantry soldiers

**mustermasters:** describes officers responsible for the muster-roll and the organisation of military training

**myddowes, mydowes:** meadows

**nacker:** knacker; a maker of horse-collars and harness (Moor)

**nayelinge:** nailing

**nayels:** nails

**oud:** wood [185]

**ought:** owed.

**pale, palles:** pale(s); timbers used to construct a wooden fence, including stakes, rails and upright bars

**pamentine, paments:** pammenting, pamments; pamments were special floor-bricks, rectangular or square

**pane, paynes:** pain(s), in the sense of the trouble taken to accomplish something [217]

**pasingers:** passengers or travellers; 'one who is upon the road' (Johnson)

**peck:** a measure of capacity for dry goods, equivalent to 2 gallons or a quarter of a bushel; peck of wheat

**peller:** pillar; the mullion of window [191]

**peneckle:** pinnacle; a small ornamental turret on a church

*per me*: Latin for 'by me'.

**phisicke:** physic or medicine

**pightell, pightle, pitell, pitlle, pittell, pyghtell:** pightle, a small enclosure or field (Latin *pictellum*)

**pining:** pinning

**plum:** plumb or lead

**Pole Monye, Poll Mony:** poll money; the Poll Tax was a national tax voted by Parliament at so much per head of adult population [252]

**preast, prest:** impressed (soldier); a man forcibly enlisted

**prentiz:** apprentice

**prese money:** money paid to impressed soldiers [183]

**precedent, presedent:** preceding, former (churchwardens).

**presentment:** describes a formal statement of facts laid before a court; to justices of the peace

**poulvering, pullerin, pullering, pullvaringe, pullveren, pulveringe (day/money):** this unusual term was used in Cratfield to describe the annual day of reckoning on or about Lady Day, 25 March. On this occasion the parish officers presented their accounts for the preceding year, and the principal inhabitants 'viewed' and 'allowed' them. The word was also used elsewhere in eastern Suffolk, for example at Dunwich (*OED*) and at Southwold (Halliwell).

**poulvers, pullerrers, pullers, pulverers:** the name given to the principal parishioners, about a dozen, who attended the annual reckoning and the dinner which followed

**Powder Treason Day:** 5 November

**pyke:** pike; a long spiked weapon used by infantry; belonging to the parish [187]

**quarrells:** quarrels; small squares of window glass, usually set diagonally

**quarterage:** quarterly payments of wages, at Lady Day, Midsummer, Michaelmas and Christmas.

**ratte, reat, ratted:** rate, rated; assessed on property and levied for parochial purposes.

**rayels:** rails; usually timbers used horizontally

**recconing, reckininge, reckoninge, reconing, reconinge:** reckoning or reckoning day, when the accounts of parish officers were presented for approval (see 'poulvering')

**regester:** register, registrar; a secular parochial official appointed in the Commonwealth period to register all baptisms, marriages and burials [217]

**riveing (pale):** riving; splitting or cleaving wood

**rossen:** rosin; a distillate of turpentine

**routing out:** ?rooting out of a person [211]

**sack:** describes a wine akin to sherry; 3 pints for communion [203]

**salet oyle, sallet oyle:** [of uncertain meaning]; could denote 'salad oil' used with cold food; context, however, suggests an oil to lubricate 'salets', a form of military helmet [182, 186]

**sare, sere:** sere, dry (firewood)

**sarveinge:** serving, military service

**sawars, sawers:** sawyers; those who saw timber and wood

**sawe pit, sawing pitt:** sawing pit; a long, deep pit dug in order to saw large timbers longitudinally

**scoore:** score, or twenty; of hoop staves [225]

**scrue boult:** screw bolt; a threaded bolt which could be secured by a nut; used for a bell-wheel in the church tower [192]

**seles:** sills; horizontal timbers used in buildings

**sessement:** assessment; the determination of the amount of rate or tax to be paid by individuals; refers to poor rate

**sessond:** seasoned (timber) [211]

**sewger, sewgr:** sugar

**sheers, sheires:** shears or shear-legs; three long poles fastened together at upper end, carrying tackle for raising heavy weights

**shreifes turne, shreiffes turne:** sheriff's tourn; the court leet of a county presided over by a sheriff

**sirtificat, sirtificate:** [see 'certificate']

**skabard:** scabbard or sheath for a sword

**soder, sooder:** solder; **sodering:** soldering

**sollder, souldiers, soullgers:** soldiers

**souldgrone, souldierin, soulgran, soulgren, soulgron:** soldiering; often describing sums of money paid to support soldiers

**spaires:** spars, perhaps rafters [211]

**spikens:** spikings or spike-nails; for schoolhouse [187]

**splentyarne:** an unidentified form of yarn, perhaps broken and fragmented [176]

**spring, springe:** describes the young growth of trees or shrubs; was often cut and 'laid'

**spur:** describes a short strut or stay set diagonally to support a post

**standinge:** standing; a place for a horse to stand; equivalent to modern parking

**states:** ?estates [204]

**steeple, stepell:** steeple; in Suffolk it denotes a church *tower*, with no suggestion of a spire

**stille:** stile, into churchyard [*unnumbered, for 1647–8*]

**stocke:** stock, block of wood (the basic meaning). In the Cratfield accounts, however, this word is used in four special ways: (1) stocks, for punishment [179]; (2) household goods [183]; (3) the block of heavy timber from which a church bell is hung [215]; and (4) a chimney-stock or fire-back [218]

**stocking, stoked:** denotes the fitting of a wooden stock to a church bell

**stoping in:** planting; dibbling of wheat [211]

**stoughing, stouing, stoweng, stoweing, stowing:** stowing; cutting or lopping branches from a tree (Moor)

**subsidie:** subsidy; a tax (for example, a tenth and fifteenth, or lay subsidy) granted by Parliament to the crown for a specified purpose

**surgin:** surgeon

**surplis:** surplice; a loose fitting vestment of white linen worn by clergy

**surtefficat, surteficat:** [see 'certifficate']

**sute fine:** suit fine; a fine imposed by a manorial court for being excused from attendance

**swayes:** sways; long sticks or rods used by thatchers to bind their work to the rafters (Halliwell)

**tackling:** generally denotes gear or fittings; specifically, a device for lifting heavy weights [177]

**tale wood:** talwood; wood for fuel, cut to a prescribed size

**tendance:** attendance

**thrashing:** threshing (of grain)

**tobacko, tobackoe:** tobacco; specified in Cratfield as Spanish or 'best Virginian' [SROI: FC62/A6/210 & 223]

**tow:** two

**towne:** township or vill (as in 'towne armour', 'towne armes'); not used in the sense of an *urban* community

**traineinge. traininge, trayeninges, traying:** training(s), military exercises or drill

**treminge, triming, triminge, trying:** trimming; specifically, the adjusting and balancing of church bells.

**truste:** trustee

**vardit:** verdict

**varmen:** vermin, pests ( for example, sparrows and foxes), for the killing of which the parish paid

**victualls:** victuals, food

*videlicet:* Latin meaning 'that is to say' or 'namely'

**visitors, vissiters:** visitors, for the purpose of ecclesiastical inspection and supervision

**warant, warrent:** warrant, an official document authorising the recipient to perform a specific act

**watchers:** denotes people paid to 'watch', or sentries [182]

**wedous:** widows [185]

**wein, wien, win:** wine, bought for the communion

**whit/whitt rent:** quit rent, a small sum paid by a tenant to a manorial lord in lieu of services

**wier, wyare:** wire, used in church clock

**wodd:** wood.

**wrigthing:** writing [*unnumbered, for 1639–40*]

**wrought:** worked, done; past participle of 'to work'

**w'tt paper:** ?white paper [203]

# Index

Note: an asterisk after a page-number means two or more references on that page

## A. PERSONS

Most people in this index were resident in Cratfield. Where individuals belonged elsewhere, their parish is usually indicated. Those for any reason passing through Cratfield are distinguished as 'itinerants'. Christian names have been modernised, but the original spelling has been retained for surnames.

Adams (Adames, Addames)
  Doll (Dorothy), 76, 106*, 109*, 117, 120, 124, 127
  Finett (Finet, Finit), 41, 45, 50, 52, 58, 80, 127
  Margaret, 127
  Robert, 88, 91, 98, 101, 110, 116, 120, 123, 127
  Stephen, 79, 127
  Thomas, 33, 35, 42, 43, 112, 127
  Widow, 127
  Widow Dorothy, 32, 35
  Widow Margaret, 87, 88, 89*, 91, 93*, 94*, 95, 96, 97, 100, 101, 102, 104, 107, 108*
Alding (Aldinge)
  Edward, 115, 116, 119, 127
  Goodman Edward, 122
Aldus (Alldis, Alldous, Alldus), 34, 41
  Frances, 35, 51*, 53, 58
  Francis, 33, 34, 38, 43, 45, 49, 64, 69, 71, 75, 76, 78, 82, 83, 84, 85*, 109*, 110*, 116*, 118, 119*, 125, 146, 147, 148
    tailor, 105, 128
    wife of, 112
  Francis senior, 30, 128
  Goodwife, 40
  Joan, 128
  John, 42, 97, 128
    wife of, 62, 101, 106, 109*
  Mr William, 33, 51, 54, 59
  Thomas, 97, 98, 128
  William, 18, 19, 31, 34, 40, 41, 50, 51*, 52, 57*, 58*, 59, 65, 72, 79, 97, 99, 101, 102*, 105, 108, 111, 113, 119, 120, 122, 128, 146, 148
    butcher, 118, 120, 121

junior, 66, 128
  wife of, 102, 106, 107
Alecorne, John, itinerant, 40
Allyott, Barnabas, itinerant, 53
Allyson, John, itinerant, 54
Antall (Antalls), Mr, 113, 129
Ashby, Toby, 100, 101, 112, 129
Ashton, Robert, historian, 21
Attebeg, Metrophanes, brief for, 41

Baldry (Balldry, Baldrye, Balldry)
  Edmund, 112, 123, 129
  Jeremy, 50, 129, 146
  Ralph, 113, 129, 146, 147
Banckes (Banks), Mr, 43, 46, 129
Barber, John, 147
Barfot, Michael, of Halesworth, 123
Barmby, Thomas, 70
Barnably (Barwby), Thomas, 129
Barnbes, Widow, 113
Barnby (Barnbe), Widow, 129
Barnes
  Alexander, 146, 147
  William, 146, 147
Barrow (Barrowe), Francis, 30*, 65, 67, 115, 119, 129
Basset, Richard, itinerant, 91
Baxter
  John, 18
  William, 18
Baxter, John, itinerant, 55
Baxter, William, itinerant, 55
Bedingfeild, Mr Thomas, 30*, 31, 32, 36, 42, 43, 45, 46*, 50, 60*, 61, 67*, 70, 79*, 87, 88, 96, 105, 129
Bellymyn, Margery, itinerant, 54
Bennit, Thomas of Thorpe, 48

163

## B. PLACES

All place-names, unless otherwise indicated, are in the county of Suffolk.

## C. SUBJECTS